MAYORS GONE BAD

Also by PHILIP SLAYTON

Lawyers Gone Bad: Money, Sex and Madness in Canada's Legal Profession

Mighty Judgment: How the Supreme Court of Canada Runs Your Life

Bay Street: A Novel

MAYORS GONE

BAD

PHILIP SLAYTON

VIKING

VIKING

an imprint of Penguin Canada Books Inc., a Penguin Random House Company

Published by the Penguin Group

Penguin Canada Books Inc., 90 Eglinton Avenue East, Suite 700, Toronto, Ontario, Canada M4P 2Y3

Penguin Group (USA) LLC, 375 Hudson Street, New York, New York 10014, U.S.A.
Penguin Books Ltd, 80 Strand, London WC2R 0RL, England
Penguin Ireland, 25 St Stephen's Green, Dublin 2, Ireland (a division of Penguin Books Ltd)
Penguin Group (Australia), 707 Collins Street, Melbourne, Victoria 3008, Australia
(a division of Pearson Australia Group Pty Ltd)
Penguin Books India Pvt Ltd, 11 Community Centre, Panchsheel Park, New Delhi – 110 017, India
Penguin Group (NZ), 67 Apollo Drive, Rosedale, Auckland 0632, New Zealand
(a division of Pearson New Zealand Ltd)
Penguin Books (South Africa) (Pty) Ltd, 24 Sturdee Avenue, Rosebank, Johannesburg 2196, South Africa

Penguin Books Ltd, Registered Offices: 80 Strand, London WC2R 0RL, England

First published 2015

1 2 3 4 5 6 7 8 9 10 (RRD)

Manufactured in the U.S.A.

LIBRARY AND ARCHIVES CANADA CATALOGUING IN PUBLICATION

Slayton, Philip, author
Mayors gone bad / Philip Slayton.

Includes bibliographical references and index.
ISBN 978-0-670-06830-2 (bound)

1. Mayors--Canada. 2. Misconduct in office--Canada.
3. Municipal government--Corrupt practices--Canada.
4. Political corruption--Canada. 5. Municipal government--Canada.
I. Title.

JS1714.A1S53 2015   353.4'652232140971   C2015-900941-3

eBook ISBN 978-0-14-319451-4

Visit the Penguin Canada website at www.penguin.ca

Special and corporate bulk purchase rates available; please see
www.penguin.ca/corporatesales or call 1-800-810-3104.

For Gabrielle, Victor, Max and Rosie

Sometimes I am overcome by boundless sadness and despair, and then, much to the displeasure of my staff, I give in to my unrestrained self-pity. My head feels like it's just about to burst, and I have the feeling I've gotten myself into something that I will never understand, not even partly. Then I long for my old life.

JÓN GNARR, MAYOR OF REYKJAVIK, 2010–14

CONTENTS

INTRODUCTION
THE NAKED GLADIATORS

CANADIAN MUNICIPAL GOVERNMENT is a mess. Why? Why are the citizens of our big cities so poorly served? The record is appalling. In recent years, Canada's big-city mayors have been driven from office for egregious personal behaviour. One has been criminally convicted; others currently face criminal charges or have been widely suspected of ties to organized crime. Mayors have been enmeshed in conflicts of interest and have escaped unscathed because of defective legislation. They have been investigated by the police or been the subject of judicial inquiries. How can these be the people who run our big cities? How could this happen in an advanced, politically sophisticated country full of well-educated, competent, thoughtful and law-abiding people? In May 2013, Christopher Hume of the *Toronto Star* wrote: "Municipal Canada is in shambles.... Mayors across the country are as dysfunctional a bunch as you could find."[1] Hume may have exaggerated, but not by much. Since he wrote, things have only got worse. And there is little or no accountability or transparency.

There are, of course, exceptions to this dismal picture. Not all Canadian mayors have "gone bad." And there are explanations for some of those who have. Some who got into trouble tried their best to serve the public good as they saw it. Sometimes their good intentions went bad because they didn't understand the context. If they came from a business background, they thought incorrectly that the problem with municipal government was that it wasn't run like a business. Some didn't understand the importance of avoiding even per- ceived conflicts of interest, of separating their personal interests from their government role, of being personally careful with the public purse. In some cases, they didn't know enough about municipal government. They weren't well educated. They had no particular competence. They weren't attuned to public policy. They didn't know what a mayor did; they just wanted to be one. They stumbled into a job they weren't fit to have. Larry O'Brien once told a reporter, "I fell asleep on my boat in July drinking a beer and when I woke up I was the mayor of Ottawa."[2] When I asked Peter Trent, the mayor of the Montreal enclave of Westmount, about Michael Applebaum, who was briefly mayor of Montreal and now faces criminal charges, Trent said, "The thing about him is, he's poorly educated and not very smart." Jón Gnarr, mayor of Reykjavik, Iceland, from 2010 to 2014, once said he had "the feeling I've gotten myself into something that I will never understand, not even partly," and perhaps these bad mayors felt the same. (Although Gnarr was a successful mayor.) Some are likeable. They are "people persons," fun to be with and charming—and they're the first to tell you that. You can be a likeable person but a lousy mayor.

Municipalities are a demoralized junior level of government, burdened by the unrealistic but reasonable expectations of their citizens, who often do not understand what cities can and cannot do, and as a result vote in confusion. Local government lacks the political power and financial resources to play the part it is expected to play. Even what one newspaper termed the "western triangle of mayoral goodness"—Mayors Naheed Nenshi of Calgary, Don Iveson of Edmonton and Gregor Robertson of Vancouver—has been largely impotent in the face of constitutional, financial and structural constraints, despite good intentions and flowery rhetoric. The western mayors, notwithstanding their considerable ability, have had to rely on their attractive personalities, as well as symbolic acts like creating bike lanes and promoting fitness challenges, to give the illusion of progressive leadership. The mayors of Canada, lacking swords and armour—many also without knowledge and understanding—are naked gladiators.

Some observers proclaimed December 1, 2014, the start of a new era—in Ontario, at least. On that blessed day, John Tory replaced Rob Ford as mayor of Toronto, Linda Jeffrey replaced Susan Fennell as mayor of Brampton and Bonnie Crombie replaced the beloved Hazel McCallion as mayor of Mississauga. The municipal world was ready to move ahead. A new age had dawned. But no, it hadn't. You might prefer John Tory to Rob Ford (Tory has better table manners), or Linda Jeffrey to Susan Fennell (Jeffrey is prepared to travel economy class), but Tory has no more political power than Ford had, and Jeffrey's treasury is no bigger than Fennell's was. The system remains the same.

Is there a connection between the low calibre of municipal politicians and their institutional powerlessness? Is it the unsophisticated and unaware, the inadequately educated, those insensitive to the great issues of public policy who are attracted to municipal office and then inevitably botch whatever is available to be botched? Do people of substance and intelligence realize that the game is not worth the candle and stay away? If that were so, the people running our cities would by definition be unable to rescue the places where they live. There is truth to the proposition, but not enough. Inadequate and confused people, even the venal and suspect, often fill high municipal office. But exceptional people also seek and sometimes attain the office of mayor. And sometimes they do exceptional things. Good or bad, all mayors face the same structural problems. They are constrained, hampered, hobbled and frustrated by the constitutional, economic and political reality of Canadian cities.

Canada faces a political and constitutional crisis. It has nothing to do with abolishing the Senate or giving greater autonomy to Quebec. The cities, where the overwhelming majority of Canadians live, and which provide essential services to their citizens, are in an impossible situation. Mayors have neither the political power nor the financial resources they need to do their job. There is a constitutional and political inversion—those who should be first are last; those who should be last are first. Sam Katz, the mayor of Winnipeg from 2004 to 2014, said to me when he was still in office, "Why should I have to kowtow to the province when 70 per cent of all Manitobans live in my city?"

The Canadian constitution should be renegotiated and redrawn to reflect modern reality. But that is unlikely to happen; the political forces and technical difficulties arrayed against it are too great. Constitutional change in favour of cities would require provincial governments to surrender great power. As a political matter, they will not agree to do so. Amending Canada's constitution requires the approval of the Senate and the House of Commons, and of the legislative assemblies of at least two-thirds of the provinces with at least 50 per cent of the population of all provinces. It is easy for a few provinces to block constitutional changes giving cities more independence and power.

That does not mean we are bereft of solutions. A new breed of municipal politician would make a difference. That would be a politician who treats the electorate as adults—who, in a campaign for mayor, says, "If you elect me, I will go to the provincial government on the day after my election and begin to negotiate new entrenched powers for the city. These powers will include the ability to create an income tax and a sales tax. We have to be able to pay for what we want and need." This is a candidate able to persuade the electorate of the rightness of this mature approach—one who does not rely on slogans, rhetoric and ill-considered uncosted promises. This is a candidate who understands the political capital of cities—who knows that although cities are provincial creations, the provinces cannot exist without them, and that ultimately the cities can be and should be more powerful than the provinces.

"Devo-max" is a neologism that was coined in the United Kingdom to describe full fiscal autonomy for Scotland as an alternative to independence. It is an arrangement in which a central government transfers (or "devolves") the maximum amount of authority to a junior government, while still retaining sovereignty over it. Boris Johnson, the mayor of London, argues that devo-max should apply to London and other major British cities. The current British government is sympathetic to the idea. I propose devo-max for the cities of Canada. Canadian municipal government must be rescued. It is the greatest political challenge now facing the country.

ONE
TO THE CITY

IT WAS A FEW MINUTES past six in the morning. Time to leave. Were the windows closed? The hurricane season would begin soon; in a bad storm, a lot of water could get in through a window that wasn't tightly shut. I looked out to sea. It was calm for now. I picked up my suitcase, went out of our old house, locked the front door, got into my car and left the Nova Scotia fishing village of Port Medway, population 220—one general store; two churches, Anglican and Baptist; everyone white (except for a few Mi'kmaq residents); only English spoken (except for Claude, who comes from Montreal); and my home for part of the year, a place where I know just about everybody. I headed to Halifax airport, two hours down Highway 103, one of the worst highways in the country, for a flight to Toronto.

Hours later, the Boeing 737 began its final approach to Lester B. Pearson International Airport. Toronto stretched densely and drably in all directions beneath the airplane: huge squares, formed by criss-crossing roads, of look-alike houses; flat-roofed industrial buildings cheek by jowl, hedged in by semi-trailers; skyscrapers nudging each other in the downtown distance; highways, jammed with cars, joining up at spaghetti junctions; churches, mosques, synagogues, temples, basilicas;

sprawl, size, dirt, noise; a babel of languages, colours and faces of people from all over the world; people working, scheming, stealing, making love, making deliveries, doing everything that can be imagined and some things that cannot. Who could understand a place like this? How could anyone govern such a city— with its multitude of conflicting beliefs and ambitions, its endless complexity and mystery, its alliances, rivalries and hatreds?

•••

As the monster is to Dr. Frankenstein, so the city is to the province. Section 92(8) of Canada's Constitution Act, 1867 says, "In each Province the Legislature may exclusively make Laws in relation to … Municipal Institutions in the Province." The city is the province's creation. It has the shape and powers bestowed upon it by its creator.

Every Canadian province and territory has a general municipal act that grants enumerated powers to its cities. Statutes other than the municipal act may give municipalities additional powers, or may control them in some way—for instance, a law about land-use planning could include restrictive greenbelt legislation. Some big cities are so-called charter cities, meaning they do not rely on the province's general municipal act but have their own individual legislation, their charter, which has supposedly been tailored to meet particular circumstances. Halifax, Montreal, Toronto, Winnipeg and Vancouver are charter cities. Calgary and Edmonton would like to be, and have been negotiating with the Alberta government for some time. In October 2014, Calgary and Edmonton entered into a framework agreement with the province that promised them new powers and duties by 2016. But the current premier of Alberta, Jim Prentice, has said that there is "no way" they will be given new taxation powers, thus undermining the whole process. Calgary mayor Naheed Nenshi has said, "I am the mayor of a city that has more people than five provinces.... And yet I have the exact same decision-making authority and powers at my city council as the mayor of, you know, Rosebud, Alberta. And it just doesn't work."[1]

But Mayor Nenshi is barking up the wrong tree in pursuing a traditional charter. A charter city's presumed independence is illusory. A charter is nothing more than another provincial statute, and so it can be amended by the legislature at any time, as it pleases, with or without consulting the city in question. A charter city, like any other city, is a creature of its province, subject to its creator's whims and politics and any legal restrictions it imposes. When Winnipeg mayor Sam Katz wanted to lower the speed limit around city schools to thirty kilometres an hour, he discovered that under the provincial Highway Traffic Act, only the province had the power to make such a change. The city couldn't legislate school zone limits by itself. When Vancouver needed to borrow money to build the 2010 Olympic Village, the Vancouver Charter had to be amended by the province to permit the financing. When some Toronto city councillors wanted to get rid of Mayor Rob Ford in the fall of 2013, they discovered there was no mechanism that made it possible. The province of Ontario would have to amend the 2006 City of Toronto Act, and the province wouldn't oblige. Disillusioned Torontonians looked with envy to Quebec, where 2013 legislation—Bill 10—allows a judge to suspend a municipal politician facing criminal charges, and where the 2011 municipal ethics code permits the province to suspend a mayor for ninety days, even if he or she is not facing criminal charges.

Sometimes a province, toying with a city, bestows upon it powers and correlative responsibilities the city does not want.

The province gives the city more than it can afford, more than it needs, and this is not a gift the city can refuse. The most famous example is the "downloading" of social services to Ontario cities by the government of Premier Mike Harris, a process that began in 1995 and was cynically designed to give the province room to make promised income tax cuts and the devil take the hindmost. (The effects of downloading have been partially reversed by "uploading," which began in 2008 as the result of an agreement between the cities and the province.) Downloading was part of Ontario's so-called Common Sense Revolution; it included the amalgamation of municipalities (75 per cent voted against amalgamation in a referendum, but that didn't stop Mike Harris), a policy later imitated and then partly reversed by Montreal. Amalgamation was intended to slash the cost of government, but a study in 2013 found that after amalgamation, more people than ever were working for Ontario municipalities, partly because of the effect of downloading. The amalgamation experience in Montreal was the same. Economies of scale were elusive. Costs increased. In 2001, when he was mayor of a recently amalgamated Halifax (that amalgamation happened in 1996), Peter Kelly warned, "If you're doing amalgamation to save money, don't do it." In Toronto there are still those who speak out against amalgamation and want to emulate Montreal's de-amalgamation. Mostly these people live downtown and consider themselves politically oppressed by suburban dwellers, who prefer automobiles to public transit and bike lanes. But journalist John Barber has argued that suburbanites were the real losers in amalgamation. The old Metropolitan Toronto, says Barber, "was a brilliant innovation that let localism thrive while leveraging the downtown tax base for massive, cross-border public works—focused mainly on building and servicing the suburbs."[2] The banner of de-amalgamation yet flies in parts of Toronto.

•••

Where does the money to run a city come from? Cities are as controlled and constrained in their revenues as they are in their powers. They have four basic sources of income: property taxes, user and licence fees, transfers from the provincial government (either unconditional or for particular projects), and grants from the federal government for special purposes.

In Canada, property taxation—widely and correctly regarded as inelastic, regressive (that is, taking a higher percentage of income from low-income people than from high-income people) and inequitable—amounts on average to 40 to 50 per cent of a city's revenue (in the United States, it is about 15 per cent). User and licence fees, such as bus fares, parking charges, water rates and admission charges for the municipal zoo account for about 25 per cent of revenue. Transfers from government, largely the provincial government, make up most of the rest; these transfers are mostly operating grants for social services. There is little direct financial relationship between cities and the federal government, although sometimes, under federal–provincial agreements, money transferred by a province to a municipality comes in whole or in part from the federal government, and sometimes there may be explicit tri-level financial arrangements. An example of a transfer from the federal government to municipalities via provincial governments is the federal Gas Tax Fund, which is designed to finance infrastructure.

Almost everyone agrees that the existing revenue sources for cities are grossly inadequate. In particular, they do not address the massive infrastructure deficit that exists, particularly in transportation systems. The consequence is that the cities must, on bended knee, take their begging bowls to the province, and indirectly to the federal government as well. They must make the begging-bowl trip frequently. And they may be going to a provincial government that is itself broke and depends upon transfer payments from the Government of Canada—Nova Scotia, say, or even Ontario. Municipal grovelling for funds can take many forms. A common request is a percentage point of the provincial sales tax. Compelling arguments that municipalities should levy income taxes or collect their own sales taxes are ignored by the provinces. (Some Quebec municipalities, including Montreal, used to have a sales tax, but the province ended this practice in 1965. The grants that replaced the sales taxes ended in 1980.)

Take Winnipeg as an example. On May 18, 2007, Bartley Kives of the *Winnipeg Free Press* wrote, "City council continues to quietly seethe about city-provincial relations, especially when it comes to three areas: money, the power to spend that money and recognition of the city's role as Manitoba's primary economic engine. Last week, Winnipeg Mayor Sam Katz broke with his long-standing policy of going through diplomatic channels by using the media to relay a message to all three major Manitoba political parties: The city wants a single grant from the province every year instead of receiving $158 million in dribs and drabs tied to specific projects."[3] On May 22, 2007, the NDP was re-elected as Manitoba's provincial government. Mayor Katz's single-grant proposal, a modest request in the scheme of things, was completely ignored. Six long years later, the mayors of Manitoba's largest urban centres were still singing the same tune, and condemning the provincial government for failing to address their infrastructure priorities.[4]

This story is commonplace and never changes. In June 2004, at the National Forum on Economic Growth of Big Cities in Canada, twenty-two big-city mayors proposed comprehensive partnership agreements between levels of government and each big city. These agreements were to address, among other things, the revenue needs of the big cities. But the proposal fell on deaf ears. What a surprise! Ten years later, in 2014, Naheed Nenshi observed: "Citizens of Calgary send to our provincial government $4 billion a year more than we receive back in services from the provincial government. To the federal government we send $10 billion a year. That's the fiscal imbalance in this country. We're not asking for a handout. When you see me and my fellow mayors with our hands out, we're not asking for a handout, we're asking for a small tax rebate."[5]

Senior levels of government will always make the cities dangle on the end of a string and pay a substantial price for any concessions they are grudgingly given. The provinces are vigilant in guarding their political and economic control of municipalities. If they let go of these fiefdoms, they would be dramatically diminished. What would be left of a province if you took away its cities? A quaint rural hinterland. For the most part, the provinces look with horror upon the possibility—raised from time to time by people of good faith, and by cities themselves—of urban areas acquiring some kind of constitutional independence, of major cities becoming "city-provinces."

Quebec might become an exception to this sorry tale of dependence. In April 2014, the new Liberal government announced that Montreal and Quebec City would be given "special status," with more autonomy over issues like social housing and transportation, and with increased revenue to match that greater autonomy. (Montreal had been pushing this idea since at least 2006, when Mayor Gérald Tremblay presented a position paper on the subject to Premier Jean Charest.) Municipal Affairs Minister Pierre Moreau said in April 2014 that he was open to creating a charter to give all municipalities greater powers and new sources of revenue.[6] He said he was amenable to recognizing municipalities as independent governments. He said the process would take at least two years, and a committee of experts would determine what powers and funds would be transferred to Montreal. Moreau seems more sympathetic toward his province's big cities than Premier Jim Prentice of Alberta. We shall see. Perhaps, in Quebec and Alberta, the granting of "new powers and duties" will amount to nothing more than downloading disguised. There is always that danger.

It's an uneasy threesome—the city, the province and the federal government. Each eyes the others nervously, vying for voters, competing for power and money. The city always seems to lose. What else would you expect? The city is a puppet. The province is the puppet master. The federal government hides in the wings, a voyeur.

•••

Who would want to try to run a city? Why would anyone want to be a big-city mayor? Cities are extraordinarily complex and face great and conflicting demands; they are constitutionally dependent on the whims of their provincial masters; they have inadequate financial resources and must resort to begging. The mayors of these political and economic cripples have no real ability to change things. Most of them belong to a so-called weak mayor system, with little or no control over either the municipal council or the city's administrative bureaucracy. The bureaucracy really runs things, and in many cases it reports directly to council, bypassing the mayor. When Joe Pennachetti, the city manager of Toronto, announced in August 2014 that he was retiring, an article in the *Toronto Star* had the headline "Toronto's Real Power Job Is Up for Grabs" and said the role Pennachetti played "is the biggest stick in the city." In November 2014, Toronto's mayor-elect, John Tory, convinced Pennachetti to postpone his retirement. After all, who else was going to run the city?

Who wants the job of mayor? Some are glory seekers. Glory seekers don't understand the position they pursue. They are fooled by the accoutrements—the title, the big desk, the flag in the corner, the chain of office, the media attention, the official car (sometimes with chauffeur), the plethora of assistants. They look forward to wielding power that, if elected, they will find non-existent. They don't understand that their political platform, if they have one, may never be implemented. They remind me of the former chief justice of California who said of his appointment, "They handed me the reins of power, but the reins weren't attached to anything."

Some who want to be mayor are office seekers. They are professional and perennial politicians, bouncing back and forth in a ballet of ambition between various levels of government, seeking to be elected in one place if they suffer setbacks in another, always looking for a political resting place. Gérald Tremblay was a member of the Quebec National Assembly and a provincial Cabinet minister before he became mayor of Montreal. Joe Fontana of London, Ontario, left federal politics, seeking what he thought would be greener pastures (they turned out to be not so green). Peter Kelly of Halifax tried but failed to secure a Conservative federal nomination and still harbours provincial or federal political ambitions (although weirdly he is now chief administrative officer of a small county in Alberta). Ottawa's Jim Watson was a city councillor and had held several provincial Cabinet positions before he ran for mayor—a job he'd held once before. Glen Murray quit as mayor of Winnipeg to run unsuccessfully for a federal parliamentary seat and is now an Ontario Cabinet minister. George Smitherman was a provincial Cabinet minister and then ran unsuccessfully for mayor of Toronto. Gregor Robertson was a member of the Legislative Assembly of British Columbia and then became mayor of Vancouver; he is now rumoured to have his eye on the federal Parliament. These once and future mayors want a home and need a job. Or perhaps they suffer from an addiction. Reykjavik's Jón Gnarr has observed, "Entering politics is kind of like taking up drugs. Politics is an environment of addiction."[7]

Some who seek the office of mayor are idealists. David Brooks of *The New York Times* writes about those who "hope that politics can transform society and provide meaning."[8] Toronto's David Crombie is an example of mayor as idealist. Inspired by Jane Jacobs, the famous left-wing urban theorist and activist, Crombie wanted community interests to trump the ambitions of property developers. It's more than thirty-five years since Crombie was Toronto's "tiny perfect mayor," but many still yearn for his kind of stewardship. The mayors of Edmonton and Vancouver are regarded by some as idealists, with their apparent devotion to high-density living, eradicating homelessness and the green agenda.

Some who want to be mayor are pragmatists. The pragmatist is often an urban policy wonk. He is interested in cities—perhaps has an abstract passion for them—and there are particular things, sometimes quite technical and complicated, that he wants to accomplish. Maybe he wants to improve public transport in some way. Or legalize basement rental suites. Or construct a network of bike lanes. Naheed Nenshi of Calgary is a pragmatist. An idealist too, perhaps. The categories can, and often do, overlap.

Maybe there is one other kind of person who sometimes seeks the job of mayor. On a visit to Montreal, I met with the admirable Linda Gyulai, who covers city hall for the *Gazette*. We had breakfast at Ben & Florentine, a café on Mansfield

Street near Place Ville Marie and not far from the newspaper's office on Sainte-Catherine. Gyulai has been doggedly covering Montreal and Laval municipal politics for many years, and she won the 2009 Michener Award for her reporting on the gross mishandling of a water management project, the largest contract in Montreal's history. I described my mayoral categories to her—glory seekers, office seekers, idealists and pragmatists. She smiled. "Maybe there's another category," she said. I asked her what it was. "Psychopaths," she replied.

•••

Mayors cannot rule, but they can lead. They can embody and articulate the aspirations of the citizenry. They can inspire. They can make people feel good about where they live. They can make them feel optimistic about the future and willing to work toward it. They can make them think. To do this, a mayor must be a person of substance and intellect, able to set an appropriate example. As David Crombie put it to me, "A mayor may not have much power, but he has *authority*. He has a bully pulpit. People listen to what he has to say *because he is the mayor*" (italics added). In our system, the mayor is the only municipal official elected city-wide—the only person who can speak for everyone. James Lightbody, a professor of political science at the University of Alberta, writes, "Being elected by all citizens presumably provides a moral suasion for the mayor's platform among the council, and the mayor can, as a result, speak for the entire community on most issues of consequence."[9] Or as journalist Edward Keenan put it, "The mayor is the personification of the city's character and mood."[10] But a mayor must be able to grasp the opportunity presented by the bully pulpit. Few can.

Of the mayors I write about in this book, Nenshi of Calgary is an example of someone who speaks to the city from the bully pulpit and makes its inhabitants feel good. This was particularly evident during the 2013 Calgary flood. Iveson of Edmonton and Robertson of Vancouver have some of this ability, but they have shown it only sporadically. No other mayor I write about has shown leadership in this sense.

One distinctive, almost defining feature of many of Canada's big-city mayors is their closeness to the citizenry. Even after Gilles Vaillancourt of Laval had resigned in disgrace, one adoring resident said, "He constantly left the refuge of city hall and engaged his fellow citizens upfront and personally, often joining them in their daily lives."[11] In some cities, a citizen is able to call the mayor directly and ask for action and get it. If you lived in Toronto and your furnace broke down at midnight, you used to be able to call Rob Ford at home and—so the fantasy went—he'd come right over (John Tory won't). If your water pipes were frozen in Winnipeg, you could call Sam Katz and he'd send out a city crew immediately to fix them (I was told this story by a grateful Winnipeg resident). When was the last time you called the prime minister or your provincial premier to complain, got through and got action? Sam Katz jokes that people would call him up all the time to complain about things he had no control over—waiting times at hospital emergency rooms, for example. "The average citizen has a pretty weak grasp of what levels of government are responsible for what," he says. Then he added, "But I always did what I could."

•••

There is little formal party politics in the cities of Canada—another reason for the political weakness of mayors—although municipal politicians often have links to provincial and federal political organizations. (In the 2014 Toronto election, Olivia Chow, formerly a New Democratic member of Parliament, was widely regarded as the NDP candidate.) Occasional attempts by national parties to enter city politics directly have failed. In some provinces (Ontario is one), local parties are banned from fielding candidates in municipal elections. But there's more than one kind of party. Larry O'Brien, mayor of Ottawa from 2006 to 2010, told me that his city had municipal party politics all right. He said that each of his twenty-three city councillors "was a member of the same party—the party of me."

Only Montreal and Vancouver have anything that looks like organized local politics. There is nothing of the kind in Halifax, Toronto, Mississauga, Brampton, Ottawa, London, Winnipeg, Calgary or Edmonton. You may be mayor of Toronto or Halifax, but you control only one vote: your own. Your fate is always to be cobbling together shifting coalitions. That might seem to be a bad way to run a government, but David Crombie—mayor of Toronto from 1972 to 1978, and widely considered to have been very successful in the job—told me that's exactly what a mayor should be doing, constantly going directly to the people and persuading them that he is right on this or that issue. David Miller, mayor of Toronto from 2003 to 2010, has expressed a similar view.

In Montreal, there have been political parties, but their principal purpose was always to promote an individual candidate. Jean Drapeau, mayor of Montreal for thirty years, formed the Civic Party in 1960; it did not survive his retirement in 1986. The Montreal Island Citizens Union, later renamed Union Montreal, was a creature of Gérald Tremblay, mayor for ten years, and was dissolved in 2013, after Tremblay resigned. The current mayor of Montreal, Denis Coderre, "led" a party called

Équipe Denis Coderre, created a few months before he ran for the office. Coderre said of this party, "It's not really a political party. When it comes to a city, it's an administration, it's not a legislature. As soon as we are elected, the political party will not exist. There will be [a] leader and all that, but it won't exist."[12] It is the same in Laval, the third-biggest city in Quebec. The party PRO des Lavallois was not a genuine party, but merely a useful vehicle for (now disgraced) Laval mayor Gilles Vaillancourt.

In Vancouver, genuine party politics has taken hold—the only Canadian city where this has happened. After the November 2014 election, six of the ten city councillors and the mayor, Gregor Robertson, were members of Vision Vancouver, a centre-left party that first elected councillors in 2005. Three councillors belonged to the centre-right Non-Partisan Association (the NPA), and one was a member of the Green Party. The NPA was formed in 1937 and has been an important political force since then. Sam Sullivan, mayor from 2005 to 2008, was a member of the NPA. If you want to run as mayor on the Vision Vancouver or NPA ticket, you must first secure that party's nomination in what is often a hotly contested battle.

Views on the value of political parties in city government are divided. Some say they stifle free speech and force council- lors to toe party lines. Others argue that many voices are better than one when it comes to advancing a larger vision, and that political parties at the municipal level promote democratic accountability. On the accountability issue, political consultant Robin Sears has noted that if Rob Ford had been elected leader of a political party, his caucus colleagues would have thrown him out early on in the Ford scandal. Preston Manning has made the same point.

Adam Vaughan, a former Toronto councillor of considerable reputation and now a Liberal member of Parliament, is totally against political parties at the city level. "My job was to represent my constituents and no one else," he told me. The former three-term mayor of Halifax, Peter Kelly, said to me that party politics in a municipality would be poison. "It is against democracy," he said. "A councillor must be independent, free to bring his constituents' views to the table." I mentioned Peter Kelly's views to David Crombie. He agreed vigorously. Sam Katz, mayor of Winnipeg, says he "believes in people, not political parties." Naheed Nenshi has frequently praised the "non-partisanship" of his city council. Views like these are in keeping with the great era of municipal reform in the latter half of the nineteenth century, although that movement was not rooted in concepts of democracy. Political scientist Andrew Sancton has written, "The most important effect of the reform movement was to convince most Canadian urban municipal voters that political parties served no purpose in municipal politics because they introduced political factors into decisions that should be based only on sound business-like and technical principles."[13]

Henry Aubin, who covered Montreal city politics for the *Gazette* for many years, believes a municipal party system promotes dishonesty. He told me that in his view, parties are just money-collecting machines, devoid of ideals. "They facilitate and promote corruption," he asserted. "It is much easier to corrupt a party than a bunch of individuals." Without a party, so the argument goes, there is no political machine to buy votes and deliver gifts to friends. There is no Boss Tweed of Tammany Hall, the political machine that controlled Manhattan's Democratic Party for 150 years and believed in "honest graft."[14] Former Ontario premier and member of Parliament Bob Rae, who knows something about politics, disagrees with this analysis. He says that municipal politicians without parties are "too close to the coal face. There are too few obstacles to bad behaviour. It's easy to get away with stuff." Anne Golden, former president of the Conference Board of Canada, has made a similar observation, pointing out that in the absence of political parties, there is no vetting of candidates.

James Lightbody is a strong and cogent advocate for political parties in municipal government.[15] He argues that the traditional case against municipal party politics is weak. That case, he writes, pivots around four points. The first is that party politics leads inescapably to corruption. But, Lightbody writes, any corruption in Canadian cities has been quite independent of the presence or absence of local parties; there's no apparent connection between the two. The second line of attack on city party politics is that "there is no 'Liberal' or 'Conservative' way to pave a street." (Naheed Nenshi is a particular fan of this argument.) Lightbody replies, "It is only a question of scale that differentiates a city street from a provincial highway.… It can as easily be argued that there is no Conservative or Liberal way to conduct federal–provincial negotiations or to administer education or health care." This seems a trifle disingenuous; federal–provincial negotiations can be very much along party lines. The third standard argument is "that partisanship produces caucuses and that the real policy choices will be made in private." Lightbody responds, "All legislatures function by allowing members to settle marginal differences privately." The last point is that party organization of council work is inappropriate for smaller councils—to which Lightbody says, "Disruption is probable in any human conclave where personal and political differences exist."

Without political parties, argues Lightbody, there is no focused authority or political clarity. I agree with him. Focused authority, political clarity and discipline are essential needs of Canadian big-city governance. Only political parties can fill these needs.

•••

Contrary to myth, the participation rate in most municipal elections is relatively high. People care about what city politicians do. Most find it hard to get worked up over Canadian policy toward Somalia or what kind of fighter jets should be bought for the air force, but they can easily get agitated over poor public transit, inadequate policing, polluted harbours, bike lanes, lousy street lighting or a mayor who smokes crack cocaine. A Leger-Yahoo Canada poll reported in November 2013 that most Canadians—around 70 per cent of those eligible—had voted in their last municipal election.[16] The poll found that in all parts of Canada except Quebec, voters believe their municipal vote makes the most difference. (In Quebec, voters think provincial elections are more important.)

Here's the surprise. The Leger-Yahoo Canada poll determined that 42 per cent of Canadians are satisfied with their municipal governments, compared to 28 per cent with the federal government and 26 per cent with the provincial government. Forty-two per cent satisfied with their municipal governments? How can that be? Look at the people who are mayors, and at how they behave.

The mayor of Huntingdon, Quebec, Stéphane Gendron, was forced to apologize for saying he liked to run over newborn kittens in his car. "'Stray cats have no business on the street,' he said, raising his voice to a shout for dramatic emphasis: 'So bang! I accelerate.'"[17] Presumably Mayor Gendron thought this was funny. Andy Wells, the "gruff and outspoken" mayor of St. John's from 1997 to 2008, called David Suzuki and Al Gore "junk scientists" and was nominated by Rick Mercer as "Craziest Mayor in Canada." Mayor Keith Hobbs of Thunder Bay marked the 2012 International Day for the Elimination of

Racial Discrimination by apologizing for racist remarks he had made in the past. Cornwall (Ontario) mayor Bob Kilger, a former NHL lineman and Liberal member of Parliament (and nicknamed Bare Ass Bob for reasons unknown), has been accused of conflict of interest (the fire department hired his son) and threw the owner of a local news website out of a council meeting for refusing to change out of a shirt showing the mayor's face on a milk carton. Sam Sullivan, Vancouver mayor from 2005 to 2008, was kept busy explaining why, before he became mayor, he gave a prostitute money for heroin and allowed a man to smoke crack in his van. He told the *Vancouver Sun* that he'd checked out his situation with the city clerk, and "he confirmed I could still be the mayor if I was in jail and I could get day passes for the council meetings."[18] Sylvie St-Jean, mayor of the Montreal suburb of Boisbriand from 2005 to 2009, was arrested in February 2011 and pleaded guilty to four fraud-related charges. Richard Marcotte was mayor of Mascouche, another Montreal bedroom community, from 1992 until 2012. He was arrested in April 2012 at Montreal's Pierre Elliott Trudeau International Airport as he arrived back from a Cuban vacation. He resigned in November of that year, faced with a variety of fraud, breach of trust, corruption and conspiracy charges connected with the construction industry. "It's 22 years of my life I am leaving," Marcotte said. "What was Mascouche 22 years ago? I was the mastermind of the city's development."[19]

The more distant past was not much better. Ed McKitka, mayor of Surrey, B.C., from 1975 to 1977, went to prison for breach of trust. He was subsequently convicted of sexually assaulting teenage girls while on parole. An alderman once called McKitka "the south end of a northbound horse." Perhaps the most famous Canadian rogue mayor—at least until Rob Ford—was William Hawrelak, mayor of Edmonton on and off in the 1950s, 1960s and 1970s. Hawrelak—known as Wild

Bill—was twice removed from office for gaining personally from land transactions involving the city, including attempts to influence the zoning of land he owned. One commentator wrote of Hawrelak's "inability, or unwillingness, to draw a line between his political and business interests."[20] He died in office.

Meanwhile, Nathalie Simon, mayor of the Montreal suburb of Châteauguay, was hailed as a hero in 2013 when she reported an attempted bribe to the police. In an interview with a reporter, Simon said, "It's sad that an honest act can be seen as the exception, as a gesture of courage. I was a little taken aback, but I guess the tendency these days is to blame elected officials for every ill."[21] Robert Lafrenière, head of the provincial anti-corruption squad, held a news conference to praise Ms. Simon. "It's a rarity," he said.

Bad as all this seems, it is nothing compared to the recent record of mayors in the United States. In November 2013, during the Rob Ford scandal, the *Huffington Post* ran an article entitled "24 U.S. Mayors Who Prove We're Also Better Than Canada at Electing Embarrassing Officials."[22] The roll call is extraordinary. It includes Bob Filner of San Diego, who was sentenced to three months of house arrest and three years of probation for harassing women during his term as mayor; Kwame Kilpatrick, who in 2013 was sentenced to twenty-eight years in prison for corruption, extortion and fraud committed while he was mayor of Detroit; Sheila Dixon, who resigned as mayor of Baltimore in 2010 after being found guilty of using retail store gift cards that had been designated for poor families; and Larry Guidi, mayor of Hawthorne, California, who stole a commercial food mixer from a local school district so that he could make pizza dough at home.

In February 2014, the former mayor of New Orleans, Ray Nagin, was found guilty in federal court on twenty counts of bribery, money laundering and fraud. In July, he was sentenced to ten years in prison. Nagin had awarded city contracts to businessmen who in exchange gave him cash, trips and other gifts. In March 2014, Patrick Cannon, the mayor of Charlotte, North Carolina, resigned after he was arrested on public corruption charges. In June 2014, the mayor of San Marino, California, Dennis Kneier, resigned after he was caught on a security camera throwing a bag of dog excrement onto a neighbour's yard. (The mayor was upset by the neighbour's opposition to a proposed dog park.)

On June 25, 2014, Vincent "Buddy" Cianci, one-time mayor of Providence, Rhode Island, announced he was going to run again. *The Economist* reported:

> Mr. Cianci's previous stints as mayor ended badly. In 1984, after a decade on the job, he had to resign when he was convicted of assaulting a man with a cigarette, an ashtray and a log. In 1990 he convinced voters to give him another shot, and did much to spruce up the city centre. But in 2002 he was brought down by a federal racketeering probe that landed him in prison for nearly five years. To add insult to injury, a musical based on his life premiered off-Broadway in 2003, featuring catchy numbers like "The Ass You Have to Kiss Today" and "The Armpit of New England" (an unkind reference to Providence).[23]

Campbell Robertson of *The New York Times* has pointed out that scandal does not always result in a politician's defeat at the polls. "All across the country," he writes, "politicians have faced opponents tainted by scandal, some of them seemingly muddied beyond saving, and have gone on to lose."[24]

Why can scandal-tainted candidates still win elections? It is because the worlds of politics and entertainment have converged. To succeed, politicians must entertain. If they are not amusing or compelling, they will be punished at the polls. However competent a candidate may be—however far-seeing her policies and proposals—she is likely to fail if she is dull. However foolish a candidate may be—however silly his ideas—he will succeed if he becomes a celebrity, grabs headlines and makes us laugh. The height of political achievement is to be a guest on Jon Stewart's *Daily Show* or to banter live with Jimmy Kimmel; it doesn't matter that your television appearance shows you in a bad light, provided those watching it have fun.

Entertainers become politicians. Reykjavik's Jón Gnarr was a former punk rocker and stand-up comedian, and he created a TV series when his career in municipal politics was over. Italian comic Beppe Grillo founded the Five Star Movement, which won 26 per cent of the vote for the Chamber of Deputies in the 2013 Italian election, making it the largest single party in the chamber. Boris Johnson, mayor of London, is often thought of as principally a comedian, albeit an amateur. American humorist Calvin Trillin has written, "There was a time when I thought that some slightly eccentric mayors were being elected in large American cities partly because the voters, figuring that large American cities were ungovernable anyway, decided that they might as well put someone in city hall who was at least entertaining."[25]

And politicians become entertainers. Why should we be surprised? One of the most perceptive comments about politics and the media came from the television critic of the *Globe and Mail*, John Doyle. He compared an interview of Lindsay Lohan by Oprah Winfrey to Matt Galloway's CBC Radio interview of Rob Ford. "The two events illustrate how traditional, firm narratives reported and spread by traditional news media have been shattered," Doyle wrote. "[Ford] knows … that in the chaos of the Internet age, a lot of people don't know or care what's real or what's merely sensational half-truths or biased opinion."[26] Anne Golden has made a similar point in discussing the Rob Ford phenomenon. Ford's appeal, she argues, aligns with contemporary cultural standards. His language and exploits, which once would have been seen as highly offensive, are now acceptable, even appealing. In the age of the Internet, when raunchiness and foulness of the most intimate kind are everywhere, people just don't get embarrassed the way they once did.[27]

The worlds of politics and entertainment converge in many ways. Thom Ernst of the *Toronto Star* wrote, in an article on mayors and the movies, "Here are 10 films featuring polarizing mayors to help us make the transition until Ford returns or a new scandal averts our attention."[28] Ernst's list includes *Beau James* (1957), a biopic of New York's real-life mayor Jimmy Walker (served 1926–32), who resigned under suspicions of corruption and being an accessory to murder (with Bob Hope improbably in the lead role); *How the Grinch Stole Christmas* (2000), featuring the arrogant and manipulative mayor of Whoville; *The Toxic Avenger* (1984), which has a mayor who "masterminds a reign of terror that allows criminals and psychopaths to run wild"; and *City Hall* (1996), in which "being mayor of one of the world's greatest cities is merely a stepping stone towards a higher office." In the acclaimed Russian film *Leviathan* (2014), a village mayor is "a large man fuelled by vodka, paranoia and a huge sense of entitlement" and "conducts civic affairs like a gangster."[29]

Rob Ford has even spawned fan fiction. Robin Spano, a mystery writer from British Columbia, has published *High Times at City Hall* on Toronto-based Wattpad, a social publishing platform that aspires to be the YouTube of writing. (Spano asks,

"Who is Rob Ford when the cameras are off and the microphones aren't aimed at his face?") Monologist Mike Daisey has created a piece called *Dreaming of Rob Ford*. Says Daisey: "What I'm interested in is the dynamic of how the media and the public interact with a man we used to think of as a political figure who suddenly becomes a pop culture phenomenon.... What suddenly made Rob Ford the major media story in North America?... People pretend that he's just amusing, that he's a punching bag, a fool, a jester, but he's more than that. He's the backbeat, he's the bass line of the story that says we're letting the media decide what we're going to think about people."[30]

And there is an abundance of stage plays about the former mayor of Toronto. Brett McCaig created *Rob Ford the Musical: Birth of a Ford Nation* at Toronto's Factory Theatre. McCaig said, "The whole story is huge, so we thought, 'How do you make that even bigger?' and the next thing is, of course, singing and dancing."[31] There's the 2011 Toronto Fringe Festival's *Accidental Death of an Anarchist by the Coward Rob Ford*; the University of Toronto's Faculty of Music 2012 production of *Rob Ford: The Opera*; Theatre Passe Muraille's 2012 *It's a Wonderful Toronto*; David Ferry's 2014 *One Wild Night*; and Jason Hall's 2014 *21 Things You Should Know About Toronto's Crack-Smoking Mayor*. There are rumours that Alec Baldwin is developing a new cable television program in which he will play a Rob Ford–like mayor of New York City.

•••

In an ideal world, the concentration of population, wealth and power found in cities would be recognized in the constitution of Canada by giving municipalities an independent status. Such constitutional reform eclipses in importance other reforms suggested from time to time, such as abolition of the Senate. How much sense does it make for Prince Edward Island to have standing and powers not possessed by the city of Toronto? Yet this issue is little talked about, and is not on any serious political agenda.

Constitutions are not sacred. Jeffrey Toobin of the *New Yorker* reminds us that Thomas Jefferson believed any constitution should expire after nineteen years, which he elaborately calculated to be the span of a generation.[32] In a 1789 letter to James Madison, Jefferson wrote: "No society can make a perpetual constitution, or even a perpetual law. The earth belongs always to the living generation. They may manage it then, and what proceeds from it, as they please, during their usufruct. They are masters too of their own persons, and consequently may govern them as they please."[33] But the provinces would have to agree to enhance and entrench the status of cities, and they are not inclined to do so, for it would eviscerate them. Recognizing and empowering cities by reform of the constitution cannot be achieved, let alone having mayors rule the world, as one recent book proposes.[34]

But some things *can* be done. All major Canadian cities should become *real* charter cities, with specific city-by-city provincial legislation giving them greater powers and more autonomy than they now possess. These charters should be carefully and publicly debated and negotiated. It should be possible to amend a charter only with the specific and formal agreement of the city concerned—a kind of entrenchment; such a provision would give the city the autonomy and political power it needs. City charters should mandate new ways of collecting and generating revenue—notably through income taxes, retail sales taxes and the issuing of debt instruments with few restrictions—increasing the desperately inadequate revenue base of municipalities and releasing them from financial servitude.

As author Alan Broadbent has written, "To tax is to govern. Without an independent and adequate ability to raise the money to pay for the things that the city needs and wants, a government can never meet the expectations of its citizens."[35] In an interview, Toronto councillor Adam Vaughan argued that cities are essentially property managers and derive most of their revenue from real estate; to give cities an income tax, he asserted, would make it less necessary for them to pursue dubious development. Finally, political parties must enter the city arena, giving the municipal political process structure and discipline.

If these changes are made, the cities of Canada will have some sort of future and the job of mayor will be worth having. But before we sketch the future as it should be, let's take a figurative trip across Canada, from the Maritimes to the West Coast, zigzagging a little, dropping in on mayors past and present to see what's been going on. First we visit Peter Kelly, mayor of Halifax, Canada's fourteenth-largest city, from 2000 to 2012, and now chief administrative officer of Westlock County, Alberta, population seven thousand.

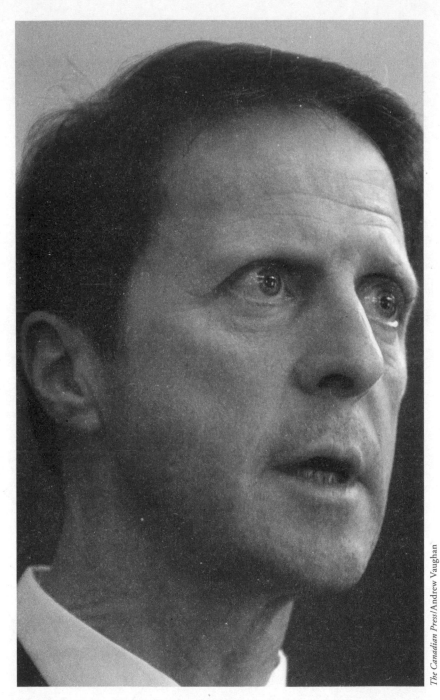

The Canadian Press/Andrew Vaughan

Peter Kelly, former mayor of Halifax, called himself a workaholic and often slept on the floor of his office. He declined to run again after a financial scandal involving a deceased friend's estate.

TWO
PETER KELLY OF HALIFAX
"Lessons Were Learned."

PETER KELLY was hard to find. I finally reached him by asking his lawyers to forward an email. After quite a while, I got a reply. We arranged to meet at Toronto's Pearson airport; he had a few hours' layover on his way to Calgary at the end of December 2013. Kelly came walking quickly through the arrivals door, a boyish-looking, slim middle-aged man in jeans. We went to a chicken restaurant on the departures level—I took the escalator, but Kelly vigorously bounded up the stairs alongside—and talked for two hours about his twelve years as mayor of Halifax. He was pleasant and easy, but he had few ideas and little vision. How could he have been mayor of a big city (and a smaller one before that), I wondered, and not have much that was interesting to say about municipal government? Perhaps I asked the wrong questions.

When it was time for him to leave, to resume his travel westward, I asked why he was going to Calgary. "To see my son," he said. "The one I recently discovered I have. He's thirty-six now." I asked how long he would be there. "I don't know," said Kelly. "Possibly weeks. My son doesn't even know I'm coming. I've rented a room at the other end of town from his place. I'll just go and knock on his door." Good luck, I said.

He gave me a bone-crushing handshake and we went our separate ways.

•••

Why does Tim Bousquet, a well-known Halifax investigative reporter, despise Peter Kelly? In May 2012, when Kelly was still mayor of Halifax, Bousquet wrote in *The Coast*, a free weekly newspaper: "Mayor Peter Kelly is a disgrace to the city of Halifax.… He has repeatedly dishonoured council and has destroyed the reputation of city government.… In years past, it was perhaps possible to think of Kelly as a bumbling fool. But the curtain has been pulled back, exposing Kelly for what he truly is—a calculating grifter."[1]

One evening in October 2013, I had dinner with Tim Bousquet at Edna's, a small restaurant on Gottingen Street in downtown Halifax, near the offices of *The Coast*. It was a Wednesday night, the week's newspaper had just been put to bed and Bousquet said he was exhausted. "I'm working on a really big story about the Halifax police," he told me. "It's wearing me out." Bousquet, now in his early fifties, came to Halifax from Chico, California, in 2004, and started writing for *The Coast* in 2006. He quickly established a reputation as a hard-driving traditional investigative journalist, an ink-stained shit-disturber, one of the very few left. "When I first clapped eyes on Kelly, he seemed familiar," Bousquet said. "I thought, I've seen this guy before; there's something familiar about him. I've seen guys like him in the States. Then I realized: I know what he is! He's a grifter!" Bousquet looked around the restaurant, which was pretty full. "We'd better lower our voices," he said, glancing at nearby tables. He leaned back in his chair and drank some wine.

Bousquet was not the only well-known Nova Scotia journalist who regularly attacked Kelly when he was mayor. Two heavyweight political commentators, Laura Fraser and Dan Leger of the *Chronicle Herald*, the major daily newspaper in the region, were charter members of the anti-Kelly chorus. Little favourable about the mayor appeared in any media while he was in office, particularly in his later years as chief magistrate. The pile-on struck me as odd and unattractive. Why did journalists hate Kelly so much? He may have been unimpressive, but he was hardly malevolent. Despite the extreme criticism, Peter Kelly struggled on, apparently buoyed by ego and sense of position, sometimes asserting himself in crazy ways, his judgment often askew, his decisions misguided, his political trajectory downward, a lonely and awkward protagonist in a minor tragedy, a sad and yet—to me, at least—strangely sympathetic figure.

•••

Peter Kelly was the mayor of the Halifax Regional Municipality (HRM) from 2000 to 2012, making him the longest-serving mayor in the history of the city. In 2000, Kelly got 55 per cent of the vote, running on a vague "back to basics" platform. He told me he was euphoric when he won. In 2004, he got an extraordinary 82 per cent of the vote. "It was because I'm a people person," he said. "The voters get that." In 2008, his percentage dropped to 53 per cent.

Kelly was born in 1956. He has a diploma in hospitality management from the Nova Scotia Community College and a master of business administration from Saint Mary's University. He briefly attended Guelph University in Ontario, but says he was thrown out after one year because "my social life was too active." He had a long political career before he became mayor of Halifax, beginning as a Bedford town councillor in 1985 (Bedford is near Halifax); he was elected mayor of Bedford in 1991. In 1995, Bedford became part of the newly amalgamated Halifax Regional Municipality, and Kelly was elected Bedford's councillor.

While Kelly was mayor of HRM, he sometimes slept on the floor of his office. "When you're sleeping on the floor," he said, "that's certainly a signal that maybe the balance is not there, but it's easy just to throw down a cushion and blanket and away you go."[2] He frequently told reporters that he worked ninety hours a week or more. "I'm a workaholic," he told me. "When I was in the hospitality industry, I worked 105 hours a week." He had a shower installed in the mayor's office suite. Maybe he worked all the time and slept on the floor and showered in his office because he was not welcome at home. He and his wife, Nancy, with whom he has two sons, split up during his tenure as mayor. He told me that Nancy made him promise not to answer the telephone when they were having supper with the kids, but he did it anyway. "I was mayor," he said. "I couldn't just let the telephone ring and ring." Recently Kelly discovered a third son, from a relationship he had in his early twenties; this was the son he was going to visit in Calgary when I met him at Pearson airport.

The mayor's behaviour often seemed odd. Sometimes he conducted interviews standing up, although his office had a comfortable sitting area. He sent memos to Halifax city councillors telling them to drink less alcohol. He was criticized for skateboarding without a helmet on Halifax Common (he fell off the skateboard but was unscathed). He went swimming in Halifax Harbour to show that cleanup attempts had been successful.[3] He was stopped at Halifax airport when security staff found a bullet in his bag. "Mr. Kelly said he found the bullet several weeks ago near City Hall in downtown Halifax and had every intention of turning it over to Halifax Regional Police, but simply forgot. Mr. Kelly explained: 'I had my briefcase bag in my office at the time and threw the bullet in the bag and, unfortunately, forgot about it until airport security found it this morning.'"[4]

Some saw Peter Kelly as amiable and bumbling, others as goofy and downright weird; some—like Tim Bousquet—considered him venal, corrupt and arrogant. One commentator wrote, "The mayor has a certain nebbish charm that appeals to voters. His humble, Everyman demeanour is punctuated by a slight stutter."[5] Bousquet admits that Kelly has a "nice guy, Nova Scotia, aw shucks" image, and that the stutter helped him politically.

Once he left office, in October 2012, Peter Kelly pretty much disappeared from public view. He closed his Twitter and Facebook accounts. He was spotted at the Sobey's grocery store in Mill Cove, near his hometown of Bedford. He has a pension of $75,000 a year from the city of Halifax. He said he was doing some consulting assignments. He was looking around for good opportunities. He said he hadn't given up on politics. He said people kept asking him to run for something. He said maybe he'd run in the next federal election, for the Conservatives or perhaps the Liberals. Maybe he'd run provincially. Or maybe, he told me, just maybe, he'd run for mayor of Halifax in 2016.

•••

The Halifax Regional Municipality has a population of about 400,000. It's the capital of Nova Scotia and the cultural centre of Atlantic Canada. It's full of well-known post-secondary educational institutions—Dalhousie, Mount Saint Vincent, Saint Mary's, the Nova Scotia College of Art and Design, and

King's College. The Canadian navy's Maritime Forces Atlantic (MARLANT), with its eighteen ships and submarines, is the city's single largest employer. But most people know Halifax not for its universities or cultural delights or military muscle, but for two things that happened a century ago: in 1912, the *Titanic* sank seven hundred kilometres southeast of the city (many of those who died are buried in three Halifax cemeteries; their graves are a major tourist destination), and in 1917, the city was levelled when a cargo ship laden with explosives collided with another ship in upper Halifax Harbour, setting off an explosion of unprecedented ferocity. In some ways, Halifax's identity, its place in the popular imagination of those who live elsewhere, remains fixed in the past, drawn from these two great historical events so often memorialized in books and movies, one ship sinking and another blowing up.

"Halifax is the best place to live in Canada—no, the world." That's what Peter Kelly said on his now-closed Twitter account. When it comes to Canada, he may have a point (not so much, perhaps, if you're talking about the entire world). For part of the year, I live on Nova Scotia's South Shore and visit Halifax from time to time, driving for an hour and a half up Highway 103, ranked the second most dangerous highway in Canada by the Canadian Automobile Association. Halifax has a sense of history and tradition—unlike Vancouver, its maritime cousin, which gives the impression of having popped up yesterday. It is reasonably prosperous, the only part of Nova Scotia that is (the population of the province has been dwindling as people leave to find work elsewhere). Halifax is the right size—big enough to offer whatever you want, small enough not to be overwhelming. It's sophisticated and attractive and easy to live in, although like other Canadian cities, it has fallen victim to poor planning and second-rate modern architecture. There is a pleasant boardwalk along the harbour, where you can look at old ships, buy BeaverTails and visit the Maritime Museum of the Atlantic and the Canadian Museum of Immigration at Pier 21, but the boardwalk is dotted with bunker-like hotels and overlooked by hideous office high-rises, and at one end is a horrible spaghetti junction of highway overpasses.

Is Halifax a "world-class city," to use the appalling expression beloved by local politicians and often invoked by Peter Kelly when he was mayor? Tim Bousquet answered that question in his normal no-holds-barred way: "Nova Scotia has a provincialism that's typical of colonial outposts: a sad need for outside validation, a craving for attention from the wider world.... The phrase 'world-class' shows up 442 different places on halifax.ca, the city's website, in documents dating from the formation of HRM in 1996, right up to last week."[6] Bousquet reports that David Miller, former mayor of Toronto, says the phrase "world-class city" is "both meaningless and demeaning.... When you say 'world-class' you're really saying something like, 'Well, we actually really don't like what we are, we want to try to be something else.'"

I asked Marq de Villiers, a well-known writer and winner of a Governor General's Literary Award who now lives in Nova Scotia, what he thought about calling Halifax a world-class city. He wrote, "It's stupid, but it doesn't have anything to do with what Halifax actually is, which is a small city of no world consequence, but that is quite interesting but could be better, and has a chance to do better when they tear down the Barrington interchange, make more parking and ... aaarrgh, doesn't matter."

•••

On February 16, 2012, *The Coast* published Bousquet's lengthy account of Peter Kelly's role as executor of the estate of Mary

Thibeault.[7] Peter Kelly and Mary Thibeault had been friends for a long time. When he was a boy, Kelly mowed the lawn at Prince's Lodge, the Bedford motel owned by Thibeault and her husband. In 1998, some years after her husband died, Thibeault sold the motel and moved to St. Petersburg, Florida. She died in her mobile home in December 2004 at the age of ninety-one. Kelly was both a beneficiary and the executor of the will. Twelve other people, and five charities, were also beneficiaries.

Shortly after Thibeault's death, and before he submitted an inventory of her property to the court as required by the Nova Scotia Probate Act, Kelly transferred $161,587.12 from the estate to himself. He claimed that Thibeault told him she wanted him and one of his sons to have $150,000 as a gift, and that the balance of the money was to cover expenses he had incurred as executor. The inventory filed in court by Kelly makes no mention of the transfer. For a long time, he failed to notify beneficiaries of Thibeault's estate of their inheritance, as required by law, and no distribution from the estate was made until more than four years after her death.

One week after Tim Bousquet's story appeared in *The Coast*, Kelly announced he would not run for re-election in November. "It's an acknowledgment that I screwed up personally," he said. A week later, he returned $145,000 to the estate. Several heirs petitioned the probate court to have him removed as executor. Their filing said, "We believe that Peter Kelly has not acted in the best interest of the estate and his lack of effort on his part shows disrespect for Mary E. Thibeault's final wishes." In September 2012, a judge removed Kelly as executor and ordered that an accounting of the estate be produced by October 1 (Kelly complied). Another beneficiary was appointed as the new executor.

On March 11, 2013, the tenacious Bousquet wrote his last story about Mayor Kelly and the Thibeault estate. "Eight years, three months and four days after Mary Thibeault died, Peter Kelly is now free of her estate,"[8] the story began. A confidential mediation between Kelly and the heirs had produced a settlement that the judge approved. To the puzzlement of many, the police said there would be no criminal investigation. Wrote Bousquet: "Has justice been served? Well, certainly not for the two heirs who have died in the eight years since Thibeault's death, never receiving their full inheritance. Other heirs have not died, but have aged considerably—one is now over 100 years old—and missed out on their inheritances when perhaps they could've made better use of them.... Then there are the charities, some of which are due at least $60,000, which they certainly could have used over the long years while Kelly mishandled the estate."

The Thibeault scandal stripped Peter Kelly of the moral authority that a democratic politician needs to govern. He was seen as untrustworthy. The people person was finished as mayor, and he knew it.

•••

Blame it on the Black Eyed Peas.

Halifax and Moncton have competed heavily for rock concerts in recent years. What rock concerts do for a city is unclear, but city fathers think they are a good idea. The Rolling Stones came to Halifax's North Common in 2006, but after that Moncton's Magnetic Hill got the upper hand as a concert venue. Halifax-boosters didn't like being bested by Moncton. It made Peter Kelly particularly unhappy. He felt that a world-class city like Halifax should have big rock and roll concerts. The mayor became actively involved in trying to acquire artists for Halifax, writing to agents and promoters to ask for help in signing performers, and forwarding concert ideas suggested by the public.[9] On November 13, 2007, he wrote to Creative Events Group, referring to the pressure that the HRM council was under to announce "a MAJOR rock and roll concert before the end of November."

In 2008, without informing the city's lawyer or bringing the matter before council, Kelly arranged for the city to advance substantial sums to Power Promotional Events, run by concert promoter Harold MacKay. Power needed the money to pay upfront expenses for concerts that were being planned. Repayment of the advances was partially contingent on ticket sales, which would have to be considerable for the city to get a full refund. Harold MacKay chased after U2, Bruce Springsteen and Celine Dion, but none of them came to Halifax. He was successful in getting Keith Urban to perform in 2008, and KISS and Paul McCartney in 2009, but the attendance figures for all three concerts were surprisingly poor. (About half as many tickets as expected were sold for the Paul McCartney concert.) Exactly how the losses were covered and what happened to those city advances is unclear, but it is certain that after the concerts, Power Promotional was in a parlous financial state.

On July 24, 2010, the Black Eyed Peas performed on Halifax Common. Again, the crowd was unexpectedly thin. Rumour had it that only five thousand tickets were sold. Many were given away in a careless fashion. Some were thrown onto a local beach, to be picked up by swimmers and sunbathers. A lot of people who didn't have tickets were let into the concert for nothing in a desperate attempt to save face. The city lost $360,000 on an unrefunded advance to Harold MacKay. In October 2010, Power Promotional went out of business. In March 2011, a city staffer leaked information about the Black Eyed Peas debacle to a city councillor. The city's auditor general, Larry Munroe, was brought into the picture. On June 7, he reported on what was now called the "concert loan scandal," or "cash for concerts."[10]

The auditor general's comments about Peter Kelly and senior Halifax officials, and the way they ignored proper financial procedures, were measured but damning. He said, "A number of individuals with senior roles in their organizations operated outside of their roles." He described official thinking that was "fundamentally flawed and reflects the culture of organizations which appear to lack an attitude of questioning, follow-up or accountability at the highest levels." He wrote,

> It is our thought, given the level of experience and involvement of Mr. Anstey [the city's acting chief administrative officer, and a lawyer] and Mayor Kelly in the public sector, each of these individuals should have known something out of the ordinary was occurring and should have asked more questions to determine if what they were contemplating and/or doing was appropriate, especially given the method of arranging for payments to be made to Power Promotional Events.... The overriding business culture of HRM does not always or consistently appear to be one of inquisitiveness, questioning or challenging of actions which do not appear reasonable. Simply put, one of the root causes for why this happened can be explained by understanding the HRM culture around these types of transactions.

Wayne Anstey resigned when the report was published. Many said he took the fall for the mayor, although no one understood why he should. Peter Kelly says Anstey should have told him that cash for concerts was improper but failed to do so. On June 21,

2011, council considered a vote to suspend the mayor, but it was defeated. The council meeting was a mess. "Councillors described a tense scene in the chamber. Some refused to vote and others said they couldn't support the motion without time to learn more about its effects. One veteran called the scene the worst he'd ever witnessed. Another said the city's government was self-destructing."[11] As for Kelly, his comment was, "Certainly, I stumbled in my enthusiasm in trying to secure concerts and big-name acts here, but lessons were learned."[12] Bousquet wrote, "Kelly worked with a small cabal of fellow conspirators to work around the city's normal financial controls ... in violation of the city charter."[13] Kelly told me that in the cash-for-concerts affair, he was "naive, stupid, I just didn't understand what was going on."

Word has it that Kelly was preparing to run federally as a Conservative candidate in Bedford—polling had been done and the results looked promising—but the concerts-for-cash scandal killed his candidacy. The Conservative Party wouldn't touch him.

•••

Halifax had its own version of the Occupy movement, the 2011 international protest against social inequality. In the fall of that year, a hundred or so angry people pitched tents downtown, in Grand Parade and Victoria Park. Kelly says he was sympathetic to the protesters' complaints and aims, but told them that their strategy and tactics were wrong. "I went there and I told them that instead of pitching tents, they should buy one share in big corporations and go to annual shareholders' meetings and complain there."

Sympathetic to their cause or not, Kelly decided the protesters had to be gone by Remembrance Day, November 11. No doubt many Haligonians felt the same way. Traditionally, Remembrance Day ceremonies are held on the Grand Parade. It's a solemn occasion, with no place for troublemakers. A secret council meeting to discuss what was to be done was held on November 8; it is not clear what happened at the meeting (even the councillors disagree about what was decided). What seems certain is that Kelly misled the protesters and the public about his intentions. He'd sent conciliatory signals that he intended to resolve things personally, but he had decided to do whatever it took, however drastic, to get rid of the protesters.

There was torrential rain in Halifax on Remembrance Day 2011. The police suddenly moved in on the wet encampments, ripping down tents and dragging occupiers through the mud. Fourteen were arrested and charged with obstruction of justice. The charges were later dropped. Dan Leger wrote in the *Chronicle Herald*, "Again, deception, cover-up and misdirection seem to be the hallmarks of Kelly's operating style. He evidently thinks that everything short of a provable lie is OK.... Kelly apparently misled the protesters, the public and even the veterans. Called on it, he shifted the blame to his hapless council and the police department. And while the cops were just doing their jobs, city councillors were played as patsies. Kelly had deceived them once again."[14]

It was the November 8 secret council meeting that stuck in people's craw. It seemed undemocratic and arrogant. Why would the council operate in secrecy? There was an outcry. Mayor Kelly, who by November had chaired an estimated twenty-five closed-door council meetings in 2011 alone, got the message. His office issued a press release on November 29: "Mayor Peter Kelly today called on Council and HRM staff to change the way business is conducted so that in-camera meetings become the exception, rather than the rule.... '[Residents] are, quite rightly, demanding more openness, transparency and accountability in government,' Mayor Kelly said.... 'Public debate is the very air that democracy breaths [sic].... We must open our windows as wide as possible to achieve that kind of ventilation.'"

Tim Bousquet wasn't impressed. The press release, he said, "was met with a round of laughter, disbelief and ridicule.... My own guffaws echoed through the office, right across the street and through the bar, for hours and hours.... The gut-busting, drink-spewing, pants-peeing chortling comes from the naked audacity of Kelly's claim to be worried about excess secrecy."[15]

•••

Not everyone thinks Peter Kelly was a bad mayor. "He does as good a job as anyone else," said one Halifax resident, Terry Lahey. "No one's going to change the world, they'll only tell you they can. He was sincere."[16] Gloria McCluskey, an HRM councillor, has said, "I have never met a more honest person than Peter Kelly.... He doesn't even claim mileage or meals half the time."[17] The Twittersphere was also forgiving. "Thank you very much for your dedication to our city," wrote one supporter. "Be proud of the time, effort, and love that you've put into it."

There were undoubted achievements during his mayoralty. In 2001 he founded the Atlantic Mayors' Congress, a twice-annual meeting of municipal leaders from across the Atlantic provinces to discuss common problems. He's proud of how he handled the September 2003 Hurricane Juan crisis and the huge February 2004 blizzard known as White Juan. "I was down at the Emergency Management Office all the time," he told me. "I answered the telephones. Being out front is key if you're mayor." A $333-million sewage treatment system came into operation in 2008, ending the daily dumping of 181 million litres of raw sewage into Halifax Harbour, but it's not clear how much credit Kelly can legitimately take for that—it was underway before 2000, when he became mayor. A more substantial Kelly achievement was the successful hosting of the 2011 Canada Winter Games, which left behind a sports facility and other useful infrastructure. Kelly promoted a much-needed urban design plan for downtown Halifax known as "HRMbyDesign." And in 2010, most interesting of all, he apologized for the razing of the black community of Africville in the 1960s to make way for a bridge; the city gave the black community $3 million to accompany the apology. Although his diction and grammar were not perfect, Mayor Kelly's speech was emotional and affecting. It was his finest hour as mayor of Halifax.[18] Kelly himself points to it as one of the best things he did. "It was the high point," he says.

•••

"The point is that Peter Kelly had no political convictions," said Tim Bousquet as we finished our meal at Edna's. The next day I talked to Stephen Kimber, long-time Halifax journalist and author, and a professor of journalism at King's College. He agreed with Bousquet. "Kelly just wanted to be mayor," Kimber told me. "Once he got there, he had no idea what to do. It's the curse of Canadian politics. They want the office but don't know what to do with it." Kelly himself doesn't seem to be much interested in political convictions or principles, except for one thing: "I'm a people person," he says. "It's all about the people, connecting with the people. You've got to bring the views of your constituents to the table. That's democracy. That's what matters. It's people that matter."

•••

Tim Bousquet left *The Coast* in March 2014. In June he started a feisty online investigative newspaper called the *Halifax Examiner*. On July 2, 2014, he published a story about Peter Kelly. With only slightly restrained glee, Bousquet reported that Kelly had a new job, working at a pest control company owned by a former employee of the mayor's office. "Residents say Kelly has shown up at their apartment buildings donned in protective gear and carrying a tank, spraying for bugs." On September 4 there was another Bousquet story about Kelly. The former mayor was no longer spraying for bugs. He had been hired as the chief administrative officer of Westlock County, Alberta. His annual salary was reported to be $140,000.

Bousquet telephoned a Westlock councillor to ask what he thought about Kelly's financial scandals. The councillor hadn't heard anything about them. But the county reeve quickly called Bousquet back and said he knew all about it. "Is there to be no mercy for Mr. Kelly?" asked one reader, commenting on Bousquet's article. "Now it is time to let go," wrote another. But Bousquet wasn't letting go. On September 5, he reported on a statement Kelly gave the *Westlock News*. Part of the statement was about concerts for cash. "This is classic Kelly: mischaracterize events, blame someone else, say 'lessons were learned,' and move on to the always-bright future," wrote Bousquet. "Anyone who points at the misdeeds and wants accountability is a 'naysayer' caught in the past, and 'it's time to move on.'" Commenting on the Thibeault estate, Kelly told the *Westlock News*, "The probate has signed off on it.... All funds were there, so at the end of the day the matter is closed and signed off and there is nothing outstanding." Bousquet's reaction? "Well, yea. Only after seven years. Only after a major expose in a newspaper revealed his chicanery.

Only after a court removed Kelly as executor. Only after the other heirs demanded full accountability. Sure, yea, the court signed off on the deal."[19] Bousquet remained relentless. On September 11, 2014, he reported that the *Westlock News* asked in a poll, "Did Westlock County council do its due diligence in the hiring of Peter Kelly?" Eighty-eight per cent of respondents answered no.

•••

Peter Kelly has left the world-class city of Halifax, the best place to live in Canada or perhaps even the entire world, and has gone to live in Westlock, Alberta, a small town on the Great Plains, a little to the north of Edmonton. I sent him an email, asking what the move was all about. He replied: "My adventure to the other side is one I had thought about often. Not many have seen and understand both the political and administrative side. But I bring all of that and more to the table; of which all has value." Maybe so, but Kelly was quickly in trouble again. Apparently envisaging sweeping changes in the governance and administration of Westlock, he sent a letter to the county's employees offering them all a severance package. Through their union, the employees filed a complaint with the Alberta Labour Relations Board, saying, among other things, that Kelly had violated the collective agreement. Lou Arab, a representative of the Canadian Union of Public Employees, said, "This idea of 'I'm coming in from Halifax where I've screwed everything up and I'm going to tell you how you're screwing everything up,' it's sort of offensive."[20]

Peter Kelly as mayor seemed quite beyond his depth. Likeable Larry O'Brien, the man who told a reporter, "I fell asleep on my boat in July drinking a beer and when I woke up I was mayor of Ottawa," was likewise confused and inept much of the time he spent at city hall. Larry O'Brien, full of fun, was my next call.

Ottawa mayor Larry O'Brien reacts after being acquitted in 2008 on influence peddling and bribery charges.

THREE

LARRY O'BRIEN OF OTTAWA
"It Wouldn't Be as Much Fun without Me."

I GOT INTO A TAXI at Ottawa airport and gave a downtown address. It was January 2014, and a cold day. The driver looked at me in the rear-view mirror as he pulled away. "That's a nice building," he said. "You live there?" I said I was just visiting someone. "Larry O'Brien. He used to be mayor." The driver nodded. "I see him walking his dog all the time. I like him." The cab went past the place where I had lived in 1969, when I was a law clerk at the Supreme Court of Canada. That was the year the National Arts Centre opened. Sparks Street had recently been closed to traffic and turned into a chic pedestrian mall. In those days, Ottawa was a parochial government town. Today the original National Arts Centre is old hat (a big make-over is planned), the Sparks Street Mall shabby; Ottawa, some would say, is still parochial and a company town.

O'Brien's condominium is across the street from the Château Laurier Hotel. The *Ottawa Citizen* says of the building that "nowhere in the city is there such a concentration of cash and clout under one terraced roof."[1] O'Brien and his wife, Colleen McBride, live on the eighth floor, in a large and immaculately furnished apartment. He and I sat in the living room, over-looking Rideau Street. He told me what it had been like to be a controversial mayor of Ottawa. Later we continued the conversation over lunch at the Metropolitain Brasserie, a burger joint downstairs.

At first, O'Brien hadn't wanted to see me. Some weeks before we met, I sent an email saying I was writing a book about municipal politics and would like to talk to him. Initially he said yes, but then he had second thoughts: "I just read a bit about your book—'Lawyers Gone Mad' [*sic*] and before we meet I have some concerns.... I am having second thoughts and do not want to feed myself to a lion.... I went into politics without experience and I had my head handed to me on a plate and as I have always said—if you are in a deep hole, the[n] first stop digging." I tried to allay his fears, and pointed out that there would be a chapter about him whether or not we talked. Maybe it would be better if we got together? "OK Philip," he emailed back, adding, "BTW you have a choice—address me as Larry or your Worship:-)"

When we eventually sat down to chat, O'Brien threw caution to the winds, in a mixture of bravado and bitterness.

•••

Some of the time, Larry O'Brien is full of energy, replete with self-confidence, good-humoured, flushed with his success as a businessman, revelling in being a multi-millionaire. Other times, he seems hesitant, self-doubting, unhappy, preoccupied with his rocky political career. Always, he is brash, an extrovert, given to speaking (and Tweeting) without thinking about it very much. During the January 23, 2012, Republican presidential candidates debate in Florida, he Tweeted, "The spics are getting way too much airtime!"

O'Brien is easy to like. Even his political opponents and hard-bitten investigative reporters, who believe he was a terrible mayor, seem to harbour a furtive affection for him, grinning when they see his bald head and big smile. He loves his wealth and spends money with insouciance. An early dream was to own a Mercedes with leather seats. Today he owns 11 per cent of Calabogie Motorsports, a racetrack near Ottawa, where he races a Mustang. He has chartered a plane to fly friends to the Super Bowl. He has that fancy condominium downtown. His Brockville, Ontario, cottage has handcrafted mahogany front doors and an entire wall of floor-to-ceiling windows. He also has a place in Miami.

Larry O'Brien was born in 1949. His father was a used car salesman and unsuccessful entrepreneur. As a boy, Larry had a paper route, delivering the now-defunct *Ottawa Journal* rather than the *Ottawa Citizen*, a newspaper he later came to detest. In 1972, he graduated from Algonquin College, an Ottawa polytechnic that teaches applied arts and technology, and focuses on "workplace needs." He worked for various Ottawa hi-tech companies over the next several years.

O'Brien started his own company, Insta-Call Ltd., a pager-rental business, in 1979. It quickly went bankrupt. He has written, with his usual candour, "Insta-Call was an ill-conceived idea that was executed in a sloppy manner and resulted in total, absolute financial, emotional and social failure."[2] In 1982 he founded Calian, a quality-assurance consulting company that became the principal source of his considerable wealth. Calian went public in 1993, after a decade of growth fuelled by the acquisition of other small companies. O'Brien was chief executive officer until 2005 (with a hiatus in 2000). In 2006 he sold part of his stake for a reputed $16 million. When he became mayor, he apparently still owned about 6 per cent of the shares of Calian, earning dividends of about $250,000 a year. He resigned from the Calian board in 2012 but is still a shareholder. "I think I'm the biggest non-institutional shareholder in the company," he told me. Today, Calian has annual sales in excess of $200 million and over two thousand employees, and it's a major supplier to the federal government.

O'Brien told the *Ottawa Citizen*, "What drove me through the years was personal security. My parents never did well financially and I developed a very deep drive to achieve success—both social and economic."[3] He finds solace in religion. O'Brien, who describes himself as "a man of faith," is a Catholic with an interest in Buddhism, and he prays daily.

In 1983, O'Brien married Debbie Green. "He was so handsome, so flirtatious," she has said. In 2008, the *Ottawa Citizen* described Green as "an heiress to a family fortune, a prominent philanthropist, tireless fundraiser and popular fixture of Ottawa high society."[4] Her parents were dog food manufacturers who sold their business to Loblaws. O'Brien and Green have two sons. They divorced in 1995, but remain close friends. The *Ottawa Citizen* reported, "When Mr. O'Brien fell ill with a rare form of blood poisoning in 2004, she converted a space on the first floor of her sprawling home along the Ottawa River into a hospital room where he convalesced for several months. Ms. O'Brien also worked on her ex-husband's successful 2006 mayoral bid, organizing dinners at her home to raise money for his campaign." On November 13, 2006—election night—Debbie joined O'Brien and his girlfriend, Ottawa real estate agent Colleen McBride, to watch the results on television in O'Brien's condominium. In 2008, O'Brien married Colleen. "Just marrying my angel," he told reporters.[5]

•••

Why did Larry O'Brien want to be mayor of Ottawa? Perhaps he was a glory seeker. He'd built a successful business. Now what? Time for something new and big. The title of mayor sounds good, and the chain of office looks impressive hanging around your neck. And being mayor gives you something to do. "I collect experiences," he told me. "And I liked the idea of being mayor. I thought I may as well go for a job where I can start at the top." But part of it was also ideology. If government was run like a business, everyone would be better off, O'Brien believed—and he knew how to run a business.

Larry O'Brien was elected mayor in 2006 on the usual right-wing platform. He promised a tax freeze (a common promise for a right-wing mayoralty candidate). "Zero means zero," he proclaimed, over and over again. He said he would "fight waste." Sound familiar? He was against a proposed light rapid transit project. He wanted a new convention centre. "The premise of his candidacy ... was that city hall was out of control and he was the man to bring the bureaucracy and the left-wing politicians to heel. It was about money, money, money."[6] O'Brien loved campaigning. "It was loads of fun," he said. "I had a natural knack for campaigning. I had no fear. I was the alternative to a bad status quo." He won 47 per cent of the vote, easily defeating the incumbent mayor, Bob Chiarelli.

Running for mayor was O'Brien's first foray into politics. "I don't think I was ready," he later told a reporter for *Maclean's*. "You know, the first city council meeting I saw with my own eyes, I was, in fact, chairing."[7] But political inexperience was part of his appeal. "He had a disrespect for politicians when he came in," said long-time councillor Rick Chiarelli (Bob Chiarelli's second cousin) a few months after the election. "And that's part of why he got elected, because people wanted someone who wasn't political. But I think he's started to develop respect. The year has been a big pile of poop, but we're starting to see a pony in there somewhere."

There were serious reservations about O'Brien right from the start. Ken Gray, a seasoned and hard-headed reporter known as "Bulldog," wrote in the *Ottawa Citizen* less than a month after O'Brien was elected: "Mr. O'Brien, a highly intelligent fellow, might be able to speak the broad platitudes required for the sound-bite world of the election campaign, but other councillors, and veteran journalists, know that he is not even at the rookie stage in his grasp of municipal affairs."[8] Gray reported that during a pre-election meeting at the *Citizen*, "journalists were unable to discover his light-rail position and on other issues he just skated and waffled. It was an abysmal performance."

O'Brien told me that the night he won the election, his first reaction was an urge to vomit. "I thought, What have I done? I know nothing about this stuff. How can I be mayor? I'm guilty of reckless abandon." It reminded me of Jón Gnarr's comment about getting himself into a situation he would never understand. O'Brien didn't even realize that he'd been elected to a four-year term. He thought he was mayor for three years until someone told him different.

•••

Big trouble wasn't long in coming for the new mayor. In February 2007, two months after he took office, Terry Kilrea, another 2006 mayoralty candidate, told the *Ottawa Citizen* that O'Brien had offered to cover his campaign expenses if he dropped out of the race and supported O'Brien. O'Brien denied the allegation. On March 27, the Ontario Provincial Police Anti-Rackets Branch launched an investigation into whether O'Brien had solicited Kilrea's withdrawal from the mayoralty race, and whether he had tried to have Kilrea appointed to the Parole Board of Canada to get him out of the way. (To avoid a conflict of interest, the

Ottawa police force had stepped aside.) On April 3, 2007, O'Brien was interviewed by the OPP.[9] An intense investigation followed. In December 2007, he was charged with breaching the influence-peddling and bribery sections of the Criminal Code.[10] On January 7, 2008, just back from a Florida vacation, he was booked and fingerprinted. "I feel like a rock star," he said, with characteristic bravado and self-confidence. "It must be a bigger story than I thought."[11]

His nine-week trial took place in May and June 2008. (O'Brien had the good sense to step aside as mayor for the duration.) There were dozens of witnesses. In his August 5 judgment acquitting O'Brien, Mr. Justice Douglas Cunningham of the Ontario Superior Court laid out the facts.[12] The crucial event was a meeting between Kilrea and O'Brien in a coffee shop on July 12, 2006. Over lattes, each tried to convince the other not to run. Wrote Justice Cunningham, "To use Mr. O'Brien's rather crude description, the discussion involved 'big swinging dicks.'" There was some discussion about the possibility of a Parole Board of Canada appointment for Kilrea, but, said Justice Cunningham, "It is not an offence to want an opponent to withdraw from a political race, nor is it an offence to encourage an opponent to seek alternative employment. Were this an offence, there would be a need for many more jails." The judge was also not impressed by Kilrea's credibility. "From 2003 until this trial began," he wrote, "Mr. Kilrea has proved to be a master of manipulating the media and keeping his name in the spotlight." Mayor O'Brien was more convincing:

> There are many portions of Mr. O'Brien's evidence
> that I do believe.... I believe that from the after-
> noon of July 12, 2006, Mr. O'Brien took no further
> steps to suggest he had influence with the govern-

ment that might get Mr. Kilrea an appointment. Did Mr. O'Brien want Mr. Kilrea out of the race? He most certainly did. Did Mr. O'Brien, in his own words, feed Mr. Kilrea some "bullshit" from time to time? He most certainly did. But the bottom line is that Mr. O'Brien very early on was aware any quid pro quo arrangement was wrong and probably illegal.

Larry O'Brien's legal fees were estimated to be about $750,000. Michael Edelson, O'Brien's lawyer, said, "My client was fortunate enough to have the resources to mount a very, very strong defence. He's a gutsy guy.... Not everyone has the determination and the guts to do it. He does."[13] In an interview with the *Ottawa Citizen*, O'Brien said, "I just can't tell you how many people over the last two months have stopped me on the street, have gone out of their way to tell me what they believed, which was that there was nothing to this.... I'm regularly getting e-mails from ... members of the clergy. Just last Sunday I met someone who is at St. George's Anglican church and the congregation prayed for the mayor of Ottawa."[14] His support was ecumenical.

But not everyone was celebrating O'Brien's acquittal. Ottawa's gay newspaper, the *Daily Xtra*, wrote, "It turns out that influence peddling isn't going to be the nail in Mayor Larry O'Brien's political coffin. No, it's going to be influence *piddling*—the mayor has pissed away a lot of goodwill, failed to keep his promises (which were, to be frank, pie-in-the-sky anyway), and failed to remain a likeable public figure."[15]

Larry O'Brien told me that his criminal trial was "life-altering." He said, "I was humiliated." He said the whole experience was "dreadful." You had to feel sorry for him.

•••

But Terry Kilrea wasn't O'Brien's only problem. Right from the start, his administration was the gang that couldn't shoot straight. A big part of the problem was the autocratic way the mayor ran things. Councillor Chiarelli said, "The mayor's idea of a committee was a committee of one. He was accustomed to owning a company and considering only his views. He believed he was the CEO of the Corporation of Ottawa and he was running it like Calian."[16] Early on, O'Brien publicly criticized councillors, accusing them of whining (a favourite criticism levelled at people who oppose him) and being lazy. He wanted the obedience that employees give to the boss, and he didn't like to compromise.

In June 2007, O'Brien's chief of staff, Walter Robinson, quit. Gossip had it that O'Brien wouldn't listen to him, particularly when Robinson didn't agree with the mayor. Robinson told a reporter, "Larry has a focused business background, which is not my 20 years of experience on the political side." O'Brien said he and Robinson were two "Alpha males" with "style differences," and it had become clear that the two approaches were not compatible.[17] In March 2008, O'Brien's executive assistant resigned after pretending to be somebody else on a radio call-in show. When that happened, Councillor Chiarelli said, "This makes the mayor's office look goofy, and goofy is not the impression you want to give when you are trying to look less Mickey Mouse."[18]

In June 2008, just before he married Colleen, O'Brien severely criticized a number of "tax-and-spend councillors" on his blog.[19] "Completely ill-advised," said the ubiquitous Rick Chiarelli. Councillor Gord Hunter said O'Brien's comments were "unfair, unbalanced." Councillor Peggy Feltmate said, "He's saying we're stupid and he's going to show us the light. Well, all I see him leading us into is a tunnel of darkness." Councillor Alex Cullen said, "For all his bravado, he has yet to show council one original idea." O'Brien took time out from his wedding duties to comment. "I think it's been a very good couple of months," he declared, "and things are moving in the right direction."

O'Brien often said, "I'm a lot of fun. You have to give me that. It wouldn't be as much fun without me." Hanging on his office wall was a city road sign that read "Swaggerville."

•••

In October 2010, as he was running for re-election, O'Brien visited the editorial board of the *Ottawa Citizen*. The newspaper reported on his visit under the headline "I Was a Lousy Mayor." O'Brien told the editorial board he wasn't certain if he was the worst mayor Ottawa had ever had, but he knew he was pretty bad. "People believe and recognize that the first two years of my mayoralty were a complete—and quite frankly, self-diagnosed as a complete—disaster. I probably made every single major political mistake that was possible…. I think I even made quite a few mistakes that, quite frankly, were impossible to replicate," he said. But despite it all, O'Brien was characteristically upbeat with the editorial board. "I am a changed man. The old Larry is gone, probably never to come back again—and [that's] probably a good thing."[20] Journalist Nancy Macdonald, writing in *Maclean's*, observed, "What was remarkable was that this was not an exit speech, but a campaign speech."[21] O'Brien told me he'd realized as he walked out of the newspaper's office that "I'd fucked myself. I could just see the headline they were going to write. I just couldn't get the hang of press relations. I shouldn't have said that stuff."

"The press were very unfair to Larry," Colleen says. "Here's an example. Larry's chauffeur when he was mayor asked Larry if he could walk the dog when he was waiting for Larry—he

needed the exercise, he'd just been diagnosed with diabetes—
and Larry said, 'Sure, go ahead.' Then one day, there's a photo
in the paper of Len walking the dog and someone says it's an
improper use of the taxpayers' money!"

Larry told me that these days he never reads the newspapers.
Never.

•••

There were twenty candidates for mayor in the October 25,
2010, Ottawa municipal election. One of them was Larry
O'Brien. O'Brien's campaign was a replay of 2006. He promised
a freeze on property taxes and city spending. But the voters
were no longer believers. O'Brien got sixty-five thousand votes,
about 24 per cent of the ballots cast. Jim Watson got twice as
many and was elected mayor.

Watson is the antithesis of O'Brien: a career politician, a
quintessential office seeker who has bounced around from one
elected position to another. He was an Ottawa city councillor
and mayor of the city from 1997 to 2000. In 2003, he was
elected as a Liberal to represent Ottawa West–Nepean in the
Ontario legislature; he was re-elected in 2007. Watson held
several provincial Cabinet positions, including minister of
municipal affairs and housing. When I asked O'Brien how
his relations with the provincial government were while he
was mayor, he laughed. "How do you think they were? The
minister of municipal affairs wanted my job." Watson resigned
from Cabinet to run against O'Brien. Strangely, the two men
seem to be friendly—now at least.

The *Globe and Mail* thought there were several obvious
reasons for O'Brien's defeat.[22] In the 2006 campaign, he had
promised there would be no property tax increases in his first

term in office; in fact, taxes went up 14 per cent. (Fees for recreational services also went up, in some cases by 40 per cent.) He presided over the longest transit strike in the city's history. The city lost $100 million on a light rail contract that O'Brien first voted for and then helped cancel. And he campaigned in a sloppy and petty way, abandoning his natural bonhomie and becoming petulant. He said Jim Watson could not take criticism and whined like a girl. "Suck it up, princess," O'Brien told him. The *Globe* commented, "The election results suggest Ottawa voters had sucked as much as they could take of Mr. O'Brien."

O'Brien said his 2010 campaign was a "disaster." Why did he lose so badly? There was only one reason: "It was that criminal trial. In this town, you couldn't win after a thing like that. It didn't matter that I was acquitted, that I was totally vindicated."

•••

Politicians, even ex-politicians, always claim a lot for themselves. O'Brien, a boastful man (he has used the word "cocky" to describe himself), is no exception. When he ran for re-election, he claimed credit for the construction of Ottawa's new convention centre, the redevelopment plan for Lansdowne Park, the postponement of the proposed north–south light rail plan (championed by his predecessor, Bob Chiarelli) in favour of an east–west plan, the funding of the new LRT plan, the untangling of the city's financial reporting, and the cleanup of the Ottawa River. Most of these claims are dubious. The convention centre project was well underway before O'Brien became mayor. He had little to do with the Lansdowne Park project. It was unclear why an east–west LRT line should be constructed before a north–south line (but even so, the contractual penalties of postponing the north–south line were substantial). As for his 2006 "zero means zero" election promise, property taxes went up considerably, while he was mayor (a whopping 4.9 per cent in 2008, although he blamed that on a "surprise attack" by "treacherous" councillors). O'Brien's reaction to the tax hike? "This is too good of a city to let a stubborn position of mine affect the quality of life for citizens."[23]

In 2013, Larry O'Brien published a book called *Ethical Entrepreneurship: A Guide to Surviving the Coming Economic Crisis*. It's chatty and amusing, surprisingly well written for a book of its kind, and may even contain some good advice. There is, of course, a lot of boasting: "My success in business has enabled me to help raise two children, create thousands of jobs, meet fabulous people, shake hands with several US presidents, dine with prime ministers, travel as an official state visitor of Canada, play golf at Augusta, almost buy the Ottawa Rough Riders, be blessed by the Dalai Lama and then be elected the fifty-eighth mayor of Ottawa."[24] The book dwells on the bankruptcy of his first business venture and what he learnt from that failure. Most interesting of all are O'Brien's reflections on the differences between business and politics. He writes, "All of the skills I developed over a lifetime in business were of no practical use to me in the field of politics…. The differences between practical politics and ethical business are chilling."[25] Politics, he continues, is "based [not] on values but on short-term profits. After years of training as an ethical entrepreneur I found myself in a world where I simply could not function."[26] And that, he sometimes says, with conviction, is the real reason he lost the election in 2010.

•••

Before we met, Larry O'Brien sent me what he described as a five-step plan to fix municipal government. It's an extraordinary document—sketchy, bizarre and muddled—but at least it shows that O'Brien has thought about the fundamentals of municipal government (many mayors have not), albeit in an unusual fashion. It begins with a list of "barriers to good governance in cities." These include professional politicians who get elected at a higher salary than their qualifications allow, and who spend all their energies trying to get re-elected; a dysfunctional political structure, particularly the absence of real power at the municipal level; no sustainable funding model; inflated worker costs and lack of management control because of unions; and lack of citizen involvement in municipal problem-solving. Sensible observers could agree with most or all of that; O'Brien is right about the problems. Then his plan proposes "practical options" that address these barriers. This is when his thinking becomes curious. He writes: "I suggest we eliminate municipal politics completely and hand the added responsibility of Councilors [sic] to the local MPP's.... The purpose of my approach to city governance is to take real issues closer [to] the people through the elimination of an entire level of ineffective government—municipal." This seems wacky at first, but maybe it's not. When I mentioned to David Crombie the idea of giving provincial legislatures hands-on responsibility for municipalities, the former mayor of Toronto thought it had some merit. "Those guys [provincial politicians] have had a pass for too long," he told me. The actual five steps of the O'Brien plan are these:

1. Reduce salaries of municipal politi-
    cians, except for the mayor, to zero.

2. Decertify public sector unions.

3. Reduce public sector salaries and
    pensions.

4. Create citizen task forces for direct
    citizen participation.

5. Directly involve MPPs and federal
    senators in municipal governance.

"As you can read," O'Brien concluded, "they are big changes that will not be adopted by little minds."

•••

I asked Larry O'Brien whether he had liked being mayor. "Well," he said, "it depends which part of it you're talking about. The protocol part was great. I was mayor of the capital city of a G8 country. Everybody who came to town came to see me.... [But] I hated the political part. I messed that up. In business, you hope everyone else is as successful as you are, and if they are, it's good for you. But in politics, everyone wants you to fail."

These days, O'Brien is heavily involved in what he calls the "virtual currency revolution." His LinkedIn profile says, "I get up every morning excited to call on my experience in business and politics to work on Bitcoin and related technologies." But he admits to having been changed by his time in office—and not in a good way. "Today, I feel like I'm toxic," he told me. "I've lost whatever influence I ever had. I'm scarred. I'm bitter and disillusioned. A lot of people won't return my calls. They threw me under the bus. I've been fucked." Then he looked at me and smiled a big smile. "You know what? I still like having fun."

Larry and Colleen saw me downstairs to a waiting taxi. As it pulled away, I looked back. They were both waving energetically. O'Brien still had a wide grin. Talking to him had been fun. I liked him.

Now it was time to circle back a bit. Off to Montreal.

Mayor of Montreal Gérard Tremblay speaks to reporters in October 2012, two weeks before he resigned amid allegations of widespread corruption in his administration.

FOUR
GÉRALD TREMBLAY OF MONTREAL
"My Last Act of Love."

ON MONDAY, DECEMBER 3, 2012, Revenu Québec agents in unmarked cars descended on a pizza joint in the Montreal suburb of Blainville. The restaurant's owner—burly, cigar-chomping Lino Zambito, who prided himself on having hair like Jay Leno's—had not paid his provincial taxes. The revenue agents seized whatever they could cart away and disappeared down the highway.

Things soon got worse for Zambito. In May 2013, he had heart surgery. His doctors told him he had to lead a less stressful life, but he couldn't manage that. In June, he filed for bankruptcy, owing about $2 million to creditors, including insurance companies, the taxman, his mother and the city of Montreal for funds allegedly obtained by fraud. Fraud? What was that all about? Before he was a restaurateur, Zambito had been in the construction business; he owned a company called Infrabec, which fixed water and sewage pipes. In May 2013, the soon-to-be-arrested mayor of Montreal, Michael Applebaum, said the city wanted Zambito to return $300,000 in phony Infrabec charges—known in this crazy corrupt world as "false extras."

Lino Zambito wasn't just a dubious guy with good hair who had once been in the construction business and then ran an unsuccessful pizzeria. In the early autumn of 2012, already convicted of electoral fraud and facing criminal charges over a water-purification contract in the town of Boisbriand, he had been a star witness before the Charbonneau Commission, a provincial inquiry investigating the awarding and management of public contracts in the construction industry. Zambito testified that beginning in 2005, he had paid 3 per cent of every municipal contract his company won to Mayor Gérald Tremblay's Union Montreal party. He alleged that city employees at every level were in on the scheme. He said that he had paid money to all Quebec political parties, with the biggest gifts reserved for the Liberals (who were then in power). He testified that payments had also been made to the Mafia, with envelopes full of cash handed over at the Consenza Social Club, a strip-mall café that was the headquarters of the Rizzuto clan. He said, "I manipulated public tenders, corrupted people, but the system existed. If I wanted to work in construction I didn't have the choice."[1] Shortly after he started testifying before the commission, Zambito and his family were put under police protection. Sûreté du Québec cruisers were prominently parked outside his house.

Calls quickly went out for the resignation of Mayor Tremblay. "My conscience is clear," he said, insisting he knew nothing about corruption or illegal financing of political parties. "The decision on my political future will never, never be linked to what you're hearing nowadays," Tremblay told reporters. "Is there corruption or collusion at the city of Montreal? The answer is yes, but it has been going on for decades."[2]

In her October 31, 2012, inaugural address, newly elected Quebec premier Pauline Marois attacked corruption in government. She had no sympathy for Gérald Tremblay. On Saturday, November 3, the telephone rang in Tremblay's house. The premier was on the line. She asked Tremblay, "Have you finished your reflection?" Tremblay had lost the support of the Quebec government. After he hung up from Marois, sitting at his kitchen table, he drafted his resignation. On Monday, November 5, in the Hall of Honour at city hall, Tremblay announced that he was leaving, a year before his mandate expired. He said he had no choice. "When I was a young man, my father told me never to get into politics because it was dirty and would destroy me," he said. Tremblay claimed he had been the victim of an unbearable injustice. Crooks within his circle had betrayed him. His resignation, he told reporters, was "my last act of love for the best interests of our Montreal."

In April 2013, Tremblay told the Charbonneau Commission that he had known nothing of the corruption at city hall. "I am just as shocked as you about the revelations before the commission," he told Madam Justice France Charbonneau. Few believed him. When he got home from testifying, he noticed that the lug nuts on his car wheels had been loosened. Maybe someone was trying to kill him. Tremblay, like Zambito before him, was placed under police protection.

Shortly after his testimony, Tremblay went on a pilgrimage to the Cathedral of Santiago de Compostela in Spain. "I didn't have anything to ask forgiveness for," he said in a radio interview afterward. "I had nothing to ask of God. I just wanted to thank him."

•••

The night Tremblay resigned as mayor, Paul Wells wrote in *Maclean's*: "I get the impression that even reporters who've followed the Montreal municipal cesspool for years will be amazed if it is ever established, as it has not yet been for sure, that Tremblay himself was crooked. He is basically a nice guy.

But if you take what he said tonight at its face he was one of the most gobsmackingly naive fools ever to wander the crumbling boulevards of Canada's second metropolis."[3] A few days later, Lysiane Gagnon, a distinguished Quebec journalist, described him this way: "A soft-spoken, devout Christian who wore rose-coloured glasses and hated controversy, Mr. Tremblay has the perpetually surprised look of someone who floats through space, unable to realize that the world is a dangerous place and that some people are wicked—a strange behaviour for a Harvard Business School graduate. Cartoonists paint him as a wide-eyed deer stunned by car lights in the middle of the road."[4] Another well-known journalist, Martin Patriquin, later called Tremblay "a nebbish technocrat, a one-time cabinet minister and perfumist, who lives in Outremont and drives a Volvo."[5] Shortly after he was elected mayor, Linda Gyulai of the *Gazette* said Tremblay "has the mien of a Milquetoast, the magnetism of drying paint and wouldn't be called fiery unless he held a lit match in one hand and tinder too close in the other."[6]

A gobsmackingly naive fool? A wide-eyed deer stunned by car lights? A nebbish technocrat? A milquetoast? Tremblay was not always regarded with such derision. Once, he was a contender. A 1992 *Toronto Star* story, written when he was Quebec's industry minister, reported:

> Looking every bit the corporate go-getter in double-breasted suits and cropped blond hair, Tremblay, 49, strides at high speed down the halls of the legislature, pausing to give rapid-fire answers to a journalist's question. With the fervor and energy of a fundamentalist preacher, he has been pushing the need to overhaul a Quebec economy in crisis.... Labor and man-

agement joined to praise the strategy and the man behind it. "He understands the problems very quickly, goes to the heart of the matter, doesn't bother with the fine details and gets things done," says Richard Le Hir, head of the Quebec Manufacturers' Association. Gérald Larose, a sovereigntist labor leader and no friend of the Liberal government, calls Tremblay "imaginative and audacious."[7]

•••

Gérald Tremblay was born in Ottawa in September 1942. His family moved to Montreal, to a duplex in Notre-Dame-de-Grâce (known as NDG), when he was four years old. When he was a child, Gérald was known as Jerry. He had three brothers. The children had a conventional Catholic upbringing. His father, Georges Albert, was a lawyer who worked for the National Parole Board. Georges Albert, who died in 1982, wanted Jerry to become a judge. His mother, Rollande, died in 2009 at the age of ninety-eight.

Tremblay seemed to know from an early age what he wanted to do in life, and it wasn't to become a judge. He has said he intended from the age of fifteen to be a politician. He has also said that when he met Suzanne, the woman who became his wife, he knew right away she was the woman for him. Gérald Tremblay was a man who decided what was important firmly and early, and then followed through. His brother Marcel, who became a Montreal city councillor, has described him as a "very programmed" guy who had his life mapped out like a flow chart: "He always said he'd go on to become a lawyer first; then he'd go to Harvard; then he'd become a millionaire, or at least financially secure; and then he'd go into politics."[8] Another brother, Michel, had a different perspective: "He's not there for money and he's not there for glory. He's got this deep conviction that he can bring about change."[9]

Tremblay earned a bachelor of arts degree from the Université de Montréal in 1962 and went to work for four years as a credit analyst at Dun & Bradstreet. In 1969, he obtained a law degree from the University of Ottawa, living in the basement of his parents' house (they had moved back to Ottawa in 1965). He was admitted to the Quebec bar in 1970. In 1972, he graduated from Harvard University with an MBA, financing his studies on borrowed money. He was scrupulously following the flow chart. Now it was time to make a million dollars. Tremblay became a businessman and entrepreneur.

Tremblay married Suzanne Tailleur in 1979. (The press sometimes refers to Suzanne as Tremblay's second wife; a first wife is never mentioned and her name cannot be found.) When he was mayor, Suzanne Tailleur was described in the gossip columns as "fab first lady," "ever-elegant," "first lady of chic," "power girl," "first lady of joy," "first lady of fun," "beautiful" and "vibrant." Gérald and Suzanne adopted twins in 1983. In 1985, they bought a country place with 105 acres in Saint-Hippolyte, near Montreal. Later, Tremblay—a devout Catholic—built a chapel on the property and called it Marie-Reine-des-Coeurs. A picture of his private country chapel hung in his city hall office.

The Tremblays were the first Quebec franchisees of Dans un Jardin, a French bath and skin-care business. (He's often been called a "perfumist" or a "perfume merchant.") In 1986, they sold five Dans un Jardin franchises and the Auberge Champêtre, a Laurentians hotel that Tremblay had bought some time before, for what has been described as "a tidy profit." Now financially independent, Tremblay could follow the plan and turn his attention to politics. He'd had the itch for a long time. In 1985, he'd tried but failed to get the Quebec Liberal nomination in the riding of Rousseau. But his second try at politics was successful.

In 1989, Tremblay was elected the member of the Quebec National Assembly for Outremont, where he and Suzanne lived, and was appointed minister of industry, commerce, science and technology in the Liberal government of Robert Bourassa. As industry minister, his big idea was to provide substantial provincial financial support to key growth sectors, so-called clusters, such as the aerospace and pharmaceutical industries. He was influenced by the writings of American popular economists Robert Reich and Michael E. Porter.

Political observers said Tremblay was positioning himself to succeed Bourassa. Speculation about his leadership ambitions increased when it became known, in late 1992, that Bourassa had had a recurrence of skin cancer and was seriously ill. But not everybody was enthusiastic about Tremblay as leader. In May 1993, as Bourassa's health worsened and speculation intensified, a reporter wrote, "Industry Minister Gérald Tremblay, once considered the dauphin of the Liberal Party, is being written off by insiders as a snob who 'was born with a silver spoon in his mouth,' a man who surrounds himself with a clique of personal friends from the same milieu. Tremblay has little support from the rank and file."[10] But when Bourassa announced his resignation in September, Tremblay seemed like a viable candidate, and at the end of the month it looked as if he would run. By early October, however, he had decided that Treasury Board President Daniel Johnson was unbeatable and announced that he was not a candidate. His written statement was tinged with bitterness. The *Toronto Star* described the bizarre announcement in this way: "He said Quebec has become an 'every-man-for-himself' society plagued by tax evasion, cigarette smuggling, black market labor, abuses and trickery. Lobbies and special-interest groups 'have become extremely powerful and force the government into decisions which ignore the true needs of Quebecers.... The population's generalized exasperation with politics, this every-man-for-himself philosophy, the abandonment of any sense of duty, none of this can last long without threatening the very foundations of our society.'"[11]

Tremblay was re-elected to the National Assembly in September 1994, when the Jacques Parizeau–led Parti Québécois came to power, and he became industry critic. "It feels good," he said on election night. But it didn't feel *that* good. His heart wasn't in it. He missed the power and prestige of a Cabinet position and resigned in 1996. At his farewell press conference in an Outremont restaurant, he said, speaking portentously in the third person, "Gérald Tremblay is not a person who can play an important role in the opposition. That is my problem." He seemed to be yesterday's man. He went back to business.

But soon a political opportunity came his way. In December 2000, the Parti Québécois government of Lucien Bouchard passed Bill 170, amalgamating the twenty-eight municipalities of the Island of Montreal as of January 1, 2002. "One Island, One City" became the mantra. Montreal suburban mayors, who didn't want to lose their autonomy and power, were incensed. Mayors of anglophone suburbs were especially worried that amalgamation into one predominantly French city would threaten English rights and institutions. The mayors were particularly angry with Montreal mayor Pierre Bourque, a horticulturist who had vigorously championed amalgamation. They wanted someone who was opposed to amalgamation to run against him—to punish him—in the November 2001 municipal election. Someone suggested Gérald Tremblay. After all, he was a prominent member of the Quebec Liberal Party (now led by Jean Charest), which had said that if it won the next election, it would allow the suburbs to de-amalgamate.

A group of suburban mayors approached Tremblay to see if he was interested. Why not? On February 27, 2001, at a tepid rally in Old Montreal, Tremblay declared himself a candidate under the banner of the Montreal Island Citizens Union. The mayors of Verdun, Côte Saint-Luc, Hampstead, Beaconsfield and Saint-Léonard stood at his side. (Frank Zampino, then mayor of Saint-Léonard, a city that has been called a moral cesspool by some journalists, had a disastrous role to play in Tremblay's subsequent career.) "He isn't the most colourful candidate in the history of Montreal municipal politics," wrote Mike Boone in the *Gazette*. "He's the kind of guy you'd want in your foxhole—especially if you were there to measure soil erosion."[12]

"It's goodbye to the gardener and hello to the lawyer," wrote Jeff Heinrich in the *Gazette* on the morning of November 5, 2001, the day after the municipal election. Tremblay, with 49 per cent of the vote, had won forty-one seats. Bourque got 44 per cent of the ballots and thirty-one seats. Tremblay triumphed in the anti-amalgamation suburbs; the town of Dorval voted for Tremblay by a margin of seven to one, and Westmount, Côte Saint-Luc and Hampstead by thirteen to one. Forty-six per cent of those eligible voted. The percentages of those voting were much higher in the suburbs than downtown.

•••

Political scientist Andrew Sancton, in his book *Canadian Local Government*, calls amalgamation "the most dramatic form of provincial intervention in urban government arrangements."[13]

Provincial governments generally like amalgamation, because it reduces the number of governments and the duplication of services, and makes life easier and less costly for those in charge of the province. Or so they expect. But as Sancton points out, in the case of Montreal the Parti Québécois government had complicated feelings: "For the Quebec government, the concern was that an amalgamated city of Montreal would have only a razor-thin francophone majority and could conceivably be captured politically by declared non-sovereignists."[14]

The big city at the centre of an amalgamation—Montreal, say, or Toronto—likes the idea in principle, seeing it as an extension of its power. For the city, amalgamation is annexation without the use of armies, a way of getting suburbanites to pay a greater share of city-centre costs. Linguistic and political groups—evaluating amalgamation on how it advances their particular interests—may see things very differently. An English-speaking Montreal suburb, for example, may be afraid that amalgamation with a predominantly French-speaking core city will diminish its rights. Left-leaning inhabitants of downtown Toronto may be concerned that amalgamation with right-leaning suburbs will dilute their influence and have unpleasant political consequences.

It was his stand against amalgamation that made Tremblay mayor of Montreal, but things started to look different to him once he had achieved office. Amalgamation is heady wine for the mayor of an amalgamated city. It gives him more power over more people, and more money to spend. In the 2003 provincial election campaign, Jean Charest reiterated his promise to allow suburbs to de-amalgamate if they wanted to. Tremblay tried to talk him out of it. In March 2003, a month before the election, he visited Charest in Quebec City. The *Gazette* reported that Tremblay told the Liberal leader that they needn't revisit a "sterile and divisive" debate. "I have no intention of being distracted by these discussions. We are here to affirm our desire to get on with building our new cities," said Tremblay.[15] Charest won the election, and he had to fulfill his promise to provide a de-amalgamation mechanism. It was to be by means of a referendum for each municipality. The referenda were held on June 30, 2004, and Tremblay fought vigorously for the "no" side. The *Gazette* reported: "Montreal Mayor Gérald Tremblay's pro-megacity campaign didn't have a moment's rest in the hours leading up to the vote. Yesterday, he met with the city's large Lebanese community. He campaigned in St. Laurent, Côte St. Luc, LaSalle."[16]

Fifteen municipalities within the amalgamated city of Montreal voted in favour of de-amalgamation.[17] Their decision took effect January 1, 2006. Views differ on the results of the partial de-amalgamation. Andrew Sancton, generally an opponent of amalgamation, has suggested that de-amalgamation was a disaster: "De-amalgamation has meant nothing in practice; amalgamated municipalities have been needlessly dismembered; and the resulting system of inter-municipal relationships is both incomprehensible and hopelessly undemocratic."[18] Municipal government on the Island of Montreal is now Byzantine in the extreme. Linda Gyulai has described Montreal municipal elections as "a kind of local version of *So You Think You Can Dance*, only the process to pick a winner appears more complicated than audience voting, the U.S. Electoral College and the Academy Awards ballot system combined."[19]

Voters on both sides of the debate could hardly have failed to notice that Tremblay had made a classic flip-flop for reasons of political expediency. Yet in 2005, running once more against Pierre Bourque, he was re-elected mayor, beating his opponent by more than fifty thousand votes, with only about a third of the electorate bothering to cast a ballot. His victory party was subdued. The *Gazette* wrote, "The atmosphere in the room was muted. Only about 200 supporters milled about, clapping and launching into a half-hearted version of a victory song."[20] Doubts about his sincerity and integrity lingered. Was this a man who could be trusted?

In 2009 Tremblay won for the third time. By then, there was much talk about corruption in city hall. In his campaign, Tremblay had said he was trying to clean it up. In 2010, he told Adam McDowell of the *National Post*: "It's a complex situation. There are allegations of collusion and corruption. When I was informed of situations, I called the police.... People ask me, 'How come it took so long?' It took so long because people don't have proof, they have rumours. And rumours are not the way police can investigate. You need proof."[21]

In conversation with McDowell, Tremblay also touched on personal matters. He said he liked to go to his place in Saint-Hippolyte and chop firewood. And he talked about what he was reading: "The book I'm on now is *Team of Rivals*.... It's about the political genius of Abraham Lincoln.... I started and I can't stop. It's what you go through to be in a position of influence, where you can make a difference."

A difference? "His mayoralty is built upon deceit," wrote Henry Aubin in the *Gazette* just before Tremblay resigned in 2012.[22] Aubin, who didn't seem to think Tremblay and Abraham Lincoln were cut from the same cloth, hadn't forgotten the flip-flop on amalgamation. "What goes around comes around," he wrote. "Today, Tremblay needs the public's trust. Sorry. He's forfeited it."

Tremblay's main defence when he testified at the Charbonneau Commission was that in his eleven years as mayor, he didn't notice much that was unsavoury and nobody brought bad behaviour to his attention—at least not often, or not convincingly enough that he felt he had to act. One journalist described his testimony as "a strange mixture of denials and mea culpas."[23] When stories surfaced in September 2014 that redacted portions of a police affidavit in support of a search warrant alleged that Tremblay had known about corruption at city hall, Richard Bergeron, a city councillor and leader of the municipal party Projet Montréal, commented, "I believed in his good faith, but also in his blindness."[24] Peggy Curran of the *Gazette* asked, "What would you rather be, a hapless dupe or a willing ostrich?"[25]

Even when something odd did come to Tremblay's attention, he was strangely accepting of whatever it was. In his November 5, 2012, resignation speech, he mentioned that right after he was first elected, in 2001, the city manager told him there were rumours about "brown envelopes" circulating in some departments. "I asked him what he had done. His response was that he asked for evidence but no one had ever given him any."[26] That was good enough for Tremblay.

•••

In 2007, Montreal offered a $355-million contract—the biggest in the city's history—to install water meters in buildings and control valves on the city's underground water network. The person in charge of awarding the contract was Frank Zampino, chair of Montreal's executive committee, former mayor of Saint-Léonard and long-time Tremblay ally. The contract went to GENIeau, a company partly owned by Antonio Accurso, who went on to be a star witness at the Charbonneau Commission. Zampino and Tony Accurso were friends; Zampino had been aboard Accurso's yacht, the *Touch*, for two trips to the Caribbean, and once went with him on a junket to Las Vegas. Accurso had hosted many other powerful and influential people on the yacht, which had four garishly decorated bedrooms and a hot tub, including former Montreal city manager Robert Abdallah; Richard Marcotte, former mayor of the Montreal suburb of Mascouche; and Mick Jagger. (The *Touch* was sold in August 2014 for a rumoured $5 million.)

In May 2008, Zampino left the mayor's office and went to work for another company involved in the water-meter deal. Tremblay, in tears, said of his departure, "I cannot hide the fact that I sincerely regret this decision."[27] In 2009, just before the election, Tremblay cancelled the GENIeau contract when the Canada Revenue Agency announced that it was investigating the company for tax fraud. In a 2014 radio interview, the mayor, apparently referring to Zampino, compared himself this time not to Abraham Lincoln but to Jesus Christ: "There were 12 [apostles]. There was one person who betrayed him. At the executive committee, I had 12 people and one person betrayed me."[28]

Bernard Trépanier, the director of financing for Union Montreal, Tremblay's party, was known as "Mr. Three Per Cent." Allegedly it was Trépanier who collected the money skimmed off construction contracts awarded by the city. Tremblay fired Trépanier in 2006. Charbonneau Commission lawyer Paul Crépeau told the commission that Trépanier was let go because Tremblay discovered he had attempted to extort $1 million from a shopping centre developer. Apparently Tremblay mentioned the matter to the chief of police, but let it drop when the chief showed no interest. Crépeau further alleged that when Trépanier was fired, he "left with four months' pay, $25,000 in severance and shoeboxes filled with $100 bills, then set up shop in a new office and continued working for the party as if nothing had happened."[29]

The rot went right to the heart of the Tremblay administration. In May 2012, Zampino and Trépanier, along with six other people—including Martial Fillion, who had been Tremblay's chief of staff (Fillion has since died)—were arrested on fraud and conspiracy charges. It was alleged that they had rigged the sale of city-owned land to a company called Construction Frank Catania at a highly favourable price—the so-called Faubourg Contrecoeur deal of 2007. The land had a municipal evaluation of $31 million but was sold for $4.4 million for a housing project.

Tony Accurso and Frank Catania were friends. An investigation by the *Gazette* concluded, "Construction Frank Catania and Louisbourg [a company controlled by Accurso] rarely bid on the same contracts, they won the same proportion of the contracts they bid on and almost the same dollar value, and certain companies regularly came in last or near-last in the bidding."[30] There were internal city reports that flagged suspicious activity in the construction industry, but Tremblay told the Charbonneau Commission he never saw them.

Accurso wasn't Catania's only friend. The Catania family socialized with the Rizzutos, leaders of the Montreal Mafia. The Charbonneau Commission was shown a 2004 surveillance video of Frank Catania sitting at a table at the Consenza Social Club as Nicolo Rizzuto stuffed thousands of dollars into his socks.

•••

Henry Aubin left the *Gazette* in the summer of 2013, after more than forty years as a distinguished columnist. He often wrote about the city of Montreal. He often wrote about Gérald Tremblay, whom he didn't like.

In May 2013, Aubin took a parting shot at Tremblay the perfumist, commenting on his appearance in front the Charbonneau Commission a few days earlier:

Perfumes are all about producing an illusion: They make something seem more appealing than it really is. And that was the former perfume merchant's effective role at Montreal city hall: His pleasant, bon-chic-bon-genre personality served to hide a bad smell and make things appear falsely sweet. Tremblay was still performing that role as he appeared before the commission. Before speaking, he even crossed himself. There he sat, wearing a tasteful suit, Ivy League pinstriped shirt, old-school horn-rimmed glasses—the very picture of a proper grad of the Harvard Business School. An image-maker's dream: benign-looking, avuncular, pious. Mr. Upright. The perfect cover, whether he knew it or not, for a crooked system.... It will take authentic moral leadership to get Montreal out of this mess.[31]

Henry Aubin must have been a very disappointed man. When Mayor Tremblay resigned, after years of top-to-bottom corruption and ineffectual leadership, Michael Applebaum took his place. Moral leadership? It was not long before Mayor Applebaum was taken away in handcuffs.

Montreal mayor Michael Applebaum resigned after eight months in office when he was arrested and charged with fraud and other crimes.

FIVE
MICHAEL APPLEBAUM OF MONTREAL
"I Have Never Taken a Penny from Anybody."

A CITY MIRED in corruption and scandal. A mayor implicated in the mess and forced to resign. Montreal in crisis. A cry for moral leadership. Who will step forward?

In November 2012, long-time councillor Michael Applebaum succeeded the severely compromised Gérald Tremblay. I heard Applebaum on CBC Radio shortly after he became mayor. He said the right things. He sounded sincere. He seemed plausible. For a brief moment, it looked as if things might get better in Montreal. And then, not long after he was chosen, the police came for Michael Applebaum.

Applebaum had always fancied himself, first and foremost, a businessman, someone who knew how to make money, somebody who was bound to be rich one day. He was born to Orthodox Jewish parents in 1963 in the Montreal borough of Saint-Laurent. He graduated from Sir Winston Churchill High School in 1980 and then went to Dawson College. The Applebaum family had for many years owned a shoe store on Notre-Dame Street, between China Boy Café and the Corona Meat Market. Michael started working in the store when he was a boy. While he was at Dawson College and still working in the shoe store, he was seized by the entrepreneurial spirit and opened a jeans outlet. His objective, he said later, "was to become a very wealthy individual in business." He didn't bother to graduate from Dawson College. "I quit because the teacher in commerce was coming late. I told him very clearly that if you come late one more time, you have nothing to teach me, because in business you must be on time."[1]

In 1993, the *Gazette* described Applebaums as a store with staying power. "Since 1913 this shoppers' landmark has dispensed cheaper shoes of every kind.... Applebaums remains in the same family, with third-generation Michael Applebaum in charge."[2] Much later, Michael told reporter Ingrid Peritz, "I've been in business, and it doesn't matter if you steal a dollar or you steal $100,000. You're not allowed to take a penny. I've always said to my employees that if you find a dollar on the floor in this business, it's not yours, it's the business's money. You have to turn it in."[3]

•••

Michael Applebaum came to public attention in 1993, when the thirty-one-year-old led a local citizen effort to keep the skating rink in Snowdon's MacDonald Park open. The city of Montreal wanted to close the rink (and many others) to save money. Applebaum lived on Earnscliffe Avenue in Notre-Dame-de-Grâce, across from MacDonald Park. In the wintertime, his three children liked to skate there. NDG, as the locals call it, is a pleasant and comfortable middle-class neighbourhood with solid houses and big trees. I lived there in the 1970s, when I taught law at McGill University, in a semi-detached house on Vendôme Avenue, across the street from the poet Louis Dudek.

In 1994, now known as the "rink activist," Applebaum ran for Montreal city council in the riding of NDG. He won narrowly, after a recount. In 1998 and subsequent elections, he was re-elected easily. In 2001, he supported Gérald Tremblay's bid for mayor, standing on the Marché Bonsecours stage with other politicians on February 27 when Tremblay limply announced his candidacy. After Tremblay's victory, Applebaum was named an associate member of the city's powerful and secretive executive committee, which was chaired by Saint-Léonard mayor Frank Zampino of later infamy.

In 2005, Applebaum was elected mayor of Côte-des-Neiges–Notre-Dame-de-Grâce (the two were merged in 2002 to form Montreal's biggest borough). Under Montreal's extremely complicated system of post-demerger government, Applebaum sat on city council as mayor of the borough. In 2009, prospering politically, he became a full member of Montreal's important executive committee. In April 2011, Tremblay named him chair of the committee and gave him the finance portfolio. Applebaum was now a powerful man.

During his political rise, Applebaum became a real estate agent to supplement his meagre income as a politician, brushing off suggestions that there might be a conflict of interest. He told a reporter for the *Canadian Jewish News*, "In my first year, I sold 48 properties, which was the second-highest in that office. It's a question of being focused."[4] He told the same reporter that he was proud of his Jewish heritage, and that he was "conscious of Jewish values such as being a good family man, working hard, volunteering and performing daily mitzvot." (Mitzvot are commandments understood by Jews to have come from God, but the word is often used to describe any good deed.) Of Applebaum's promotion to the city's finance portfolio, Linda Gyulai of the *Gazette* wrote, "The move baffled municipal observers, who point out that as a real estate agent with no background in finance or business, Applebaum is an unlikely choice to put in charge of a $4.5-billion municipal budget and run the executive committee that's in charge [of] a city of 23,000 employees."[5]

Applebaum's big chance came in November 2012, when Tremblay resigned as mayor. But the Union Montreal caucus didn't find a Jewish anglophone with imperfect French very appealing and chose Richard Deschamps as its candidate to succeed Tremblay. Applebaum, showing considerable political shrewdness, promptly quit the party to sit as an independent and resigned as chairman of the city's executive committee as well. Nine other councillors quit Union Montreal with him. The resignations were strategic, but Applebaum tried to make it sound as if he were acting out of principle, complaining about the executive committee's refusals to make public a damning report on city contracts and to reduce the 2013 property tax hike.

Applebaum rushed about soliciting support from the opposition parties, Vision Montréal and Projet Montréal, describing himself as an "independent candidate" for mayor. The canny strategy worked. On November 16, council chose him as mayor by a margin of two votes. He was forty-nine years old, the first anglophone mayor of Montreal in a century, and the first Jewish mayor ever.

Michael Applebaum was sworn in on November 19, 2012, two weeks after Tremblay had left in disgrace. The ceremony was in the Hall of Honour, the very place where his predecessor had given his resignation speech. Portraits of the mayors of Montreal hang in the hall. Now there were more portraits to add. The Hall of Honour has marble from Italy, art deco lamps from Paris, hand-carved ceilings and stained-glass windows. Standing in these splendid surroundings, Applebaum proclaimed, "Today, I promise you sincerely to erase this stain upon our city." There to hear him make this promise was his eighty-nine-year-old father, Moishe; his mother, Ray; his wife of twenty-eight years, Merle; and his three children. Lysiane Gagnon wrote in the *Globe and Mail*, "Mr. Applebaum will bring a breath of fresh air.... The mayor intends to work with the provincial government to prevent corruption and recover 'stolen money' lost to Mafia-linked practices."[6]

•••

Right from the start there was something odd about Applebaum and a fantastic quality to his mayoralty. Ingrid Peritz commented in the *Globe and Mail*, "This month, Mr. Applebaum became the first anglophone in a century, the first Jewish person ever—and likely the only unicyclist and hypnotist—to ascend to the mayor's chair."[7] Applebaum told Peritz, "I can show you tapes of me hypnotizing people and making them bark, or sing like Michael Jackson." And how did he become a unicyclist? "When I was 13, 14, I had a two-wheel bike and it got stolen. And I was very upset and I said, 'I'm going to get something that no one can ride so no one is going to want to steal it.'"

It wasn't long before trouble was brewing. Rumours circulated about Applebaum's real estate dealings while he was mayor of Côte-des-Neiges–Notre-Dame-de-Grâce. There was talk of Applebaum having ties to the underworld. Reporters asked questions about a 2003 Union Montreal fundraiser he had attended at La Cantina, a restaurant partly owned by Federico del Peschio and said to be frequented by drug traffickers and the Mafia. In 2009 del Peschio, described as "a prominent member of the Mob,"[8] was gunned down in the parking lot behind the restaurant. Del Peschio and known Montreal Mob boss Nicolo Rizzuto had once served time together in a Venezuelan jail on drug charges.

The unravelling gathered speed. Exactly three months after Applebaum became mayor, on Tuesday, February 19, 2013, at 4:07 in the afternoon, police cars pulled up to the back door of Montreal's city hall.[9] Armed with search warrants, officers from the provincial Unité permanente anticorruption (UPAC) began an unprecedented raid. Nine other locations were searched simultaneously, including the Côte-des-Neiges–Notre-Dame-de-Grâce city hall. Richard Bergeron, an opposition leader who was supposed to meet Mayor Applebaum at 4:15 to discuss a floral exhibition, "arrived at the mayor's office to find it full of 'authority figures' and deduced the meeting would not be happening." At 4:20, the fire alarm sounded and a voice on the emergency loudspeakers told everyone to leave the building. At 4:22, councillors and city employees received an email ordering them to leave the building because of "exceptional circumstances." Some people were stopped by the police for questioning as they attempted to leave. A UPAC spokeswoman said they were investigating possible fraud, forgery and breach of trust. There were more raids in the weeks to come. The Côte-des-Neiges–Notre-Dame-de-Grâce borough offices were raided again on March 6 (along with the offices of some other boroughs), and yet again on May 22.

On Monday, June 17, 2013, just after six o'clock in the morning, Applebaum was arrested at his house. The mayor of the great city of Montreal was taken away in handcuffs. There were fourteen charges against him, including fraud against the government, conspiracy to commit breach of trust and conspiracy to commit municipal corruption. The main allegations involved supposed bribes paid in exchange for approval of two real estate projects in Côte-des-Neiges—the NDG Sports Centre and the Onyx condo project at the foot of Mount Royal. Later reports suggested that investigators were looking at as many as ten real estate deals between 2002 and 2012. Jack Todd wrote in the

Gazette, "When Michael Applebaum was arrested on corruption charges almost before he had taken office, high politics had degenerated into low comedy: If not for the perpetual distraction of a drunken, obese, abusive crackhead running Canada's largest city down the 401, Montreal would have been fodder for the late-night comics."[10]

Applebaum was released at about 4 P.M., after nine hours of questioning by police. He told reporters "no comment" as he left the police station. The next day, at a news conference, once more in the Hall of Honour, Applebaum resigned. "I have never taken a penny from anybody," he said. On June 25, Laurent Blanchard, who had been appointed chairman of the executive committee by Applebaum, was chosen as interim mayor by city council. He served until the election of Denis Coderre on November 3, 2013.

There was a lot of schadenfreude elsewhere in Canada. Sophie Cousineau of the *Globe and Mail* commented: "It's a twisted contest between *The Globe*'s Montreal bureau and the Toronto newsroom: Who gets the front page with the most insanely crazy municipal politics? So on Monday Montreal came from behind and won. Hands down."[11] Vancouver's *Province* said, "Vancouver Mayor Gregor Robertson has his fair share of critics, including this newspaper. But perhaps we should all be relieved he's running the show given what's happening in other big Canadian cities."[12]

Applebaum received $267,000 in severance pay from the city of Montreal. He will keep this money even if found guilty. When he became mayor, he told an interviewer, "I'm a simple kind of fella. I go home, I have a wife, I have kids, I take out the garbage, I do the laundry, I do the shopping. Yes, there's a lot on my shoulders. But I haven't changed over the years."[13]

•••

Michael Applebaum was a municipal politician for twenty years. What did he accomplish? As a citizen, early on, he helped keep a skating rink open; that was his finest hour. As a councillor, he fought for safer playgrounds, a ban on pesticide use in parks, better snow removal and garbage collection, and fewer restrictions on street food vendors. He fought against fraudulent use of loony-sized washers in parking meters, drivers who don't stop at red lights and Karla Homolka coming to live in NDG (she didn't). As a member of Montreal's executive committee, he was "in charge of" urban planning, housing, citizen services and borough relations, but it's hard to identify anything memorable that he accomplished. As chair of the executive committee, he ran the city's finance portfolio and pursued the usual crowd-pleasing budget cuts. "I have a responsibility to manage the finances of the city of Montreal," he was quoted as saying. "I'm not happy that people are saying Applebaum's a big, bad man. But I sleep well at night."[14] As mayor, in ironic initiatives, he created an advisory board to recommend measures to counter corruption and formed the Escouade de protection de l'intégrité municipale (EPIM), an anti-corruption squad to investigate the city.

Now Michael Applebaum spends his time trying to stay out of jail. As Henry Aubin, long-time municipal affairs reporter for the *Gazette*, told me, Applebaum's story shows that it's not just francophones who are corrupt. When I asked Peter Trent, the mayor of Westmount, about Applebaum, he said, "The thing about him is, he's poorly educated and not very smart." (That may be the best explanation of them all.) A friend who knows Applebaum told me, "If he stole money, he wasn't very good at it. The Applebaums live in a pretty crummy duplex." Linda

Gyulai of the *Gazette* said, "The funny thing about him was he started out as an idealist—the rink stuff and all that—and turned into a sneaky, conniving son of a bitch."

•••

I went to Montreal's city hall to see the Hall of Honour, the place where mayors traditionally give their resignation speeches when they leave in disgrace. I looked at the mayoral portraits hanging in a corridor adjacent to the hall. The most recent was a small and undistinguished photograph of Pierre Bourque, who left office in 2001.

As I wandered about, the only other people in the hall were a couple of security guards and a cleaner, chatting and laughing together. I went up to them.

"Excuse me, are there portraits of the mayors who came after Bourque—you know, Tremblay and Applebaum?"

"They're not up yet," I was told. "We have to hang three: Tremblay, Applebaum and Blanchard."

"Blanchard? But wasn't he mayor for only three or four months?"

"In this town," said one of the security guards, "we hang your portrait even if you've been mayor for only one day."

And they all laughed some more.

Laval mayor Gilles Vaillancourt announces his resignation in November 2012. Months later he was arrested and charged with gangsterism, money laundering, fraud and corruption.

SIX
GILLES VAILLANCOURT OF LAVAL
"It Looks Like It Is Good."

MONTREAL may have been bad, but Laval was worse. Montreal's Gérald Tremblay has not been criminally charged, leaving him free to go on a pilgrimage to the Cathedral of Santiago de Compostela and read books at his Saint-Hippolyte estate. Perhaps he was only a hapless dupe, or a willing ostrich. Michael Applebaum, Tremblay's successor, has been charged with crimes, but Applebaum was only an embarrassing cipher, a footnote to the Tremblay regime, dragged off the stage shortly after he walked onto it. But the situation in Laval was different. There, for the years when Gilles Vaillancourt was mayor, corruption contaminated municipal government from top to bottom, permeating every pore.

Gilles Vaillancourt—King of Laval, the Boss, mayor for life, consummate politician, superb administrator, urban visionary, populist, autocrat, walking contradiction, the man who transformed Laval from a few farmers' fields into Quebec's third or maybe second (it depends on how you count) biggest city, unbeatable in an election, loved by everybody, master of all he surveyed, monster of politics, gangster, fraudster, crook, hauled in handcuffs before a judge ...

A 2011 *Maclean's* article about Vaillancourt said, "He bears a passing resemblance to jazz crooner Mel Tormé and has barely blinking blue eyes and a low, raspy voice that he uses sparingly. Vaillancourt seems at once an incarnation of folksy politician and intense combatant who has fought (and won) all his life."[1] Bill Tierney, the former mayor of Sainte-Anne-de-Bellevue, had a different take: "He knew where all the bodies were buried because he'd probably buried most of them."[2]

•••

Gilles Vaillancourt was born in 1941 and raised on Île Jésus, which is north of the Island of Montreal across the Rivière des Prairies. In 1965, fourteen tiny, semi-rural municipalities on the island were forcibly amalgamated by the provincial government into the city of Laval. The amalgamation angered those who wanted to hang on to their rural lifestyle and resented the high-handedness of the provincial government. Vaillancourt has said that the controversial merger was what got him interested in politics.

Vaillancourt studied business administration. He married Francine in 1965, the year of the municipal merger that piqued his political curiosity. The couple had a daughter in 1968. He ran the family furniture store started by his father. In 1973, he became a city councillor. In November 1989, he was elected mayor (he had already been in the job a few months, having been appointed in June to replace an ailing Claude Lefebvre). He led a party called the Parti du ralliement officiel des Lavallois, known as PRO des Lavallois.

Vaillancourt's electoral success was stunning. In 1989, he had almost twice as many votes as the runner-up. During that campaign, popularly known as the Battle of the Billboards, he pledged to rezone agricultural land to make it available for development, and to bring the Montreal metro to Laval within five years. In the 1993 election, despite persistent conflict-of-interest allegations, Vaillancourt won by almost three votes to one over his closest opponent, and PRO des Lavallois members were elected to twenty-three of twenty-four council seats. In 1997, he suffered a setback (by his standards), winning only 41 per cent of the vote and sixteen seats; he might have lost altogether, but two opposition parties split the anti-Vaillancourt vote. In 2001, running against Daniel Lefebvre, son of the man he replaced as mayor, and Philippe Garceau, he got 57 per cent of the vote and his party won every seat on the council; the press described the campaign as lacklustre and bland. In 2005, Vaillancourt won an astonishing 75 per cent of the vote and his party claimed all the council seats; his opponents this time included a man who went on a forty-four-day fast during the campaign, a former actor who was a stand-in for John Travolta in the film *Battlefield Earth*, and an eighteen-year-old college student acting on a dare from a professor (to everyone's surprise, she won 17 per cent of the vote). In 2009, he had 61 per cent of the vote—still remarkable by any measure—and once more won all the council seats. During the 2009 campaign, he told a journalist, "Each campaign I like to spend six months getting to visit at least 30,000 homes.... I do it to find out if what I'm doing is good. And so far, it looks like it is good."[3]

No one could stand up to Gilles Vaillancourt. Philippe Garceau said he wouldn't waste his money trying to run against Vaillancourt again. "He's unbeatable," he declared. Journalist Jean-Claude Grenier said in 2005, "There is no one that will beat Vaillancourt. He's a monster of politics in Laval."[4] Journalist David Johnston wrote in the *Gazette* in 2009 that Vaillancourt "presides over his constituency with the majesterial [*sic*] bearing of an old-style Quebec parish priest."[5] As the mayor himself said, "It looks like it is good."

•••

Before Vaillancourt's regime crumbled into scandal and failure, many were quick to point out that under his rule, Laval went from fourteen semi-rural villages to a prosperous and industrialized city of 400,000 people attracting more than a billion dollars a year of private and public investment. The modern Laval—the Vaillancourt Laval—has shopping malls, a major hospital, a satellite campus of Université de Montréal and three new metro stations (Cartier, de la Concorde and Montmorency). The metro stations alone, opened three months ahead of schedule on April 28, 2007, by Premier Jean Charest, were considered a triumph. They cost $675 million.

But not everyone applauded the way in which Vaillancourt promoted development of the city. A July 2013 story in the *Gazette* noted, "There is mounting evidence that the city's growth was carried out at the expense of people … who possess expansive properties and no political connections…. What has raised alarm among residents and observers is the way politicians have worked hand in hand with real estate developers."[6] Henry Aubin of the *Gazette* describes Laval today as "terrible, a wasteland. There is no downtown. There are no sidewalks." To Aubin, Vaillancourt promoted the worst kind of urban sprawl: "He had an anti-metropolitan spirit. He was for the suburbs. He was anti-Montreal." Laval became the Mississauga of Quebec.

Nonetheless, the general feeling about Vaillancourt was extremely positive for a long time. In 2008, Aubin picked Vaillancourt as his person of the year. Wrote Aubin: "Even his fiercest critics admit he does two things brilliantly. First ... he continuously extracts stunning largesse from senior levels of government. Second, even though his suburb has a quarter as many people as Montreal, he arguably wields as much political influence over the region as Montreal Mayor Gérald Tremblay."[7] Aubin offered as proof a new bridge from Montreal to Laval, the three provincially financed metro stations and a variety of impressive municipal projects. "The 67-year-old mayor is the gold standard of municipal chauvinism." Aubin, who now thinks differently, still told me grudgingly, "Vaillancourt was extremely competent."

•••

It was white envelopes that started the trouble for Gilles Vaillancourt.

On Monday, November 15, 2010, following a twelve-month investigation by reporter Christian Latreille, Radio-Canada interviewed Serge Ménard, a Bloc Québécois member of Parliament, former Quebec minister of justice and all-around "good guy" according to his supporters. Ménard told Radio-Canada that in 1993 Vaillancourt had tried to give him a white envelope containing $10,000 in cash as a contribution to Ménard's first political campaign.[8] He said he refused it. (Quebec's Election Act sets a limit of $3,000 on contributions to provincial candidates, and so the attempted contribution was potentially illegal.) A similar accusation was quickly made, on the same day, by Vincent Auclair, a Laval member of the National Assembly. Auclair, a lawyer, said that in 2002, Vaillancourt had also offered him a white envelope stuffed with cash. Henry Aubin has described the white envelope incidents as an example of *"immobilisme moral."* He wrote: "Ménard is a perfect example of what's wrong with Quebec politics. He himself is a man well-known for his personal integrity. He might not let the grimy world of politics contaminate him personally (he says he rejected the cash-stuffed envelope), yet his failure to take action against it shows that he accepts the existence of that world."[9]

David Johnston of the *Gazette* described November 16, the day after the Ménard interview, as the longest day in the long career of the mayor of Montreal's largest suburb. "As Gilles Vaillancourt drove east along du Souvenir Blvd. shortly after 8 A.M. and turned south into the parking lot beside Laval's city hall," Johnston wrote, "he peered out the passenger side of his car window and noticed something unusual. A Radio-Canada van. It had been parked there since 6 A.M., hoping to catch an unsuspecting mayor.... Seeing what looked to him like a media stakeout, Vaillancourt took a circuitous route around the back of city hall and disappeared for the next seven hours."[10]

When Vaillancourt finally appeared that afternoon for a press conference, he denied the white envelopes allegation. "There are lots of white envelopes in my office.... Mr. Auclair says, 'There was an envelope.' I will tell you that every new political candidate who comes into my office I give a nice little document to, a document I have written myself, entitled 'How to Do Door to Door Campaigning.' And with that, I tell them, they should be able to get elected." And then Vaillancourt left the press conference, no doubt confident that a silly story about white envelopes could not shake his grip on public life.

Laval police chief Jean-Pierre Gariépy later said of the allegations, "That was the beginning of the investigations and with the buildup of pressure from the public and the media, it was like a train gaining speed and the government finally put all its resources into this investigation."[11] The Sûreté du Québec began looking into the affair. Vaillancourt was forced to resign from the Hydro-Québec board and as vice-chairman of the Union des municipalités du Québec (UMQ), a powerful post. Fresh allegations started to surface. The *Montreal Gazette* reported that a contract for the city's new police station went to a firm that employed the mayor's daughter, and a contract for the interior design of the station went to a firm that employed his brother.[12] The police were everywhere. Suddenly the Boss, the King of Laval, was on the run.

•••

On Thursday, October 4, 2012, UPAC, the provincial anti-corruption unit, raided Laval city hall and Gilles Vaillancourt's house (leaving behind hidden microphones). In the days following the raid, UPAC seized bank accounts and safety deposit boxes belonging to Vaillancourt. On October 12, Lino Zambito testified before the Charbonneau Commission that entrepreneurs who had contracts with the city of Laval were expected to hand over 2.5 per cent to the mayor.[13] On October 24, Vaillancourt went on sick leave. On November 9, five days after Gérald Tremblay resigned as mayor of Montreal, Vaillancourt resigned as mayor of Laval, after twenty-three years in office. He gave his resignation speech at city hall, under police guard. Many still adored him. Savas Fortis, an anglophone alderman, wrote in a local newspaper: "The corruption allegations are flying but many voters still love him.… His popularity is firmly rooted in the fact that unlike most elected officials, he constantly left the refuge of city hall and engaged his fellow citizens upfront and personally, often joining them in their daily lives."[14]

On May 9, 2013, Vaillancourt was arrested by UPAC and charged with twelve counts of gangsterism (the Criminal Code defines gangsterism as three or more individuals participating in an organization whose main purpose is to engage in crime), money laundering, fraud and corruption. He was taken in handcuffs before a Superior Court judge. Thirty-six Laval business-people, lawyers, city officials, engineers, construction bosses and Vaillancourt supporters were arrested at the same time.

The facts started to come out in testimony before the Charbonneau Commission. On May 22, 2013, retired engineer Roger Desbois testified that in 2003, he was recruited by city manager Claude Asselin to act as a bagman for PRO des Lavallois. He explained that his job was to keep track of rigged municipal contracts and collect a 2 per cent kickback from the winning construction company on each project.[15] The money was distributed among a variety of people who were in on the scheme. It is alleged that Vaillancourt smuggled about $15 million into Swiss bank accounts, using minors as mules to take the cash to Europe.[16] On May 30, Jean Bertrand— the official agent for PRO des Lavallois between 1984 and 2013, and one of those arrested on May 9—told the Charbonneau Commission that for at least two decades, "almost every PRO des Lavallois councillor has participated in what is known as the 'straw man' scheme—contributing financially to their own party via several small cheques in the name of family members (respecting the limits set out by the law) and then accepting a lump sum of cash from local engineering firms as reimburse-ment."[17] Bertrand, a lawyer, said that he told councillors this practice was illegal, and that Vaillancourt was aware of it.

As I write, the case against Gilles Vaillancourt is wending its way through the courts of Quebec, slow as molasses. The Crown prosecutor says members of Vaillancourt's "inner circle" will testify against him, including the former Laval city manager, Gaétan Turbide, and the former assistant city manager, Jean Roberge. It is said that Vaillancourt is being protected by the provincial Liberal Party, although no one can explain how or why that is being done. In September 2014, the new mayor of Laval, Marc Demers, announced the city was going to sue Vaillancourt in an attempt to recover money that was used illegally.

•••

There was an odd and ominous coda to the Vaillancourt story just before the municipal elections of October 2013. In August, Vaillancourt met Claire Le Bel, a candidate to replace him as mayor of Laval, offered her cash and told her that Marc Demers's legs would be broken. Le Bel secretly recorded her conversation with Vaillancourt, and eventually, days before the election, took the recording to Radio-Canada. The *Globe and Mail* reported: "Mr. Vaillancourt even told Ms. Le Bel 'a new system is already in place' to replace the kickback, bribery and bid-fixing regime he is accused of running when he was mayor. 'You know, even if there's a new law, even if everyone says, 'My hands are now clean, I'm now clean,' the reality is there's already another system,' he said in an excerpt aired by Radio-Canada."[18] Shortly after Le Bel made the recording public, her campaign manager, Rény Gagnon, "was forced to pull over on a Montreal freeway because of a flat tire. He was approached by two men, beaten and told to keep his mouth shut."

It is a tragic tale, far from over, of government perverted and citizens betrayed. Tragedy turned to farce when Alexandre Duplessis succeeded Gilles Vaillancourt as mayor of Laval.

Alexandre Duplessis, implicated in a sex scandal, resigned as mayor of Laval after being in office for less than a year.

SEVEN
ALEXANDRE DUPLESSIS OF LAVAL
"Will She Be Dressed Sexily?"

GILLES VAILLANCOURT resigned on November 9, 2012. His party, PRO des Lavallois, was disbanded almost immediately at the request of the twenty councillors who belonged to it. They announced they would now sit as independents. PRO des Lavallois was Vaillancourt's party, and there was no reason for it to exist after he was gone.

The Laval council, now crammed full of independents, held a vote to pick an interim mayor on November 23. Alexandre Duplessis, first elected in 2005 and appointed by Vaillancourt to the executive committee in 2009, got fifteen votes, his opponent only three. Generally regarded as Vaillancourt's anointed successor, the forty-two-year-old chartered accountant, one-time bus company executive and father of two had once considered the older man his mentor. Now he sought distance from his predecessor. "It will be completely different," Duplessis said in his victory speech. "You will see the management of the city will completely change…. We must use all means to show our fellow citizens they have rightly placed their trust in us."[1] He said he planned to run for mayor in 2013. He was considering starting a new party, to be called the Duplessis Party.

•••

On Friday, June 14, 2013, thirty-two-year-old Julie Cadieux and forty-four-year-old Nathalie Paquin drove to a chalet in the Laurentians, north of Montreal. Julie was a prostitute. Nathalie was her driver. The chalet was owned by Alexandre Duplessis.

According to news reports, Duplessis had sent 110 text messages to an escort service to arrange the get-together. He had requested a "30-year-old, 5-foot-8, 130-pound, 34 DD, blond with green eyes." He had asked, "Will she be dressed sexily? High heels?"[2] Later, the owner of the escort service was interviewed on television. "She said the customer asked if he could wear women's underwear, and whether the escort enjoyed white wine," according to the *Canadian Press*. "When the woman's employee finally found the cottage after getting lost, they dressed up together, put on high boots, and did makeup.... 'He really wanted to spend an evening as if they were girlfriends,' said the agency boss."[3]

There are at least two distinct accounts of what happened at the chalet in the Laurentians. One is that when Cadieux and Paquin got there, they immediately recognized their client as the mayor of Laval, and Duplessis, alarmed at having been identified, sent them on their way. Another version says there was a dispute over whether Duplessis should pay Cadieux's $160-an-hour rate for time spent on a boat ride. What seems clear is that there was an argument over money. In the days to follow, Cadieux and Paquin demanded sizeable and increasing amounts of cash, and threatened to go public about the encounter if Duplessis didn't pay up. He went to the police. Cadieux and Paquin were charged with extortion. The story quickly became widely known. Just after the July 29 television interview with the escort agency owner, Duplessis resigned as mayor—for other reasons.

•••

On May 30, 2013, Jean Bertrand, former official agent for PRO des Lavallois, told the Charbonneau Commission that Duplessis and members of his family had written cheques to the party and were then reimbursed in cash by companies winning city contracts, thereby circumventing Quebec law, which prohibits corporate giving to political parties.[4] The next day, Duplessis gave a press conference. "Squinting into the bright sunlight as a dozen cameras captured his every blink and tick, Duplessis planted his feet, smiled awkwardly and began to speak," wrote Monique Muise in the *Gazette*. "What followed was a brief and somewhat hurried address referencing 'transitional solutions' and 'extraordinary contexts,' but the bottom line was this: Laval would become a ward of the province. Duplessis wouldn't be running for office again."[5] On June 3, the government of Quebec put Laval into trusteeship, ostensibly at the request of Duplessis. Florent Gagné, a former provincial deputy minister and once head of the Sûreté du Québec, was now in charge, along with two administrative judges from the Quebec Municipal Commission. Any decisions of the municipal council would require approval of the trustees in order to be implemented. The trustees could impose their own decisions, had to approve the city's budget and could hire and fire city employees.

And then, later that month, there was the problem with the hookers. It was all too much. By the end of July, Alexandre Duplessis was gone. In March 2014, his LinkedIn profile said that he was "*disponible*" and looking for a "*nouveau défi professionnel.*" Today he works for a propane supply company.

On November 3, 2013, Laval elected a new mayor, Marc Demers, a former policeman. One of Demers's earliest cases, in the 1980s, was a fraud investigation of a city councillor called Gilles Vaillancourt. In the middle of his investigation, he was taken off the case and promoted to homicide.[6] That was the way things worked in those days.

The Canadian Press/Joe Bryksa

Sam Katz announcing in 2004 that he will run for mayor of Winnipeg. He left in 2014 under what the *Winnipeg Free Press* called "a haze of disappointment."

EIGHT
SAM KATZ OF WINNIPEG
"Who Wants It? Who Needs It?"

THE OLD WINNIPEG city hall, a Victorian gingerbread edifice, was built in 1866 and torn down in 1962, replaced by what many think is the ugliest public building in Canada. I went there in September 2014, on a cold day with the wind blowing mightily at the nearby corner of Portage and Main, to see Mayor Sam Katz. His office was on the second floor. I was a bit early and waited in a large and formal antechamber at the top of the stairs. In a glass case was a model of the beautiful old city hall. The building around me was strangely quiet. There was only the occasional click of high heels on a marble floor. Suddenly there was an explosion of energy and Sam Katz bounded up the stairs. He waved at me. "Come in, come in!" he said with a big smile.

Katz is in his mid-sixties. He is an ebullient, intelligent and good-humoured man, immediately likeable. When I talked to him, he was in the last few weeks of his decade-long mayoralty, having decided not to run in the October election. I asked him, Had it been worth it? "That's a good question," he said, and grinned.

•••

In December 2010, Sam Katz hosted a Christmas lunch at
Hu's Asian Bistro. He invited city councillors and department
heads and their families. The meal, with tip, cost $3,084.35.
The city paid for it. That didn't seem unreasonable. It was, after
all, an official function of sorts, a Christmas party for the folks
at city hall.

But there was a problem: Sam Katz owned Hu's. Reporters
found out about the lunch under freedom-of-information legislation. They questioned its propriety. It seemed wrong for city
funds to go to a restaurant owned by the mayor. They asked Katz
about it. He missed the point, or pretended to. He talked about
how much those attending had enjoyed the meal. "They love
Asian Bistro," he said. "Talk to them. Some of them actually take
food home from those events."[1]

Joe Chan, the manager of Cathay House, a Chinese restaurant in Winnipeg's east end, was particularly upset about the
lunch at Hu's. He said the mayor was guilty of a breach of
trust. He said that the Manitoba Municipal Conflict of Interest
Act had been breached, and that the office of mayor should be
vacated. He filed a declaration saying so in the Court of
Queen's Bench. Chan is a mysterious character and his motives
were not clear. Did someone put him up to it? There were
clumsy procedural errors in his motion, and it was eventually
withdrawn. Then Winnipeg human rights lawyer and well-
known idealist David Matas stepped in. Matas's motive *was* evident: he wanted to strike out against what he saw as municipal
corruption.

Madam Justice Brenda Keyser heard the case in April 2013.
Robert Tapper, Sam Katz's lawyer and a part-time international
boxing judge, told the court, "This case is not about corruption. This case is not about democracy. This case is about a
Christmas party. It's trivial. It's a Christmas party, for crying out

loud."[2] David Matas had a different view. He argued, perhaps a trifle sententiously, that the mayor knew he owned Hu's Asian Bistro, knew the invitations for the party came from his office, knew the city was paying for the party and knew the conflict-of-interest rules.

Justice Keyser decided that the conflict-of-interest legislation did not apply to social gatherings, but she didn't sympathize with either of the parties before her. She ordered Chan to pay $10,000 in Katz's legal expenses. As for Katz, she said that although he had not broken the law, he had exhibited bad political and ethical behaviour, and would be judged by the public in the 2014 civic election. Katz's only comment? "It's now history and we move forward."

But for Chan and Matas, lunch at Hu's wasn't history—not quite yet. They continued their quixotic fight. They appealed the decision to the Manitoba Court of Appeal, which in September 2013 upheld Katz's acquittal. It said that the Manitoba Municipal Conflict of Interest Act *did* apply to social gatherings, contrary to what the trial judge had found, but that there was no evidence Katz was involved in the decision to hold the lunch at his restaurant. Chan and Matas applied to the Supreme Court of Canada for leave to appeal, but the Supreme Court didn't oblige.

It seems like a lot of trouble over a festive lunch. As Robert Tapper, the mayor's counsel, said, "It's a Christmas party, for crying out loud." But some thought the lunch at Hu's was indicative of the mayor's conduct over a long period. Sam Katz was accused many times of being insensitive to conflicts of interest. Sometimes the issues—surrounding complex real estate transactions, for example—were hard to grasp. But everyone understands lunch. To some, lunch at Hu's seemed to encapsulate the way the mayor confused his personal interests with those of the city of Winnipeg. Maybe Katz, as the judge suggested, would be judged harshly by the public in the 2014 election—on lunch at Hu's and other mistakes.

•••

My family moved from London, England, to Winnipeg in 1954. In 1965, I graduated from the University of Manitoba and went back to England for a while. I have never lived in Winnipeg again, but I visit there from time to time. Some things have changed dramatically since the 1950s and 1960s, but others remain the same. Eaton's and the Hudson's Bay Company, which in the old days dominated the Winnipeg retail trade with huge downtown stores, live on largely in memory (there is still a downtown Hudson's Bay store, but in a very reduced state). The University of Manitoba, which had five thousand students when I graduated, now has thirty thousand. But my old neighbourhood, River Heights in the south end, looks much the same as it did before, almost as if frozen in time. It's still leafy and quiet and middle class, although in this chaotic world, residents may feel less confident and secure than their counterparts who lived there fifty years ago and delighted in polishing their Oldsmobiles on a summer Sunday afternoon.

Our house was on Oak Street. Our neighbour across the street was Lionel Orlikow, who taught me Grade 10 geography at Kelvin High School. His son John now represents River Heights on city council. Stephen Juba was the mayor for most of the time I lived in Winnipeg. He was a colourful politician who drove a yellow Cadillac, smoked cigars and was a proud Ukrainian Canadian. He was first elected mayor in 1957, and stayed in office for twenty years. The consensus is that Juba is the finest mayor Winnipeg ever had, certainly in recent times. In 2009, the *Winnipeg Free Press* asked its readers to name Winnipeg's greatest mayor of the past fifty years. Forty-four per cent voted for Juba, and 23 per cent for Glen Murray. Bill Norrie got 16 per cent, followed by Sam Katz with 11 per cent. Juba "put 'Peg on the map," said one reader.[3] Sam Katz, a great admirer of Steve Juba's, told me he was a people person, "just like me."

Steve Juba's biggest achievement was bringing the 1967 Pan Am Games to Winnipeg. Peter Warren, one-time city editor of the long-defunct *Winnipeg Tribune*, explained how it began: "Mayor Daley [of Chicago] had just announced Chicago had Pan Am [in 1959], and he told Steve you should get Pan Am, too. So when he got off the plane, he was so excited I asked him why. And he said Chicago had Pan Am, and he'd like to see Winnipeg get Pan Am, too. He said it would be great to see Pan Am Airlines at Winnipeg airport. That's how it all started."[4]

It was Steve Juba, by the way, who pushed the hardest to demolish the beautiful old city hall building.

•••

Sam Katz was born on August 20, 1951, in Rehovot, Israel. His parents were Holocaust survivors. His father lost a previous wife and children in the Holocaust, but never spoke of them. The Katz family came to Canada when Sam was six months old. His father was a baker and worked the night shift. His mother was a clerk in another bakery.

Sam graduated from West Kildonan Collegiate. He earned a bachelor of arts in economics from the University of Manitoba. He went to dental school, but dropped out after the first year. He tried accountancy and law, but they didn't work out either. At age twenty-three, he opened a clothing store in Brandon, Manitoba.

A little while after that, he set up Showtime Productions, a concert promotion company, with his friend and roommate, Bruce Rathbone. His successful career as an enthusiastic and flamboyant entrepreneur had begun. He credits some of his success to Winnipeg. "I love Winnipeg," he says. "That's why I wanted to be mayor—to give something back to the city that gave so much to me."

In 1994, Katz purchased an expansion franchise in baseball's Northern League and named the team the Winnipeg Goldeyes. The Goldeyes won the league championship that year. The *Globe and Mail* called Katz "the effervescent Mr. Winnipeg— entrepreneur, promoter, ideas man, wheeler-dealer, sports mogul." The account went on: "He is president of the Winnipeg Thunder of the National Basketball League and principal shareholder of the Northern League's Winnipeg Goldeyes baseball club. His business, Nite Out Entertainment, owns the city's grand old Walker Theatre, [as well as] two trendy local nightclubs, and if there is a major concert in town, it's likely to be a Nite Out show. With partner Bruce (Bones) Rathbone, Nite Out Entertainment is the $20-million-a-year promotion company that brought Paul McCartney and David Bowie to this oft-maligned and isolated prairie burgh."[5] Katz told the *Globe* that he loved "doing deals." He was prominent. He was everywhere. He had excellent name recognition. He was Mr. Winnipeg. He was on every list of possible candidates for important jobs. He was, as he puts it, "living the dream."

In May 2004 the mayor of Winnipeg, Glen Murray, resigned in mid-term to run for federal Parliament (he lost). As Sam Katz tells the improbable story, he wasn't considering filling the mayoral vacancy, but one day seven pastors visited him in the Winnipeg Goldeyes boardroom, urged him to run and said they would pray for him. That did it. Who could resist seven pastors? Coming into the race at the last possible moment, filing hours before the deadline, he got 47 per cent of the vote and easily beat three city councillors and a member of the legislative assembly. But Katz's joy at winning seemed short-lived. Soon he was pushing back against the intense public scrutiny that comes with politics. He seemed bitter, not effervescent. These feelings didn't go away. Ten years later, he railed against "media bias" and told me, "If you can't handle criticism, stay out of this line of work."

In 2006, there was a municipal election. During the campaign, Katz was asked why he had entered public life. His answer was striking: "There's nothing to gain, and everything to lose. Very few people want to be criticized on a daily basis, and that's part of public life.... The reality is, it's because I've been successful in my other life and it's because I don't have any needs that I have the opportunity and I have the want to do something for our city."[6] He went on to say, "I don't believe you will ever again see a high-profile, successful individual run for mayor of this city. Who wants it? Who needs it? Why would you do it? Why would you open up your closet so everyone can pick through every-thing?" He used almost the same language when I talked to him in September 2014.

The 2006 campaign was a cakewalk for Katz, who focused on "a simple mantra of fixing roads, reducing crime and creating more economic opportunities."[7] He won 62 per cent of the vote. The day after the election, Sam and his wife, Baillie, began proceedings for divorce and custody of the couple's two young daughters, five-year-old Ava and nineteen-month-old Kiera.

In 2009, a poll conducted for the *Free Press* reported that 74 per cent of Winnipeggers approved of Katz's performance, suggesting "the vast majority of Winnipeggers are as enthralled with Katz as they were when he was first elected mayor."[8] In the 2010 election, running on a simple anti-crime campaign and promising fifty-nine more police officers, endorsed by the United Fire Fighters of Winnipeg and the Winnipeg Police Association, Katz had a tougher fight than in 2006, but he managed to win 55 per cent of the votes. His popularity seemed deeply entrenched, unshakeable.

•••

Paradoxically, bad publicity dogged Katz almost from the beginning. For a long time, it didn't appear to have much effect on his performance at the polls. Voters seemed amused by it all. He mostly shrugged off criticisms. "Let's move on," he would say routinely. "I look forwards, not backwards." This insouciance annoyed journalists. Was he thick-skinned, or just stupid?

The press seemed to criticize every little thing. Katz got into trouble when he called five Manitoba Olympians "beautiful females" who made him feel like Hugh Hefner. His divorce from Baillie was messy; she claimed that the Winnipeg Goldeyes baseball club (with Sam as president) had paid her $60,000 a year for doing nothing. "I was never hired by the Goldeyes or by Sam to do any work whatsoever," she said. Katz countered that she had been hired to do a job, but had "simply refused to attend work on a regular basis."[9] In 2010, Katz was filmed accidentally kicking a child in the head during a charity soccer match. The announcer screamed, "He's booted him in the face in an election year!"[10] (Katz received a yellow card but won the election.) In 2013, he was challenged by a citizen when he threw chewing gum away on the street and claimed it was lint. What concerned the complainant the most, she said, was "'the natural ease' with which the mayor initially was able to be dishonest, in the moment, about what he had done."[11]

There was even a blog, *The Black Rod*, devoted in part to vilifying the mayor on a regular basis. It was started in 2005 and has had more than 1.5 million visits. Here is part of *The Black Rod*'s comment on the transcript of Katz's March 2014 speech to the Winnipeg Chamber of Commerce: "It read as if it was cribbed from a city travel brochure. It looked like the Mayor dashed it off at the last minute on a sheet of toilet paper while sitting on the crapper. Winnipeg is great, it's got a zoo, and some American stores, and (a white elephant, aka) a human rights museum, said Mayor Sam Katz. And there's some theatres, and restaurants, and a convention centre and 'optimistic spirit.' Okay? *Gotta run*."

•••

Sam Katz's biggest problem involved conflicts of interest, not kicking children in the head or lying about lint. He saw city business from the perspective of a businessman rather than that of a public servant. "I'm still a businessman," he told me when I met him in the mayor's office. Larry O'Brien, the former mayor of Ottawa, liked that about Sam. Also a successful entrepreneur, O'Brien saw things the same way. In November 2007, the *Ottawa Citizen* reported: "Mr. O'Brien said Tuesday that after several conversations with Mr. Katz, he found the Winnipeg mayor's way of doing things a 'very good model.' Like Mr. O'Brien, Mr. Katz—a colourful, self-made millionaire businessman—went into city politics to shake things up and 'deliver fundamental change.' One of his major priorities was to get 'City Hall out of the way of business' and create an 'entrepreneurial environment' in Winnipeg."[12]

But accusations of conflict of interest dogged Katz from early in his mayoralty. "In February 2005, Salisbury House Restaurants won a call for proposals to establish a restaurant on the Esplanade Riel," reported Dan Lett of the *Winnipeg Free Press*. "Salisbury House was partly owned by David Wolinsky, a longtime friend and business associate. Katz did not recuse himself from any of the deliberations on the Esplanade Riel proposal, or the final council vote approving the deal."[13] That same year, the city bailed out the failing Burton Cummings Theatre. Katz had a financial interest in the theatre until just before the bailout, and there were suspicions that somehow he had benefited from the murky transaction. In 2006, the city extended the Winnipeg Goldeyes lease on a parking lot in what critics called a "sweetheart deal." In 2008, controversy erupted over another Goldeyes parking lot lease. The lessor this time was Riverside Park Management, a company that had itself leased the land, on very favourable terms, from the city. Sam Katz was president of Riverside. That controversy dragged on into 2009.

"Katz has been vilified for participating in city business that directly and indirectly involved longtime friends and business associates," said the *Winnipeg Free Press*. Katz remarked, "The real sad thing is that in the future, you'll never see someone come forward like me to become mayor. Nobody is going to take on the shit and abuse I've taken." In February 2009, a frustrated city council passed a resolution asking the province to create a code of conduct for elected officials and appoint a conflict-of-interest commissioner. The *Free Press* later commented, "The motion was seen as a significant defeat for Katz, who spoke against the resolution, voted against it and then, when it was passed by a 7–6 margin, complained it was all part of a witch hunt organized by the media and political opponents."[14] Mysteriously, the province declined to act on the city's request.

In 2009, questions began to be asked about the mayor's relationship with Shindico, a real estate company doing business with the city. The principals of Shindico, brothers Robert and Sandy Shindleman, were long-time friends and business associates of Katz's. The Shindlemans owned a minority interest in the Goldeyes, and were directors of the Goldeyes and Riverside Park Management. In 2012, a land-swap scheme between the city and Shindico came to light. The plan was to exchange two decommissioned fire stations and some vacant land owned by the city for some Shindico property that was to be used for a new fire-paramedic station. City assessments suggested the fire stations and vacant land together were worth much more than the Shindico site. City council commissioned an independent review by consulting firm EY (formerly Ernst & Young) of the transaction. On October 17, 2013, just before the public release of the review, Phil Sheegl, the city's chief administrative officer and a close friend of Katz's, resigned. The review concluded that contracts had been awarded to Shindico on a non-competitive basis, and that Sheegl had made deliberate moves to avoid involving city council.

Sometime before the review was released, Katz bought the Shindlemans' Goldeyes shares, and the brothers resigned as directors of both the club and Riverside Park Management. Katz announced that he had "severed his ties" with Shindico. Meanwhile, EY was given a more extensive commission by council to review the city's real estate processes and policies, focusing on significant property acquisitions, expropriations, sales, transfers and external leasing transactions over a minimum period of five years.

In August 2012, Katz bought a house in Scottsdale, Arizona, from Terri Nordstrom, the sister-in-law of Sandy Shindleman. When questioned by reporters, Katz said, "Bought a home, it's in my name, end of story. Paid fair market value."[15] In September 2012, CBC News reported that Katz had bought a shell company from Phil Sheegl (he later sold the company back to Sheegl). The company was called Duddy Enterprises. Duddy is Sam Katz's nickname, presumably derived from Mordecai Richler's fictional character Duddy Kravitz, who said, "A man without land is nobody."

In a December 2012 EKOS Research poll, commissioned by CBC News, 46 per cent of respondents said they believed Katz had definitely been involved in conflicts of interest, 33 per cent said he had probably been involved in conflicts and 70 per cent said that city council did not deal very well with conflict allegations.[16]

•••

From time to time, Sam Katz has sat down with reporters from the *Winnipeg Free Press*, Winnipeg's major daily newspaper, to talk about his accomplishments as mayor. Most of the time it was with Bartley Kives, who has closely followed Katz's career for many years. Kives began his journalistic career as a music critic in 1998, when Sam Katz was a promoter. Kives often spoke to Katz about what was going on in the music world in those days. He told me Katz was a "reliable source." The relationship between Katz and Kives has been an odd one. Kives has been a forceful critic of Katz, but I detect an underlying personal regard, even affection, for the now former mayor.

Kives told me that Katz always thought he was the smartest person in the room. He didn't care what people thought about alleged conflicts of interest. He didn't listen to advice. He didn't understand the role of a municipal leader. He mistakenly thought he could compartmentalize—be mayor one minute and a businessman the next. "He didn't get nuances," Kives said. If he could make things happen, that's all that mattered, process be damned; Kives called this a "weird commonsensical approach." After a while, according to Kives, all that really mattered to Katz was not getting caught.

But Kives also had good things to say about Katz. He was very accessible, never shying away from the press. He wanted to eliminate red tape standing in the way of business, and had some success doing that early in his mayoralty. He had an innate understanding of Winnipeg's major socio-economic problem, the plight of local aboriginal people—something Kives has written about with eloquence. And what did Katz think of Kives? "He's a very peculiar individual," he told me.

In December 2008, Kives asked Katz to name his biggest achievement during the past twelve months. "Stage 1 of rapid transit, I consider very positive. The fact the (Canadian) Museum of Human Rights will finally be starting up. A state-of-the-art indoor soccer facility ... and also some of the projects we've brought to fruition for our recreational facilities. And I guess one of the big ones is the initiatives we brought forward under urban aboriginal strategies for youth."[17] His biggest failure? "Off the top of my head, I can't think of a specific failure, per se." When Kives asked if there was anything he would have changed about the year just past, Katz expressed his recurring bitterness at the way municipal politics worked. "I just wish, at some point in time, councillors would show a little more integrity or credibility on the floor of council.... It's like every time we try to do something, there's criticism, no matter what we do. I'd like to see councillors do the right thing. And in my opinion, these people are not doing the right thing. They're hypocrites. They're not telling the truth."

In 2010, in the run-up to the October election, Kives asked Katz why Winnipeggers should vote for him. "I definitely have the expertise, the work ethic, the knowledge and I've been here for the last 25 years, 30 years, 40 years, 50 years. I haven't been out of town. I know what the problems are. I know how to identify them. But more importantly, I'm here to represent the citizens of Winnipeg, not a political party."[18]

In his December 2011 year in review, Kives asked Katz, "What are you most proud of accomplishing in 2011?" Katz answered, "The City of Winnipeg is on the global map right now. What I mean by that is everybody in North America is taking note of wonderful, positive things that are happening in our city. It started with the (Canadian) Museum for Human Rights, but then you got to look at the airport that just happened and the football stadium that's being built."[19] Meanwhile, a cross-Canada poll showed that Katz was now near the bottom when it came to mayoralty popularity, keeping company with Rob Ford and Gérald Tremblay.[20]

Katz struck a similar upbeat note in his December 2012 conversation with Kives. "We're making significant investment in our infrastructure.... We've been investing $10 million every year in community centres. When it comes to fire-paramedic stations as well as police stations, significant investment there. We're continuing to basically make sure we're taking care of one of the gems of our city, Assiniboine Park. And just recently, we made a significant announcement to address the infrastructure at Polo Park, with an investment of $30 million."[21]

In December 2013, with another election less than a year away, Katz sat down with *Free Press* reporter Aldo Santin. Santin suggested that 2013 had been a very bad year for Katz: "Your friend Phil Sheegl was blamed by the Ernst & Young audit for the mishandling of the fire-hall replacement program. Two senior public servants [Fire Chief Reid Douglas and city entomologist Taz Stuart] were dismissed under mysterious circumstances. You continue to be dogged by allegations of ethical improprieties."[22] But as always, Katz was unfazed. "A lot of that is not accurate," he asserted. "If a senior official is let go, that has nothing to do with the mayor and council; that has to do totally with the administration and human resources. We don't have any role to play in that."

In May 2014, as a new municipal election campaign sputtered into life, the *Winnipeg Sun*, in what smelled like a political obituary, listed "Five good things Katz did for Winnipeg."[23] He made good on a 2004 campaign pledge to drop the business tax; it went from 9.75 per cent to 5.7 per cent. He privatized garbage pickup, saving the city about $3 million annually. He improved recreational facilities. He hired more police, and the crime rate dropped. He promoted public–private partnerships, which delivered major projects on time and on budget. But meanwhile, the polls were recording a dramatic decrease in the mayor's popularity. A February 2014 poll gave him only 12 per cent support. The citizenry was clearly getting tired of Sam Katz. There was a sense on the street that he might not run in October 2014, or would lose if he did.

May 1 was the first day a candidate was allowed to announce his intention to run and start raising campaign funds. Katz was coy about his plans. The media continued to torment him. In late May, Tom Brodbeck of the *Winnipeg Sun* described Katz as careless and do-nothing. "Sam Katz's time in office falls somewhere between disappointing and disastrous, depending on how charitable you want to be. To say he did not live up to expectations would be an understatement. He aroused suspicion in his dealings and management style and showed contempt for openness and accountability in office. He failed us, plain and simple."[24] Then came EY's real estate management review.[25]

EY delivered the 190-page report, commissioned by council two years earlier, to city auditor Brian Whiteside on Thursday, June 19. It seems that city councillors did not get copies of the review until many days later, possibly not until July 1 or 2, although the mayor saw it almost immediately. Council discussed the report in a closed-door meeting on July 2, the same day it was released to the public. EY reviewed thirty-three transactions and found that "evidence supporting compliance with City policies, procedures, and industry practices was lacking in many instances." The report concluded: "There is no real estate transaction management framework and a lack of standardized processes. EY's testing results showed certain procedures were not performed, there was inconsistent application of informal procedures, and key documentation was not retained in transaction files. A common theme identified in the findings was a requirement to enhance governance as well as establish a formal Real Estate Transaction Management Framework and confirm appropriate roles and responsibilities." EY made seventeen detailed recommendations for improvement to the system.

Reaction was mixed and predictable. Councillors evinced dismay at EY's findings. John Orlikow issued a statement claiming the audit showed "deceit, favoritism and incompetence."[26] Katz said he was disappointed: the report, he claimed, was a review and not an audit; a genuine audit would have been based on facts, not opinions. Phil Sheegl, the city's former chief administrative officer, who resigned just in advance of the public release of the earlier EY report on the Shindico land-swap, said the new report was "a joke" and "a political witch hunt," adding that EY made no attempt to interview him. Shindico president Sandy Shindleman asked how EY could charge the city $500,000 without interviewing him or other Shindico officials about transactions involving the firm. "It's impossible for them to know what they're talking about," he said.[27]

On Friday, June 20, several days before the report was released to the public, there was a lunch-hour concert at Winnipeg's

Central Park, featuring the Winnipeg Symphony Orchestra, a Ukrainian dance troupe and a Jewish folk ensemble. Before the concert began, Sam Katz got up on stage and announced he would not run for re-election. He said later that he had lived up to every promise and commitment he had made, and that his announcement had nothing to do with the EY review. Many observers thought that Katz, a shrewd politician, had simply concluded that he couldn't win the October election. Bartley Kives wrote that the election would have turned into a massive pile-on: "A campaign featuring Katz would have been a referendum on his time in office, and the debate over that referendum wouldn't have been pretty."[28]

On July 18, the *Winnipeg Free Press* ran an editorial severely criticizing the city administration. Phil Sheegl, not Mayor Sam Katz, was the newspaper's principal target. Sheegl, it said, "has been identified as the main culprit in the mismanagement of a series of real-estate transactions that cost the city millions of dollars as a result of poor practice, circumvention of policies and processes, and favouritism to a small group in the private sector."[29] The chief administrative officer, said the newspaper, had more power than the mayor. But Sam Katz and the council did not entirely escape criticism. "The mayor and councillors are supposed to provide oversight and demand updates on important projects. The administration withheld some important documents from council, but there was an astonishing lack of curiosity among the entire group." The next day, Bartley Kives went on the attack in a column about "city hall's rotten, fetid mess."[30] He wrote about "the severe mismanagement and questionable decision-making that botched major projects, infected real estate deals and tarnished the reputation of the city.... The past five years have been a horror story."

The 2014 municipal election, now without Sam Katz, got off to a bizarre start. One mayoral candidate's wife posted a comment on Facebook about "drunken native guys" who collect welfare and harass people; this was quickly discovered and apologies were made. Another candidate posted a campaign picture in which he posed with women in bikinis. A third sent out a news release in which he misspelled his own name. A *Canadian Press* story pointed out that after all, anyone can run for mayor.[31]

•••

On October 4, 2014, the *Winnipeg Free Press* published Bartley Kives's exit interview with Sam Katz. Two old friends were parting. Katz was leaving office, wrote Kives, "with his reputation in tatters."[32] For his part, Katz accused Kives of bias, and laid the blame for everything that went wrong "at the feet of consultants, public servants and the media."

On the same day, the *Free Press* published another Sam Katz story by Kives. This one was entitled "Katz Never Dodged Media."[33] Its tone is elegiac and affectionate. "The mayor and I wound up in a relationship that was often adversarial, at times uncomfortable but never, in my estimation, marred by personal disdain," wrote Kives. "I questioned his ethics so often—in person and in print—it appeared he stopped noticing, let alone taking offence." Kives was particularly impressed by Katz's accessibility. "Katz may not answer questions," he wrote, "but he never tried to prevent journalists from asking them. For that, he earned my respect even as he proved exasperating and irascible." And—dare I say it?—Kives shows fondness for Katz. "He could also be quite likable, affecting a charming disposition even in the midst of a heated scrum." The odd couple, Kives and Katz. "I would posit I'm not alone in having a complex relationship with Katz," Kives observed. "The entire city is justified in feeling somewhat discombobulated about a mayor who arrived with so much optimism and left under a haze of disappointment.... Perhaps he truly believes he was a good mayor. Perhaps he knows he wasn't but doesn't care what anyone thinks."

In the election on October 22, 2014, three incumbent councillors were defeated and a self-described "urbanist-progressive," Tory lawyer Brian Bowman, was elected mayor by a landslide. Infrastructure, ethics and indigenous relations were the big campaign issues. In the opinion of Bartley Kives, election night amounted to a repudiation of Sam Katz's city hall.[34] Bowman is said to be a progressive, in the mould of Naheed Nenshi of Calgary and Don Iveson of Edmonton. He's also a Métis, the first indigenous mayor of Winnipeg.

Joe Fontana, former mayor of London, wipes away tears after being sentenced in his July 2014 fraud trial.

NINE

JOE FONTANA OF LONDON
"They Are Hot on My Trail and Baying for Blood."

IN MY JOURNEY from Steve Juba's Winnipeg (where I lived as a teenager) to John Tory's Toronto (where I live now), London, Ontario, was a stop along the way. I lived in London from 1977 to 1983, teaching law at the University of Western Ontario. My house was in Old North, on a quiet, leafy street near the university campus. In those days, London was a prosperous, middle-class town, dominated by the university and the life insurance and banking industries. It was a dull place—peaceful, if you prefer. For most of the time I lived there, the mayor was Al Gleeson, an Irishman known as "Big Al, the people's pal." Not much happened in London while he was in office, other than a moderately dramatic twenty-two-day strike of city workers in 1979. Not much ever happened in London; that was the feeling I had. When Big Al died in 2009, Joe Fontana, who had served on city council with him in the 1980s, said, "He was a pretty incredible guy. I'm still in shock."[1] These days, London is best known as the birthplace of Rachel McAdams (1978), Ryan Gosling (1980) and Justin Bieber (1994). Big Al is forgotten.

Not much happened in London? Maybe I just wasn't paying attention. A criminology professor at Western University (as it now calls itself) claims that in those years, London was the serial murder capital of the world. Michael Arntfield says that from 1960 to 1985, London may have had up to six active serial killers. CTV News reported, "Arntfield says the city's proximity to the highways, its stratified social class at the time, and the fact that it was culturally isolated from larger urban centres may have all been factors making the city conducive to such criminals. '(London) had a social ecology of a frontier town,' he says."[2] London didn't seem like a frontier town to me as I walked to work down tranquil streets lined with substantial brick houses, stopping off at the friendly Miles Variety Store to buy a chocolate bar before another comfortable day at the law faculty.

In recent years, things have deteriorated in London, one of the country's larger cities (population about 400,000). Businesses have closed, and the unemployment rate has been one of the highest in Ontario, bouncing back and forth between about 8 and 10 per cent. Kellogg's closed its cereal plant in 2014, and the Caterpillar locomotive plant shut down in 2012. The Conference Board of Canada estimates that London has lost eighteen thousand jobs since 2003. The losses have been not just in manufacturing but also in education and health care and other professional sectors.

The middle-class confidence, even a certain heedlessness, that was evident when I lived in London has gone. The *Globe and Mail* has described Southwestern Ontario as the province's Achilles heel. "Once the nation's industrial heartland, it is in an economic tailspin."[3] Poor municipal leadership may have had something to do with it, and as we shall see, municipal leadership has indeed been poor. But there is at least one bright spot. In May 2014, Dr. Oetker, a large German food company, opened a frozen pizza plant that employs more than one hundred people. Frozen pizza is better than nothing.

•••

London's Marconi Cultural and Banquet Centre is named after Guglielmo Marconi, the Italian who invented wireless telegraphy, won a Nobel Prize in 1909 and was an active anti-Semite and member of Mussolini's fascist movement.[4] It began in 1900 as the Marconi Club (most people in London still call it that) and has been an important part of London's Italian-Canadian community ever since. The centre describes itself on its website as "classy, upscale and affordable."

Michael Fontana and his fiancée held their wedding reception at the Marconi Club on June 4, 2005. Two hundred and sixty people attended. The arrangements were made by Michael's father, Joe Fontana, then the Liberal member of Parliament for London North Centre and federal minister of labour and housing. Fontana was a long-time member of the Marconi Club, and he had known the president, Vince Trovato, for forty years.

In October 2010, Joe Fontana was elected mayor of London. In August 2012, Chip Martin, a reporter at the *London Free Press*, received a brown envelope in the mail. The envelope had no return address. Inside were two photocopies—one of a cheque stub from Public Works Canada, dated April 6, 2005, and showing $1,700 paid for "INV 2661 Joe Fontana MP," and the second of a "provisional function contract," numbered 2661, from the Marconi Club for Michael Fontana's wedding. It looked as if Fontana had used government funds to pay for his son's wedding reception. (There has been speculation that Joe DiPietro, general manager of the Marconi Club when Michael Fontana's wedding reception took place, sent the envelope to Martin. DiPietro is close friends with Tim Best, the husband of former mayor Anne Marie DeCicco-Best, who was defeated by Fontana in 2010.)

Chip Martin broke the story.[5] Because Fontana was an MP at the time the cheque was written and was seeking reimbursement of expenses he said were incurred officially, the Board of Internal Economy, the governing body of the House of Commons, quickly asked the RCMP to investigate. A team of five investigators got to work; presumably so many officers were assigned because a well-known public figure was involved. On November 21, seven years after the wedding reception for his son, Fontana was arrested and charged with fraud under $5,000, breach of trust by a public officer and uttering forged documents.

Fontana's bizarre three-hour interrogation by Constable Shawn Devine of the RCMP was videotaped and can be seen online.[6] For several minutes Fontana is alone in the interview room, picking at his fingernails. Then Constable Devine appears, and there are formalities and, for about an hour, a lot of inconsequential chit-chat about London, Fontana's personal history and political career, his love of music, how much things cost in Nunavut. Fontana seems relaxed and forthcoming. (Later a judge described all this as an attempt by Fontana to ingratiate himself with the constable.) Then Devine goes over the case against Fontana, reviewing documents and emphasizing suspicious alterations made to the original Marconi Club contract, including the date, before it was submitted to the House of Commons for payment. "The documents tell the story, Joe," he says. Devine thinks the story is that Fontana doctored the Marconi contract, which was for a personal event, to make it appear a reimbursable political expense.

•••

On June 16, 2012, just a few months before Joe Fontana was arrested, there was another Fontana family wedding event at the

Marconi Club—this one for Ugo Joseph Fontana, known as Joe Junior, Joey or Hugo, and his fiancée, Josephine Maisano.

Joe Junior, the mayor's son by his first wife, Marilyn, was president of Trinity Global Support Foundation, a registered charity established in 2007 by Vince Ciccone, a boyhood friend of Joe Senior's from his days in Timmins. The proclaimed goal of the charity was to eradicate poverty. In 2012, Trinity Global issued $152 million in tax receipts, making it one of the biggest charitable foundations in the country. Joe Senior joined Trinity Global's board of directors in 2008, becoming chairman in 2010 when Ciccone left the board. Between 2008 and 2010, Trinity Global paid close to a million dollars to its directors and companies they controlled. It also invested $7 million in a Ciccone company that subsequently went bankrupt. Late in 2012, Fontana stepped down as chair of Trinity Global, but he remained a director. Joe Junior stayed on as president, earning about $70,000 a year.

In May 2013, following an audit, the Canada Revenue Agency revoked Trinity Global's charitable status. A damning CRA press release said in part that Trinity had devoted a significant portion of its resources to the promotion of a tax shelter; had issued tax receipts improperly and for grossly inflated amounts; had invested over $7 million in investments held by corporations related to its directors, which funds were subsequently lost (i.e., the Ciccone investment); and had improperly paid over $865,000 to individuals and corporations related to its directors.[7]

On July 12, 2012, the mayor posted an emotional, almost incoherent, "message to Londoners" on the Internet. It read in part: "The long days of summer are upon us but instead of silencing the barking dogs the heat appears to have unleashed the hounds. They are hot on my trail and baying for blood. The local daily has been pricked by the summer musings of local bloggers who sit in cool basements. They have questions. They want a confession. I have one. I sleep well at night. I am a husband and father. I am a practising Catholic. I am a Canadian, but I was not born here. I embrace my Italian heritage."[8]

In 2012, Vince Ciccone was convicted of securities violations and ordered to repay investors in the bankrupt Ciccone Group more than $15 million. At the time, Joe Fontana was reported as saying, "Vince is a friend and always will be."[9] In May 2014, Ciccone was charged with defrauding 160 investors of more than $21 million. These charges were unrelated to Trinity Global. No criminal proceedings arose from the Trinity Global mess.

Oddly, in the saga of Joe Fontana, the egregious multi-million-dollar story of Trinity Global has been eclipsed by the tale of $1,700 paid to the Marconi Club.

•••

Joe Fontana was born in 1950 in Cellara, a tiny village in southern Italy. His family moved to Timmins when he was four. Joe's father became a police officer.

Fontana went to the University of Waterloo in 1969 to study chemical engineering, but he soon left to be a drummer in a rock band. "Music is my first love," he has said. While drumming, he met his first wife, Marilyn (Ugo's mother), who already had two children from an earlier marriage. He also smoked a lot of marijuana. "I was a drummer in a rock band in the late 60s. What do you think I was doing?" he told a reporter. "I didn't exhale."[10] Marilyn and Joe moved to London in 1971. He studied briefly at the University of Western Ontario, but left to work in the insurance and real estate industries.

Fontana quickly became involved in local politics and was elected to city council in 1978. Eventually, he and Marilyn divorced. In 1986, he married Vicky; they have two children, a son and a daughter. In 1988, he was elected to the House of Commons as a member of the Liberal opposition for the riding of London North Centre. In Ottawa, he formed the rock band True Grit, with Jean Chrétien on trombone. In 1996, he became chair of the National Liberal Caucus. He has been described as "gregarious, bombastic, colourful ... always a charmer ... on the common man's side."[11]

Fontana supported Paul Martin in his ultimately successful attempt to replace Chrétien as prime minister. In 2004, he was rewarded for his loyalty and became minister of labour and housing in Martin's minority government. After Martin was defeated by Stephen Harper in 2006, Fontana, not interested in being a member of the opposition, resigned his federal seat to run for mayor of London. He was easily defeated by Anne Marie DeCicco-Best, who won 58 per cent of the vote to Fontana's 36 per cent. He blamed biased reporting by the *London Free Press* for his defeat (losers typically blame the press rather than the electorate). There is long-standing animosity between Fontana and the local London daily.

In 2010, promising a four-year tax freeze and ten thousand new jobs for the city (the standard unimaginative promises of a weak mayoralty candidate), Fontana narrowly beat DeCicco-Best, with 47 per cent of the votes to her 45 per cent. DeCicco-Best's husband, Tim Best, had been charged in 2009 with impaired driving causing bodily harm, and those charges were pending during the election. Observers felt her husband's problems with the law hurt DeCicco-Best. Tim Best was eventually convicted and went to prison for four months. Joe Fontana was the beneficiary of Tim Best's stupidity.

Fontana's popularity, such as it was, quickly waned. In a 2012 survey, 46 per cent of those surveyed said they were satisfied or somewhat satisfied with the government of London. By 2013, the number had sunk to 32 per cent. Fontana commented on the 2013 numbers with typical incoherent bluster: "I will hearken to the Canadian Parliament, I will hearken to the American Congress, people unfortunately don't have the greatest sense of confidence in their elected representatives."[12] He added that the year "has been a little weird."

Fontana couldn't put a foot right. In December 2013, Ontario ombudsman André Marin released his second annual report on local government transparency. "There is, in my view, a putrefactive decay in democracy at the municipal government level, due to the insistence on officials to continue conducting city business secretly and illegally," Marin told a press conference.[13] His report found that nineteen of ninety-six meetings investigated by his office had violated Ontario Municipal Act guidelines. Of 293 complaints received by the Ombudsman's Office, 64 were filed against London, more than against any other municipality (Sudbury was second, with 54 complaints). There were 60 complaints from London about one meeting. "Public suspicions were aroused when six councillors and the mayor gathered in the back room of a local restaurant that day—some arriving by the back door," according to the report. "Although they publicly stated that the meeting occurred by happenstance and no city business was discussed, our investigation determined that an illegal closed meeting did occur."[14]

By the beginning of 2014, an election year, public opinion was turning even more strongly against the incumbent mayor. His "state of the city" address on January 28 was a barely understandable mishmash of platitudes. Someone quipped that Joe Fontana made former Toronto mayor Mel Lastman sound like Noel Coward. Chip Martin of the *London Free Press* wrote, "Fontana likes to project an image as an ideas guy, a go-fast-guy with great visions…. He's like the magician trying to fool onlookers with the pea-in-the-pod trick."[15]

On February 7, 2014, Fontana announced he'd be running again for mayor on October 27. The auguries were not promising—a criminal trial was pending. Chip Martin wrote, on February 26, "His political horsepower is gone—that was apparent this week as council nixed initiatives he pushed hard for: the proposed performing arts centre and police spending cuts. The mayor's supporters, suggests Western University political expert Andrew Sancton, may be distancing themselves on the eve of his May 26 criminal trial as they mount re-election bids."[16]

•••

Fontana's trial before Justice Bruce Thomas of the Ontario Superior Court began on Monday, May 26, 2014, and took four days. He had earlier elected for trial by judge rather than jury.

The Crown argued that Fontana had altered the contract for his son's wedding reception at the Marconi Club to make it look like a contract for a February 25, 2005, reception for Ralph Goodale, then minister of finance. (The Goodale reception, although apparently scheduled, never happened.) Fontana admitted on the stand that, using Wite-Out and an eraser, he had changed the original document, altering the date of the event and the reason for booking the hall, substituting his signature for his wife's and writing "Original" at the top. A photocopy of the altered contract was sent by Fontana's parliamentary assistant to the House of Commons for reimbursement. The Crown said that Fontana's intention was to pocket $1,700. The money was paid by the House of Commons, but unfortunately for Fontana, the cheque was mistakenly sent to the Marconi

Club rather than to him personally. The club credited the amount against Michael's wedding.

Fontana's lawyer, Gord Cudmore, conceded that his client had altered the document, but he insisted that the $1,700 was a deposit for the Goodale reception, payable even though the reception had ultimately been cancelled. Fontana testified that he felt the Marconi Club was owed a deposit, and that $1,700 was an appropriate amount—despite the fact that the club had not asked for any money. Fontana handled the paperwork the way he did, he claimed, because he was "dumb, stupid, busy ... harried." In his eyes, he was not forging an old document but creating a new one. He couldn't be bothered to get a proper invoice from the Marconi Club. The club, he said, had made a mistake when it credited the money against the Michael Fontana wedding reception.

Justice Thomas gave judgment on Friday, June 13. Fontana was found guilty on all three charges—breach of trust, fraud and uttering a forged document. The judge didn't believe a word of Fontana's explanation. He said, "Where his evidence seeks to describe a legitimate motive for his actions related to this payment of $1,700, I reject it completely."[17] He excoriated Fontana's friend Vince Trovato, the former president of the Marconi Club, who gave evidence in Fontana's favour: "When he testified I got the feeling that Mr. Trovato was making it up as he went along."

The *London Free Press* described the decision as "the judicial equivalent of a knockout punch."[18] Fontana said he was "surprised, shocked, devastated." He resigned the following Monday, June 16. "I am taking this step out of respect for the office of the mayor, the people of London and our judicial system,"[19] he declared, and then he said nothing more, dodging the media. Later, a press release from the mayor's office quoted Fontana as saying that "he will not return to public life." A board member of the Marconi Club commented, "Ninety-nine per cent of people who are here are hardworking people. They don't give a sh— about what happens in politics." The club's general manager said, "I have no comments and I'm not interested."[20]

On July 15, Fontana was sentenced to four months of house arrest and eighteen months of probation. Addressing the judge before sentencing, he said, "Nine years ago I did something very, very stupid, very, very, very wrong. I made a big, big mistake. What's ensued since then is I've disgraced my family, my mother and father, who gave me an opportunity and spoke to me about always giving back, and my wife, my kids, my friends, my community and city and country and the very institutions that I've always respected—especially this one."[21]

•••

If you ask Fontana what he accomplished as mayor, he points to three things: job creation, property tax freezes and the World Figure Skating Championships in March 2013. The reality? Overall, jobs have been lost. Tax freezes have put the London budget under serious pressure that will have to be corrected soon by a significant tax increase (Fontana himself recognizes this is the case). Perhaps Fontana, looking for a legacy, will have to hang his hat on the figure skating championships.

As for the $1,700, there's something peculiar about that particular scandal. Why was the potentially more serious Trinity Global mess so overshadowed by the nickel-and-dime Marconi Club caper? The amount is so small; the incident violates Al Capone's maxim, "If you're gonna steal, steal big." Maybe Justice Thomas had it right when he observed, "I have long ago abandoned the notion that motive results from a logical cost–benefit analysis."

As for Joe Fontana, he's pretty much disappeared, and I don't expect we'll be hearing from him again—not speaking from the political stage, at any rate. Perhaps he'll go back to playing the drums, his first love. It's an odd end for someone who was once an important and respected public figure. But he was not smart, and he was not scrupulous, and he won't be missed.

Rob Ford was called "a plague on all your houses" kind of candidate by broadcaster Rex Murphy.

TEN

ROB FORD OF TORONTO

"To the People of This Great City, I Want to Offer a Public Apology."

IN SEPTEMBER 2014, I was in Bishkek, the capital of Kyrgyzstan. Bishkek is a remote and drab Russian-speaking city of about a million people, fifteen hours from Toronto by plane. One day in a taxi going back to my hotel, I asked the driver if he had ever heard of Rob Ford. He shook his head. "He's the mayor of Toronto," I said. The cabbie shook his head again. I was pleased. Finally, I had found a place where Ford was not famous. Not wanting to disappoint me, the cabbie worked hard to summon up some names of Western political figures. "Leetle Bush," he said, grinning. And then, a moment or two later: "Condoleezza Rice!"

Why have people voted for Rob Ford? Because he seems— to some, at least—to be Everyman. "Rob Ford is a simple man, and I am a simple man, and so I voted for him," one Torontonian told me. For a time, until they sobered up—and many have still not sobered up—Torontonians wanted their spokesman and leader to be someone whom they thought they understood, and who seemed to understand them. They didn't want a cerebral person leading their parade—a person with an elite education and progressive views; a person on a bicycle; someone who was handsome or beautiful, obviously rich, slim and trim, a metrosexual, a teetotaller who didn't eat hamburgers and played a lot of tennis. They didn't want a "perfect" person as their mayor. They were not perfect. Ford was not perfect. They voted for Ford. They voted for themselves.

Later, when the consequences of what they had done became apparent, there was regret and re-thinking by all but the fanatical. But there are many fanatics. The Ford Nation remains intact. Doug Ford, Rob's brother, came close to beating John Tory in the October 2014 mayor's race. Rob Ford himself was re-elected to city council. Their political careers are far from over.

There is a class-warfare aspect to the Ford phenomenon. A radical divide exists between Rob Ford supporters and his vociferous opponents, who loathe and despise the erstwhile mayor. This divide is often expressed in phrases like "suburbs versus downtown," or "rednecks versus snobs," or "right versus left." Ford's ascent to the mayoralty is frequently blamed on the 1998 amalgamation that made Toronto voters out of the worthy burghers of Etobicoke (where the Ford family resides), Scarborough, York, East York and North York. The amalgamation was seen by some as a cunning move by Conservative premier Mike Harris to allow the votes of the lesser people of the suburbs to swamp those of right-thinking and left-leaning urbanites. But Richard Florida, a well-known urban theorist, has argued that the divide is more complicated than suburbs versus downtown. The 2014 vote in Toronto, he says, was about economic and social classes, not simple geography, and the same was true in the Vancouver and Montreal elections.[1]

Rob Ford, the common man, famously returns his calls. Personally. He did it even when he was mayor. He was not isolated from the ordinary citizen by a phalanx of staffers. He would arrange to have someone come and fix your furnace in the middle of the night. Who knows, he might come and do it himself. He "really cares about the people" was a frequent comment made about him. David Miller, Ford's predecessor as mayor, did not come in the middle of the night to fix your furnace. Don't expect John Tory, Ford's successor, to lend a hand when appliances go wrong. Ford handed out fridge magnets; Miller did not hand out fridge magnets. So goes the narrative. Journalist Edward Keenan has astutely observed, in his book *Some Great Idea*, that Ford's "personal failings enhanced his credibility. A guy that apparently guileless, unhinged and fallible didn't seem capable of the inauthenticity most politicians seem to possess."[2]

Ford may not be a policy wonk, but he is a people wonk. He has an intuitive understanding of the individual, his strengths and weaknesses, what he cares about. Rather than debate the intricate details of transportation infrastructure (something few people are truly interested in), he swung into action and filled a pothole (something almost everybody is interested in). Keenan described what he saw one day when he followed along as the mayor visited constituents: "There was something pathetically charming about the sight of him there, soaking wet, red-faced in his wrinkled suit, getting drenched in the name of helping out those who elected him.... Rob Ford may have been a raving lunatic, but he was a raving lunatic who would come to your home and stand in the rain to ensure you'd get your fifteen minutes with the city staffer who could help you."[3]

Often, elected officials become suffused with self-importance. Become a city councillor or a member of the legislature, get a big office and staffers, vote for or against budgets of millions or billions, debate complex policy issues (or attempt to), and you become too important to stand in the rain in a wrinkled suit, too important to spend time with individuals if there isn't an election going on. Rob Ford, although full of himself, was not self-important in that way. He was a politician not of policy but of the individual. He would stand in the rain to help you.

•••

It is a dinner party in North Toronto in early June 2014. Six people are sitting at the table. Two are distinguished psychiatrists. Another is a family doctor. One is a psychologist with a Ph.D. from a famous university. My wife and I complete the party. There was a time when people at dinner parties like this talked about Conrad Black. But in June 2014, Lord Black is blessedly passé. Now we talk about Rob Ford. At this dinner party—in spite of where the guests live, their educational achievement, their social standing—the sentiment is surprisingly pro-Ford. As we talk about him, Ford is in rehab at the GreeneStone treatment facility in Bala, Ontario. GreeneStone, according to its website, "provides expert care in the treatment and recovery of those with substance abuse issues. We offer a comfortable and private environment where executives and professionals are able to find the individualized care that they need."

"The thing is," says one of the psychiatrists, "Ford's behaviour hurts himself terribly, but it doesn't hurt the city in any obvious way. How does smoking crack in your friend's basement hurt the city? What's it got to do with his being mayor? Does personal failing invalidate professional or political achievement? I don't think so."

"He's Falstaff," says the other psychiatrist, who has a particular interest in the theatre. "Shakespeare's Sir John Falstaff. A man of appetites who amuses us, a rebel to the traditions of his order. Remember, Falstaff is flawed, but everyone likes him. The audience claps when he comes on stage. They clap when Rob Ford comes on stage."

"A lot of people say he's a terrible mayor, but it's just not true," says the psychologist. "He tamed the unions. He saved the city money—not as much as he claims, but a lot. I voted for him before, and I'll vote for him again."

. The lone dissenter is the family physician. "I'm a union person," she declares. "I can't support Ford. He's a union-basher."

My wife says nothing. I murmur, "Interesting, interesting." At this dinner table, Ford has a 50 per cent approval rating, maybe more.

It's surprising who has supported Rob Ford. The wealthy chief executive officer of a multinational mining company told me he voted for Ford in 2010. "I just wanted to see what would happen," he said, perhaps a little sheepishly. A friend of mine, a lawyer with an Oxford doctorate in political science, admitted that he voted for Ford. There's more to this Ford thing than meets the eye. It isn't just suburbs versus downtown, rednecks versus intellectuals, poor versus rich. A subtle bloody-mindedness is at work. The class divides are complex. There's a nihilistic urge in play.

And my friend the distinguished psychiatrist was not the only one to spot the Falstaff in Ford. Playwright Brett McCaig, creator of a stage musical about the mayor, said, "He's very Shakespearean or operatic. He's our modern tragic hero—he rode in on his white horse, stallion, to save his village and then through his own weakness fell hard."[4]

•••

A huge amount has been written about Rob Ford. Once, not long ago, there were as many conversations and arguments about him as there are stars in the Milky Way. But as a new Toronto mayor took the stage, the Ford family psychodrama faded, at least a little, and Rob Ford began to recede in consciousness and memory.

Much of the written word has delightedly chronicled Ford's awfulness, with obligatory interspersed tut-tuts. You haven't read much that defended his attitudes and behaviour. There has been a lot of embarrassment (some of it feigned). There have been cries of outrage. There have been many references to Toronto being "Canada's largest city," to its high ranking on various international lists, to the absurdity of such a place having a mayor like Rob Ford. Moral superiority has abounded.

But voter reaction to Ford's scrapes has often been ambivalent and hard to read. Take his run-in with *Toronto Star* reporter Daniel Dale on May 2, 2012. Dale was inspecting a piece of land adjacent to the mayor's house that Ford wanted to buy from the Toronto and Region Conservation Authority. Ford said that Dale was peering over his backyard fence and taking photographs with a cellphone. The mayor came running out of his house, agitated and aggressive. Later, interviewed on television by—guess who?—Conrad Black, Ford said, "I have little kids. When a guy's taking pictures of little kids, I don't want to say the word, but you start thinking, you know, What's this guy all about?" Dale brought a libel action against Ford, but withdrew it when Ford gave a complete apology.[5] The mayor, by his own admission, was completely in the wrong, but to some the incident reinforced a "conception of the mayor as strong, powerful, someone who won't take crap—from journalists he doesn't like, from staffers who give him disagreeable advice, from unions in the midst of negotiations."[6]

Then there was the reaction to Ford's admission in November 2013 that he smoked crack cocaine. Anthony Furey of the *Toronto Sun* wrote, "The argument that this drama is damaging Toronto is total crap. This is the mayor's personal life. Any damage just hurts him." The bottom line, wrote Furey, is that some people "don't like that a fat, red-faced football coach with a working-class way about him is mayor."[7] Of course, many fat members of the working class like it just fine. Nelson Wiseman, a politics professor at the University of Toronto, commented, "The attitude of a lot of people is that, 'Look, I didn't elect this guy because he doesn't sleep around or he doesn't do crack cocaine. I elected him because I think there's a gravy train at City Hall, and that's what I care about.'"[8] Marni Soupcoff in the *Huffington Post*, comparing Ford favourably with Joe Fontana of London, wrote, "Ford has proven himself to be unpolished, undignified, inarticulate, petulant and impulsive. This displeases many people for obvious reasons, but it particularly disgusts politicians and reporters, who operate in a sphere where the opposite characteristics are considered emblematic of virtue. Yet for many voters, the more relevant questions when judging a politician are: Is he a greedy bastard and has he tried to screw me over?"[9] After all, Fontana stole taxpayers' money; Ford didn't.

Pollsters could never get a good fix on Rob Ford. Results were all over the map. One poll would contradict another, and then itself be contradicted. The biggest losers were the polling companies themselves. For a time it seemed that no matter what happened, Ford's support was rock solid, even growing. When allegations of drug use were first made in May 2013, the mayor's approval rating climbed. Marcus Gee of the *Globe and Mail* observed, "Mr. Ford's brand as the rumpled champion of the taxpayer remains strong despite all his stumbles."[10] When Toronto police announced at the beginning of November 2013 that they possessed a video showing Rob Ford smoking what was thought to be crack cocaine, the mayor's approval rating in a Forum Research poll immediately rose 5 per cent, to 44 per cent.[11] How to explain this startling result? In an op-ed piece in *The New York Times*, writer Stephen Marche posited that Ford "captures, better than anyone, the deep currents of outsider rage against the city's institutions…. Toronto is the city of Rob Ford now, an expanding hot mess, fueled by dark secrets, inarticulate desires and inchoate fury."[12] At the time, pollster John Wright pointed out that high approval ratings do not necessarily translate into electability. When people were given four ballot scenarios of declared and potential challengers in November 2013, Ford received between 19 and 24 per cent support.[13] Bob Hepburn of the *Toronto Star*, no Ford-lover he, observed in April 2014, "Ford has no growth potential in the polls; he lacks support from any major community, political, religious or academic leader; every newspaper … opposes his candidacy; and his lone main campaign message of controlling city hall spending can be easily usurped by other candidates."[14] A Forum Research poll in June 2014 reported that Ford was strongest "with voters who make less than $40,000, voters age 34 or younger, the least-educated voters, and voters in Scarborough he has long targeted with his 'subways, subways, subways' mantra. He dominated, with 49 per cent support, among people with a high school education or less."[15]

All along, Ford's political program, like his persona, was something of a joke, at least among the intelligentsia. Again, Edward Keenan put his finger on it: "The billions of dollars of waste he claimed he could cut simply did not exist. And the combination of massive tax cuts and slashed government spending appeared nonsensical when considered in combination with his insistence … that no city services would be cut, that customer service would be enhanced and that new subways would be built in sparsely populated suburban areas."[16] Keenan pointed out that Ford didn't really have an ideology. "He can sometimes look like a libertarian or a corporatist," he wrote, "but he does not cohere to the logical elements of those schools of thought. He starts from two, sometimes contradictory, premises: 1) No taxes are good taxes, and 2) The role of government is to give people what they want directly. As a corollary, he has complete faith in the 'private sector' to deliver anything that is needed."[17]

In 2010, Rob Ford, Everyman without an ideology, lacking a grasp of complex policy questions but with an electoral lock on the downtrodden and a strange appeal for bloody-minded members of the privileged classes, had been elected, to the despair of the "downtown elites." Democracy had displayed its relentless, sometimes self-defeating, brilliance. But soon, the mayoralty of Everyman became a catastrophe, and this particular expression of the democratic process was revealed as a debacle. The *Toronto Star*'s Christopher Hume wrote in October 2013, "Ford's term has been a disaster that will endure long after he has disappeared. His recklessness dealing with issues as diverse as public transit and taxes, bike lanes and vehicle registration fees, will hobble Toronto for decades to come."[18] At the end of December 2013, Hume, discussing the ice storm that paralyzed parts of the city for as much as a week, wrote, "How fitting that 2013 should end in disaster; for Toronto, the year has been one long disaster.... If it wasn't bad enough that freezing rain left more than 250,000 Torontonians without power for days, Ford left the whole city looking like some over-sized backwater inhabited by rubes too dumb to know they're being played for suckers."[19]

•••

Rob Ford returned from rehab in the Muskokas on June 30, 2014, with a sobriety coach called Bobby Marier in tow. (Marier is a recovering alcoholic and cocaine addict who in 2004 was arrested for fraud and in 2006 was charged with assault.)[20] The *Toronto Star* reported that Ford had been "disruptive" in rehab. "Mayor Rob Ford pushed and scuffled with fellow rehab residents," wrote Kevin Donovan, "and was so verbally abusive that he was kicked out of his group therapy program, according to people who have knowledge of his two-month stay at GreeneStone."[21]

On his first day back, the mayor held an invitation-only press conference, with no questions permitted, in his protocol office at 3:30 in the afternoon. Several prominent journalists, including Robyn Doolittle, author of the Ford-bashing book *Crazy Town*, were not on the list of invitees, but since there was a live audio feed, the exclusion was only symbolic. That didn't stop Royson James of the *Star* from violently attacking the media, including his own newspaper, for not boycotting the press conference. "Makes you sick," wrote James. "Grow some spine, cowards."[22]

At his press conference, Ford spoke for seventeen minutes from a carefully crafted text. He began with an extended apology:

> When I look back on some of the things I have said, some of the things I did under the influence, I'm ashamed, embarrassed and humiliated. I was wrong, and I have no one to blame but myself. I want to apologize, not just to the people of Toronto but to everyone who was hurt by my words and my actions. It was never my intention to embarrass the city or offend my fellow members of council. I deeply regret some of the personal choices I have made. I now realize that I was blind to the dangers of some of the company I kept. And those associations have ended. My commitment to living clean is now unwavering.

> To the people of this great city, I want to offer a
> public apology. I used poor judgment, and I take full
> responsibility for my actions.[23]

After the apology, Ford moved on to more familiar campaign
territory. "When I was first elected in 2010, I promised to stop
the gravy train. And that's exactly what I have done," he declared.
"We've moved away from the tax and spend ways of the past
and changed the culture at City Hall. We have reduced the size
and cost of government. And we have saved the taxpayers
hundreds of millions of dollars." He continued:

> The days of transit strikes and garbage strikes are
> now over. We've made the TTC an essential service.
> And we have contracted out garbage collection,
> saving you 80 million dollars, while improving
> service delivery.... I am keeping the City of Toronto
> accountable to you, the taxpayer. They said I couldn't
> work with the unions.... Well, I proved them wrong
> by achieving historic labour deals. Deals that are
> fair to the taxpayer and to our frontline workers.
> And most importantly, we have brought all three lev-
> els of government together to build new subways to
> Scarborough. We have come a long way, and despite
> my personal struggles, I am extremely proud of my
> public record.

Predictably, other candidates for mayor, and the media, were not
impressed. They found the apology weak, and loudly regretted
that Ford had so quickly moved on to familiar and banal
campaign rhetoric. A Forum Research poll taken two days after
the apology asked if voters were satisfied with Ford's statement.

Sixty per cent said they were not. The poll gave challengers Olivia Chow and John Tory 36 and 27 per cent of the vote, respectively, and Ford 26 per cent.[24] A Nanos Research poll taken at about the same time had substantially different results, once more raising doubts about the accuracy of all poll results. Nanos gave Tory 39.1 per cent, Chow 32.7 per cent and Ford 21.7 per cent.[25]

On July 1, Ford marched in a Canada Day parade in the city's east end. The *Canadian Press* reported that he seemed in high spirits. On July 2, in an interview with CBC's Dwight Drummond, Ford said his drug use ran the "full gamut" and "refused to say whether he would resign if he returns to drinking and using drugs."[26] Doug Ford, his brother and campaign manager, proudly announced that the mayor had trimmed down from a 52 pants size to a size 44.

The nineteenth annual Ford Fest, billed as a family-friendly barbecue with free hamburgers, was held on the evening of July 25 in Scarborough's Thomson Memorial Park. Thousands of people showed up. The *Globe and Mail*'s Ivor Tossell reported: "There formed an enormous, screaming knot of people, cellphone cameras raised above heads, and TV cameras hoisted above those. In the centre, an elderly Ford supporter in a battered Canadian Forces uniform had his arms held protectively to either side of an even tinier young woman, an LGBT protestor.... A wildly gesticulating man was screaming at the old soldier about how Liberals were turning Canada into a socialist third-world country."[27]

Campaign chaos now reigned. Public opinion polls continued to bounce all over the place. A Forum Research poll toward the end of July suggested that Ford, Tory and Chow were in a three-way tie, with Chow losing steam.[28] A Maple Leaf Strategies poll at the end of July showed Ford trailing Chow and Tory everywhere except Scarborough.[29] A Forum poll in early August showed a dramatic drop in support for Olivia Chow, and John Tory clearly in the lead.[30]

In the middle of August, a report from the University of Toronto's Institute on Municipal Finance and Government (IMFG) said that Toronto had a revenue problem, and not—as often asserted by Ford—a spending problem.[31] The report identified the core problem of municipal governments everywhere. Toronto expenditures, it said, are about the same as they were ten years ago, taking inflation and population growth into account; property taxes are low; and debt is modest and manageable. But according to the IMFG, the city would not be able to maintain its infrastructure and make necessary investments in it without new sources of revenue. "Toronto's funding shortfall for maintaining existing assets, such as transportation infrastructure, in a state of good repair will grow to nearly $2.5 billion by 2020," said the report. "Toronto Community Housing alone reports an $860 million unfunded repair bill for social housing. There is no funding available for big new proposals, such as the much-talked-about transit investments. And there is little certainty about provincial and federal transfers, which represent a third of planned infrastructure spending." This responsible note of caution, emphasizing the parlous state of the city's finances—a serious note struck amid electoral cacophony—was ignored by those campaigning for the city's highest office as they went on their merry way, promising expensive infrastructure without explaining where the money to pay for it would come from.

The Ford campaign developed a farcical side. Early in August, the mayor announced that he had received an email threatening to blow up city hall unless he resigned immediately. He called the threat "very serious" but courageously said it was "business as usual."[32] A week later, he told reporters that he had had standoffs with raccoons. "Seriously, they just look at you, and they're not scared anymore. It used to be you could yell or scream at them, [now] they just look at you. I mean, right up to my front door."[33]

As the summer wound down, John Tory seemed to be emerging as the favourite. Comfort was taken in Rosedale and Forest Hill. And then came a bombshell: a Forum Research poll at the end of August showed a significant rise in support for Ford, putting him almost neck and neck with Tory. The *Globe and Mail* reported: "The poll found that Mr. Ford's support was highest among men, those aged 18-34, residents of Etobicoke and Scarborough, people with a household income between $60,000 and $80,000 and those with a high school education or less. By contrast, support for Mr. Tory was highest among senior citizens, North York residents, voters with household incomes over $250,000 and those who have gone to graduate school. His support is almost evenly split between men and women."[34] The Forum Research president, Lorne Bozinoff, announced, "Rob Ford is on the comeback trail." An article by Dan Rath in the *Toronto Star* carried the headline "Why Rob Ford Will Win Again in Toronto."[35] Rex Murphy suggested in the *National Post* that many voters viewed ticking off Rob Ford's opponents as more pleasurable than voting for a sensible candidate. "'Normal' politics has brought these voters no comfort, and the class of people that owns 'normal' politics has brought no harvest of joy either," he wrote. "It is 'a plague on all your houses' kind of moment. And Rob Ford is 'a plague on all your houses' kind of candidate."[36]

On Labour Day, as is traditional, campaigning started to get more serious, Marcus Gee wrote in the *Globe and Mail*: "See the world's most notorious mayor act like nothing ever happened and pretend he is qualified for a second term.... See a man who has never held municipal office say he can fix the city's congestion problem in the blink of an eye. Listen as a woman tells you the touching story of how she came here as an immigrant—an immigrant, I tell you! In Toronto!—and learned to ride the TTC."[37] Toronto's transportation woes were the key campaign issue. Ford released a vague $9-billion plan to build thirty-two kilometres of subways. "You bore, bore, bore until the cows come home," he said at a news conference. Tory promoted a dubious $8-billion SmartTrack plan that relied on electrifying existing GO lines, which he said could be done in seven years; there were doubters, particularly about his proposal to partly finance the scheme with speculative tax increment financing.

On Wednesday, September 10, Rob Ford was having breakfast with Doug Ford at Perkins Restaurant in Etobicoke. He complained about severe pain in his abdomen and went to see his doctor, who sent him to Humber River Hospital. A CAT scan showed a tumour. Suddenly the tone of the campaign changed in an extraordinary way. There was an outpouring of what could almost pass for affection. John Tory said, "I want to see him back in good health as soon as possible and back where he would want to be—with us at the debating tables talking about the city we all love." Olivia Chow said, "He has a lot of people who believe in him and love him."[38] The *Globe and Mail*'s Marcus Gee, a persistent critic of Ford, wrote, in an emotional column, "He is a man.... The whole city should join in wishing for his speedy recovery."[39] Edward Keenan wrote in the *Toronto Star*, "There are parallel stories of the Rob Ford mayoralty. One of a grand debate about what kind of city we want to live in, the importance of tax rates and service levels and infrastructure. The other has been about the personal struggles of the mayor overshadowing those political debates.... When he went off to rehab and returned appearing healthy this summer, it seemed like we might finally be able to focus the election on the pressing larger issues, with a fit Ford representing his own side vigorously."[40] The terrain had shifted. Was it possible that everybody loved Everyman?

The election rules required that new candidates for municipal office officially register by two in the afternoon on Friday, September 12. The formal withdrawal of anyone already registered was subject to the same deadline. With minutes to go, Rob Ford dramatically withdrew from the mayoralty race and registered as a candidate for councillor in his old Etobicoke ward, and Doug Ford registered as a candidate for mayor. The reaction was shock and confusion. Was the mayor very ill? Was this a plan cooked up weeks in advance? What were the implications for the campaigns of John Tory and Olivia Chow? Marcus Gee continued his unlikely (and slightly backhanded) praise of Rob Ford: "Because of him, people who used to yawn at city politics now follow it with passionate interest.... In his odd, often infuriating way, he made people care about the fate of the city."[41] The irascible Heather Mallick wrote in the *Toronto Star*, "Rob Ford had a sediment of sweetness in him, a naked honesty even when he was screaming violently about his underpants."[42] Someone said to me, "Oh yeah, the Rob/Doug thing, that switcheroo is right out of the Putin/Medvedev playbook."

On Wednesday, September 17, doctors announced that Ford had a malignant liposarcoma, a rare cancerous tumour with an uncertain prognosis. Chemotherapy would begin soon. Prime Minister Stephen Harper said he was "deeply saddened." "He's a fighter," said Olivia Chow. Marcus Gee wrote, "As he faced this sudden, unexpected struggle the city was united in consternation and sympathy."[43] Now the Ford psychodrama dominated the news in a different way. The main candidates for mayor (other than Doug Ford) seemed uncertain what to do. Was criticism of Rob Ford off-limits?

Another Ford Fest was held in Scarborough on September 27. Both Rob and Doug were there. "The mayor and his brother revved up the crowd like a pair of tag-teaming Bible Belt preachers," reported Marcus Gee. But, he said, "There was something different in the air this time around: a sense of finality.... Voters will bring an end to the weird, embarrassing, fascinating, event-crammed reign of the brothers Ford in just four weeks."[44] Voters with some help from cancer, he might have said.

But the polls continued to confound. On September 29, a Forum poll gave Tory a twenty-point lead over Doug Ford, with 43 per cent of support. But on October 6 a headline in the *Toronto Star* screamed, "Doug Ford Closes on John Tory in Latest Forum Poll."[45] The newspaper breathlessly reported that Ford and Tory were "neck and neck," with 39 per cent supporting Tory and 37 per cent supporting Ford. The president of Forum Research said this was a "shocking upset." By the middle of October, Tory's lead was widening, or at least so the polls said. The emerging wisdom was that Tory would win, as votes went to him as part of a broad stop-Ford movement.

Everybody knows what happened on October 27. "Tory Takes T.O.," trumpeted the *Star* headline. John Tory received 40 per cent of the vote, Doug Ford an astounding 34 per cent (he came first in twenty wards, equalling John Tory) and Olivia Chow just 23 per cent. Sixty-one per cent of the electorate voted. "A return to normalcy," said the dailies. "A profound relief." "The start of something immeasurably better for Toronto." John Tory? "Boring as Nebraska," wrote journalist John Barber (who once, in a city hall news scrum, called Rob Ford a "fat fuck"[46]). The new mayor's great accomplishment, wrote Barber, is "putting everybody back to sleep."[47]

It all seems like a dream. Or a nightmare. Is it over? Many experienced observers say Ford Nation is as strong as ever, the social and economic divisions that propel it remain and are growing bigger, and the Fords' 2018 mayoralty campaign has already begun.

Mayor Susan Fennell of Brampton carries a copy of a Deloitte forensic audit as she leaves for a lunch break before Brampton council discusses her personal spending.

ELEVEN

SUSAN FENNELL OF BRAMPTON

"I've Had It Up to Here with the Lies, the Innuendo and the Smears."

COMPARED TO the unprecedented, bizarre and completely original scandals of Rob Ford's Toronto mayoralty, what happened in Brampton with Mayor Susan Fennell was small-time and tedious. It was the old "fiddling with expenses" thing, a common and boring peccadillo in both government and the private sector. Rob Ford's missteps were epic. Mayor Fennell's were pitiable.

When I first visited Brampton, in the early 1980s, it was a sleepy town with a picturesque main street and not much else. The population was about 150,000. Bill Davis, the premier of Ontario, lived there, a fact he mentioned in public at every opportunity, no doubt thinking it good politics to be from somewhere outside Toronto (but conveniently nearby). The biggest industry was greenhouses. But even then, thirty-plus years ago, it was clear that change was in the air. On the outskirts, farmers' fields were being replaced by subdivisions. From the highway you could see row upon row of identical brick houses, marching across the fields, encircling and asphyxiating the historic old town.

Today, conquest by subdivision is complete. Brampton has a population of over half a million. It's the ninth-largest city in

Canada, bigger than Laval, Halifax and London. It is intensely multicultural. Thirty-eight per cent of the population is South Asian, 33 per cent white, 13.5 per cent black. It is also multi-religious. Nineteen per cent of the population is Sikh, 12 per cent Hindu, 7 per cent Muslim. Eighteen per cent of the population has Punjabi as a mother tongue. The city has become a cen-tre for manufacturing, retail administration, food and beverage and business services, with a dynamic if uncontrolled economy fuelled by its proximity to Pearson International Airport and major highways. The only thing that many Torontonians see of Brampton is the distant glimpse they get from Highway 400 as they speed past, off to the Muskokas for a weekend of expensive peace.

Novelist Rohinton Mistry—born in India and celebrated in Canada and internationally—lived in Brampton for many years (now he resides in downtown Toronto). When he lived in Brampton, Mistry—not former premier Davis—was the city's most famous resident. In 2002, he was on a book tour of the United States. He cancelled the second half of the tour. "As a person of colour, he was stopped repeatedly and rudely at each airport along the way—to the point where the humiliation of both he and his wife has become unbearable," declared a press release from the writer's U.S. publisher. It must have been a shock to someone used to Brampton.

•••

Susan Fennell was the mayor of Brampton until October 2014, when she was resoundingly defeated at the polls. Fennell was first elected mayor in 2000. It was a job she had long coveted, and she revelled in it once she had it. Before becoming mayor, she had been a member of the Brampton city council and the

Peel regional council. She founded the National Women's Hockey League in 1999 and was its commissioner until 2006, shortly before it disbanded. She owns the Brampton Thunder, a member of the Canadian Women's Hockey League.

During Fennell's first campaign for the mayor's job, she was described as the heir to Mel Lastman and Hazel McCallion "for personality, pugnacity and relentless hometown promotion.... Susan Fennell is a piece of work, so gung-ho by nature she makes Norman Vincent Peale sound like a pessimist.... She has the energy of six people and could probably talk the ear off a department store mannequin."[1] Fennell was easily re-elected in 2003, beating her nearest rival by 28 per cent. In 2004, no lesser person than Jane Jacobs described Brampton as "one of the country's most cosmopolitan and economically sophisticated communities."[2] Fennell seemed to go from success to success, leading one of the most interesting and promising communities in Canada.

On September 29, 2006, Brampton's $55-million Rose Theatre opened with a glittering gala headlined by jazz pianist Diana Krall. The opening was the apogee of Fennell's political career. Her slide began almost as soon as Krall stopped playing. Another municipal election was less than two months away. During the campaign, Fennell was attacked for not controlling the relentless pace of development. She was criticized for not addressing traffic gridlock; for the lack of schools, community centres and libraries; and for the destruction of green spaces. It was said she was in thrall to property developers, who were the main funders of her campaign. She lost the endorsement of the *Toronto Star*, which for a time had been an admirer and supporter. *Star* reporter San Grewal began reporting relentlessly on Fennell's every blunder and omission, an effort that kept him busy for years and eventually helped drive her from office (Fennell blamed the newspaper for her defeat in 2014). Nevertheless, despite those bad omens, in 2006 Fennell easily handled her critics and won the election with 75 per cent of the vote—an overwhelming landslide. Thereafter, she coasted for some time, largely trouble-free, although storm clouds continued to gather.

Serious trouble finally arrived in 2010, while Fennell was campaigning for a fourth term. A San Grewal front-page story in the *Star* began, "For five years, Brampton Mayor Susan Fennell has raised hundreds of thousands of dollars from the community for a fund in her name that isn't registered as a charity, doesn't issue receipts and has never opened its books to the public."[3] The main event of the Mayor Susan Fennell Community Fund was an annual arts gala reputed to raise as much as $250,000. Most of the gala's sponsors were property development companies. No one seemed to know exactly how much money was raised or where it went. There was also the Mayor Susan Fennell Annual Golf Classic, with its long list of sponsors. For several years, this event produced a $100,000 donation to the Brampton Civic Hospital. Grewal reported on allegations that city staff and resources were improperly used to mount these two events.

Fennell dismissed accusations about the gala and the golf tournament as a smear campaign. But serious rumblings of discontent increased. Four days before the 2010 election, Royson James argued in the *Toronto Star* that Brampton developers were too cozy with politicians, including Mayor Fennell. This, said James, "breeds contempt among citizens, who question whether election campaign contributions grease the approval process at city hall."[4] Despite the attacks, Fennell again won re-election, but this time with only 51 per cent of the vote, a big drop from 2006. Pressure to reveal the community fund's financial statements intensified during the weeks that followed. In January 2011, financial statements for 2008 and 2009 were posted on the fund's website, but this limited disclosure was generally regarded as inadequate and the attacks continued.

In October 2011, the city's integrity commissioner dismissed a variety of allegations against Fennell. But things had turned permanently sour. There was constant and acrimonious squabbling at city council. Accusations against the mayor became commonplace. A 2012 audit of the Rose Theatre, which had opened to plaudits but now often sat empty, showed "revenues not accounted for, unsigned sponsorship agreements that lack proper approval and provide improper benefits, large numbers of ticket giveaways with no explanation, inadequate insurance, disregard for safety and security protocols, bylaw violations and lax financial oversight."[5] Evasion and incompetence were everywhere. The Fennell magic had disappeared.

On March 26, 2013, San Grewal reported that Fennell was the best-paid mayor in Canada (earning more than the premier of Ontario).[6] In 2012, she received $162,839 from the city of Brampton and $50,888 from the region of Peel (on whose council she automatically sits as mayor of Brampton), for a total of $213,727. She received a further $14,682 from Peel Region for serving on the Police Services Board, as well as a $23,524 car allowance. Brampton also spent $45,726 to provide her with a driver. In the fall of 2013, Fennell secretly asked city staff to stop salary payments for November and December so that her 2013 salary would not be the highest in Canada; this pay reduction was not renewed in 2014. The day after the "best-paid mayor in Canada" story appeared, the *Star* opened a new front in its attack, questioning Fennell's excessive spending on trips to China, India and the Philippines.

At the beginning of November, columnist Christopher Hume weighed in. "In her monstrous sense of entitlement," he charged, "Fennell has made it clear she has no real interest in the notion that Brampton might actually become a city rather

[than] just a place to sleep or pass through on the way somewhere else. Indeed, she depends on it remaining in an infantilized state.... [Fennell] seems to view Brampton as a personal fiefdom she can treat as she wishes."[7] Two weeks later, San Grewal was at it again, developing the expenses story using freedom-of-information requests. "Brampton Mayor Susan Fennell has expensed taxpayers over the past three years for items such as $2,160 on personalized barbecue aprons, $3,191 for a seat upgrade on a trip to India, $1,326 for Mandarin lessons and $1,500 for an orchestra performance."[8]

Soon, further reports of her travel expenses surfaced, including one that she spent $50,000 on travel in the first ten months of 2013, typically flying first class and staying in five-star hotels, such as the InterContinental in London (England), the Fairmont Château Whistler and the Château Laurier in Ottawa. Some of her hotel rooms cost $700 a night. She also claimed two dollars for an airport luggage cart and one dollar for an iTunes download. Between February 2007 and November 2013, she made thirty-nine Shoppers Drug Mart charges, for a total of almost $3,000. A *Toronto Star* editorial commented, "Unlike Toronto's crack-smoking, so-called fiscally conservative chief magistrate, the city in the northwest is saddled with a mayor who hasn't met a tax dollar she isn't ready to spend—on herself."[9]

A fed-up Brampton council moved to cut the mayor's apparently unrestricted expense account, trying to reduce her car allowance by $10,000 (this proved impossible because the lease for her Lincoln Navigator couldn't be broken) and eliminating entitlement to first-class travel. As she headed into an election year, things looked bleak for Susan Fennell. A Forum Research poll taken in January 2014 predicted she would lose to potential candidates by a wide margin. By May, another poll suggested her support was down to less than 20 per cent.

At the end of May 2014, San Grewal was back on the front page of the *Star* with another damaging story. "A man who has been living in a house belonging to Brampton Mayor Susan Fennell owns a company that has received $1.1 million in city contracts and millions of dollars to stage the mayor's annual private fundraiser," Grewal reported.[10] Malcolm Scott Ching, described in the story as a "close personal friend" of Fennell's, owns a Brampton-based event-planning and promotion firm called Meri-Mac. On July 3, San Grewal reported that "the City of Brampton has broken its own rules for purchasing and procuring goods or services 302 times since 2007. In total, $4,627,027 worth of contracts violated the city's own bylaws going back seven years, according to city documents."[11] Meri-Mac received seven of the non-compliant contracts.

In August 2014, Deloitte Canada delivered the results of a forensic audit on the expenses of the mayor and councillors.[12] Deloitte's report showed that the mayor had been in breach of city spending policies on many occasions, for a total of well over $100,000. Many of the breaches involved hotel upgrades and unnecessarily expensive air travel. Travel in breach of spending policies alone accounted for about $70,000. Other breaches included purchases of liquor and iPad apps, and the frequent downloading of cellphone IQ tests (Fennell later said those charges were a Rogers billing error). But Deloitte also found that she had not used city resources inappropriately for the community fund, the golf tournament and similar events. Deloitte said it had been given insufficient information to determine whether a number of other expenses, of both the mayor and some councillors, complied with city policies. At a meeting on August 6, council voted in favour of asking the police to undertake a criminal investigation into the spending of the mayor and several councillors. This came days after the conviction of Mayor Joe Fontana of London on fraud charges. (An Ontario Provincial Police investigation found no criminal wrongdoing by Fennell.)

"Susan Fennell doesn't get it," declared Royson James in the *Toronto Star*. "Or doesn't want to acknowledge that after 14 years as mayor, Brampton is being defined by her. And the image she portrays is not pretty. Try arrogant, entitled, over-paid, slick and engorged at the public trough."[13] Another *Star* story began, "When the talk turns to politics in Brampton these days, finding a Susan Fennell supporter is tougher than finding 'Peppy,' the city's elusive white-tailed squirrel."[14] By August, it seemed clear that Fennell, politically ruined by her own excess, had no chance of being re-elected.

In early September, Brampton's integrity commissioner found that Fennell had violated the city's code of conduct by knowingly overspending close to $200,000 on business travel. A council meeting was scheduled for September 10 to decide how to respond. The maximum penalty under the code of conduct was the loss of ninety days' pay. Fennell could also be ordered to repay the city for inappropriate expenses. But in a desperate move moments before council met, Fennell announced that she was taking legal action against the *Toronto Star*, Deloitte Canada, some councillors and the integrity commissioner. "I've had it up to here with the lies, the innuendo and the smears," she said. "I want to sweep away all the partisan garbage and get us back on track serving the people of Brampton." She said that despite it all, she was staying in the election. "I believe one of the greatest prime ministers of all time, Winston Churchill, said it best when he said, 'When you're going through hell, keep going.'"[15] A Deloitte report tabled at the September 10 meeting recommended that Fennell reimburse the city $34,118, but because of the threat of legal action, the report was not discussed by an intimidated city council. Onlookers in the council chamber yelled "Shame, shame" at Fennell.

Meanwhile, the national and international reputation of Brampton had been sinking like a stone. In 2014, *MoneySense* magazine's rating of the best Canadian cities ranked Brampton 166 out of 201 (St. Albert in Alberta was first and Port Alberni, B.C., was last). Also in 2014, the Conference Board of Canada gave Brampton a D grade for its attractiveness to skilled workers who are newcomers to Canada, and the C.D. Howe Institute ranked it third last of Canadian municipalities for budgeting accuracy.

On September 18, Fennell served a libel notice on the *Star* and four of its reporters (San Grewal, Tim Alamenciak, Royson James and Edward Keenan), alleging that the newspaper had published details of her spending "with malice and with a total disregard for the truth." At a news conference on October 24, a Fennell supporter threw coffee in the face of San Grewal. A poll at the end of September showed Fennell's support at 17 per cent and also found that 55 per cent of respondents wanted her criminally charged. Former Brampton MPP and minister of municipal affairs Linda Jeffrey, running against Fennell for mayor, looked like a sure thing with 42 per cent support. The election was Jeffrey's to lose.

On October 27, Fennell received a derisory 12 per cent of the vote, to Linda Jeffrey's 50 per cent. Fennell blamed the *Toronto Star* for her defeat. At her victory party, Jeffrey was introduced by Bill Davis, the grand old man of Brampton. But Fennell's political corpse continued to twitch. A new council meeting to discuss the expense scandal was scheduled for November 12. Once more, Fennell's response was to threaten a libel suit, this time against two city councillors and once more against the *Star*. But the meeting went ahead (Fennell did not attend because of impending spinal surgery). By a 7–3 vote, Fennell was stripped of ninety days' salary and ordered to pay back $144,150 that she had spent on an on-call limousine service. The money would be deducted from her severance pay.

As Susan Fennell slinked off into the sunset with less severance than she expected, Mississauga mayor Hazel McCallion retired after a very long time, covered in endless praise at banquet after banquet, smothered by honours. Despite the difference in treatment at the end of their reigns, in some ways Fennell and McCallion were similar. McCallion may never have misused public funds, but like Fennell, she had given developers pretty much a free hand at the cost of her city, and she had not always been scrupulous about conflicts of interest. As she packed up her office, Fennell must have thought, life isn't fair.

Mississauga mayor Hazel McCallion takes her seat during a 2010 judicial inquiry into her alleged conflicts of interest.

TWELVE

HAZEL McCALLION OF MISSISSAUGA

"I Only Wish There Had Been Clarity at the Time as to What the Rules Were."

SUSAN FENNELL left the Brampton mayor's office in defeat and disgrace. When Hazel McCallion retired as mayor of Mississauga, she left as a victorious goddess, awash in accolades. Why the difference? In some ways, their legacies are similar. Both left behind dysfunctional cities damaged by property developers and with growing fiscal worries. Both mayors also had severe ethical problems. Perhaps Hazel McCallion emerged intact because she is more likeable than Susan Fennell, and she is very good at putting her pleasing characteristics on full display. She has a knack for public relations. She is frugal, personally and as an elected official; no questionable dollars ever went into her pocket. And she is lucky. "Give me lucky generals," Napoleon once said.

If you live in downtown Toronto, Mississauga is west, beyond the horizon. It's the place where the sun sets and the voluptuous "Marilyn Monroe" condo towers rise. To get there from downtown Toronto, you have to mount the Gardiner Expressway (not an easy thing), go down the Queen Elizabeth Way and fight extraordinary traffic; it takes forever. It's a great big ugly sprawl of a place, a municipality of malls and six-lane highways, Canada's sixth-largest city. And why are you going to Mississauga anyway? Perhaps you are going there to get to Toronto's airport, which is actually in Mississauga (as Hazel McCallion often points out). Or maybe you live in downtown Toronto but work in one of the Mississauga corporate offices—for Microsoft Canada, perhaps, or Laura Secord—and are prepared to fight the awful traffic not to live in the place where you work.

Hazel McCallion was mayor of Mississauga for thirty-six years, from 1978 to 2014, when she finally retired at age ninety-three. Despite frequent claims to the contrary, McCallion was not Canada's longest-serving mayor. That title belongs to John Hamlyn, mayor of Crow Head, Newfoundland and Labrador, since 1963. Crow Head has a population of 220.

•••

She was born Hazel Journeaux in Port-Daniel West in the Gaspé on Valentine's Day 1921, the same year that the original *Bluenose* schooner was launched in Lunenburg, Nova Scotia (the *Bluenose* was wrecked in the Caribbean and abandoned in 1946). Hazel was one of five children. Her mother was a nurse; her father was in the fish-processing business and also owned a small grocery store. Orthodoxy has it that her family was frugal but not poor. Hazel likes to say that when she was a child she had only one toy.

When Hazel finished high school, she went to a secretarial school in Montreal. Soon she was working for Canadian Kellogg, an engineering firm, which sent her to Toronto to help open an office. She became president of the Anglican Young People's Association of Canada, where she met Sam McCallion, whom she married in 1951. The couple moved to Streetsville, just west of Toronto, and started a dry-cleaning business. Sam also began a printing and photography enterprise, and founded a monthly community paper called the *Streetsville Booster*. They had three children—Peter, Linda and Paul. Sam died in 1997 from Alzheimer's disease.

In 1970, McCallion was elected mayor of Streetsville. In 1974, the provincial government made Streetsville part of Mississauga (Clarkson, Port Credit and Meadowvale were also part of the amalgamation). McCallion was bitterly opposed to the merger, although critics accused her of political posturing, since it was clear the amalgamation could not be stopped. In November 1978, after serving as a Mississauga councillor for several years, she became mayor, narrowly beating the incumbent, Ron Searle.

And then, quite soon after she became mayor, came the event that made her nationally known and very special—a train derailment. On Saturday, November 10, 1979, Canadian Pacific train 54, laden with noxious chemicals, derailed near Mavis Road and Dundas Street. There was a massive fire, and chlorine escaped from tanker cars. A large part of Mississauga was evacuated. McCallion took charge, or seemed to, her every move followed by national and international media. "Her legend was born," wrote one journalist, swooning with admiration, "her brand identity of being tough and graceful under pressure fixed forever."[1] The train derailment made McCallion a national political figure. She became "an instant urban folk hero," a "goddess." She was on centre stage and used it to great effect. She sprained her ankle early in the crisis and added to the drama by hobbling around on crutches. Tom Urbaniak, McCallion's biographer, writes, "Mississauga now, finally, had a leader."[2] He also notes, "But for good fortune to redound on a leader it must be seized, Machiavelli reminds us." She was quick to seize her good fortune.

McCallion was easily re-elected every four years, without campaigning much (if at all). She regularly claimed campaign contributions of zero dollars and corresponding expenses.

She typically garnered a huge percentage of the votes cast, often over 90 per cent. But Mississauga's voter turnout has been among the lowest for municipal elections in Canada, about 25 per cent. Not all that many people have actually voted for Hazel McCallion—a fact generally ignored.

In 2014, the unthinkable happened. At age ninety-three, McCallion announced she would not run for re-election.

•••

She is known as Hurricane Hazel, the Iron Lady of Mississauga or just Hazel. She has been called "crusty," "Tabasco-tongued," "not one to avoid a cliché," "tougher than boot leather," "a pint-sized dynamo," "a force of nature." She is much admired, even loved. Politicians from senior levels of government seek her approval. They want to be photographed with her—a photograph suitable for framing. She is a superb self-publicist. She has extraordinary stamina. She likes to talk about how she's a woman of the people, up at dawn, gardening before breakfast, putting in fourteen-hour days, doing her own laundry, cooking the evening meal for any family members who happen to be around (if she's not out at a banquet or dinner meeting). She eats a lot of vegetables. She likes to fish, and has gone fishing with Rob Ford (there are photos). She calls herself "the people's mayor." She revels in being blunt. She and Don Cherry admire each other. She had a picture of Cherry hanging in her mayoral office. When she was mayor, the Toronto press atypically and routinely wrote extraordinarily sycophantic articles about her.

She is also criticized, ridiculed, even reviled. Some think her an opportunist, a gunslinger who for many years was in the pocket of big real estate developers and then changed her tune when the popular mood shifted. She does not like opposition and is partial to revenge. She can be nasty. In his generally sympathetic biography of McCallion, Tom Urbaniak offers this judgment (although he carefully distances himself by putting the words in the mouths of "critics"):

> Her critics ... have seen a "take-no-prisoners" local dictator, an opportunistic populist, a Canadian Huey Long who has stifled legitimate and open debate, who ridicules the activists and "special interests" who bother to surface, and who refuses to tolerate open criticism of her leadership.... They have criticized her lack of compassion and her anti-intellectual rhetoric. Her very practicality and rather austere demeanour may, in their view, have sapped the energy from, or pre-empted, cultural initiatives and efforts to make the city's neighbourhoods, and especially its vast commercial districts, less repetitive and sterile. She has been unable, they claim, to fully come to terms with Mississauga's growing cultural diversity.[3]

One of McCallion's most cogent and persistent critics has been Christopher Hume of the *Toronto Star*. In 2009, after McCallion announced she would run for re-election in 2010, Hume described Mississauga as the bedroom community that never woke up, a place so ill-equipped for the twenty-first century it could serve as a poster child of how not to build a city. "More than anything else, her time in office has benefited the development industry, which must have made countless millions during her tenure. Churning out subdivision after subdivision along with countless corporate campuses, builders ... have had a field day. Mississauga is their personal fiefdom as much as the mayor's."[4] In 2011, Hume wrote, "Here is the city apathy built.

Barely a city, in fact, it hardly exists outside its maker's mind, which must be why Mississaugans remain so attached to McCallion. She's all that keeps them from the suburban oblivion into which much of North America has fallen."[5]

But by 2014, after McCallion finally announced that she would not run again, even Hume was feeling kindly. He noted that she had at last become an advocate for urban density and public transit, and he even described her as "bold and brave." She had repented before it was too late. Or was it too late? "Not all Mississaugans have kept up with Hurricane Hazel," wrote Hume. "They bought into the vision she promoted all those years ago and still like it that way. To them, change is something to be avoided at all cost."[6] Even if Hazel had overcome her lack of vision, the city she created had not.

•••

The feisty and frugal Hurricane Hazel may have been beloved by her citizens, but she fell prey to the familiar bane of municipal politicians: conflict-of-interest allegations. Questionable incidents bookend her tenure and tarnish her reign. The first happened in 1981. In November of that year, Mississauga council approved releasing fifteen hundred hectares of land for residential development, substantially increasing the land's value. McCallion and her husband lived in a house on two of those hectares. They had lived there since 1951, when they got married. McCallion declared her interest but still participated in the council debate.

John Graham, a ratepayer, the former mayor of Streetsville and a political opponent of McCallion, applied to the County Court for an order declaring that she had contravened subsection 2(1) of the Municipal Conflict of Interest Act. He argued that under the provisions of the act, her seat on council was accordingly vacant. In his decision, Judge Ernest West said:

> The proscriptions of the subsection are fourfold.
> There is an obligation on a member having a
> pecuniary interest in any matter in which council
> is concerned: first, to disclose that interest as soon
> as practicable after the commencement of the
> meeting; second, to refrain from taking any part
> in the consideration or discussion of the matter;
> third, to refrain from voting on any question with
> respect to the matter, and fourth, to refrain from
> attempting in any way to influence the voting on
> the matter.... I must find that the respondent has
> breached all of them.[7]

But Judge West found that McCallion had no corrupt intent, and
that her breach of the act was an error in judgment. Therefore,
according to another section of the act, her seat was not to be
declared vacant. On appeal, the Divisional Court upheld the
decision of the County Court (except as to the awarding of costs,
which it changed to McCallion's benefit).

It was a close brush with trouble, but she emerged unscathed.
Tom Urbaniak observed: "One suspects that had she been in an
old central city—rather than a suburban city—with a full array
of television, radio, and print media, not to mention 'gotcha'
reporters, she might have been hounded to the point of contri-
tion."[8] McCallion cynically trumpeted the case as a victory, and
got away with it.

Her political opponents subsequently tried to make an issue
of the conflict-of-interest case in the 1982 election, but the voters
weren't interested and McCallion won the election in a cakewalk.

•••

The second conflict-of-interest imbroglio was far more serious.

Peter McCallion is Hazel's eldest son and the father of her only grandchild. He was born in 1953. He didn't finish high school, and his working life has been less than distinguished. He got his real estate licence in 1986; it was suspended in 2007 for failure to take required courses, and in 2009 for non-payment of fees. He has been convicted of impaired driving. He wears a black Stetson hat and cowboy boots. After his father died, he often accompanied the mayor to official functions. After his divorce, he lived with his mother for a time.

Peter was part owner of a real estate development company called World Class Developments (WCD), a firm he incorporated in February 2005. WCD had a plan to build a hotel and convention centre in central Mississauga—something Hazel felt was important for the city and had wanted for some time. In March 2005, WCD made an initial offer to buy 3.4 hectares near city hall known as the City Centre Lands. The lands were co-owned by the Ontario Municipal Employees Retirement System (OMERS) and AIM, an Alberta pension fund. In January 2007, WCD signed an agreement of purchase and sale (APS) with OMERS and AIM. Hazel McCallion, who knew in general terms of her son's interest in WCD, participated in private meetings concerning the project, had frequent dealings with OMERS and AIM, encouraged the co-owners to sign the APS and generally promoted WCD at every opportunity over a considerable period of time. When the project eventually aborted, she encouraged OMERS to pay WCD $4 million to settle outstanding legal issues. Eventually, all this came to light. Hazel's opponents and doubters were galvanized. On November 11, 2009, city council passed a resolution asking the chief justice of the Ontario

Superior Court to appoint a judge under the Municipal Act to consider conflict-of-interest and other allegations. Justice Douglas Cunningham, fresh from presiding over Ottawa mayor Larry O'Brien's trial on corruption charges, was appointed commissioner.

The inquiry cost $7 million. Justice Cunningham delivered his 403-page report, "Updating the Ethical Infrastructure," on October 3, 2011.[9] In the introduction, he summarized his view of Hazel McCallion's involvement with WCD:

> Given her son's pecuniary interest in the transaction, it was improper for the mayor to repeatedly use her public office on behalf of WCD, from the perspective both of the common law and of common sense. The mayor ought to have given the WCD project a wide berth. A member of council cannot promote the financial interests of family members and must avoid any appearance of impropriety. Citizens have a right to expect that a mayor will act impartially and without favour, as the oath of office requires. It is no answer to say that a public office holder may advantage a relative to the extent that it is in the furtherance of the greater good.

Justice Cunningham found "that the mayor knowingly used her relationship with OMERS and her public office to influence the co-owners to agree to concessions throughout this period. She knew that her son Peter stood to gain financially if the deal succeeded, and, although his interests alone may not have prompted her intervention with the co-owners, the exercise of this influence put her in a position of conflict, both real and apparent." Hazel McCallion might have been in a conflict of interest, but that didn't mean she was in breach of the law, which on this matter was woefully inadequate. Justice Cunningham made a number of specific recommendations for changing and toughening the law governing conflicts of interest and other ethical issues. So far, none of these recommendations have been implemented, although the provincial government is considering revising the Municipal Conflict of Interest Act. As well, the Ontario legislature is currently considering a bill that would give the provincial ombudsman the power to investigate a complaint filed against a municipal politician by a taxpayer.

What was Hazel McCallion's reaction to Justice Cunningham's damning and enormously expensive report? Most in her position would be chastened by the judge's blunt language and clear findings, and many would feel compelled to resign. The judge said she had behaved improperly. He said there was an appearance of impropriety. He said there was a real and apparent conflict of interest. Perhaps Hazel McCallion should have resigned, but what she did was deny. "I only wish there had been clarity at the time as to what the rules were," she said. The citizens of Mississauga seemed to agree, or perhaps they just didn't care. A Forum Research poll at the end of October 2011 gave her a 78 per cent approval rating, the highest of all big-city mayors (Naheed Nenshi of Calgary was second, with 76 per cent).[10]

But Elias Hazineh didn't want to let McCallion off the hook. In March 2013, Hazineh applied to the Superior Court for an order that McCallion be removed from office for breaching the Municipal Conflict of Interest Act (MCIA). Hazineh is a long-time friend and political associate of Carolyn Parrish, a one-time Mississauga councillor and fierce political opponent of Hazel McCallion. He is also a well-known and controversial anti-Israel activist. It is not known who put him up to the McCallion litigation, how it was funded or why he waited for over a year after the Cunningham report to proceed.

Hazineh's action focused on a 2007 Peel Region council debate on a bylaw amendment that would exempt some existing planning applications from an increase in development charges. WCD would have benefited from the exemption if its hotel project had proceeded. McCallion had participated in the debate and voted in favour of the amendment. Justice J.R. Sproat found that at the time of the vote, Hazel McCallion knew her son had an ownership interest in WCD and therefore, under the MCIA, she had a deemed financial interest in WCD, but he also found that WCD could not qualify for the exemption because it had not filed a complete site plan application by the cut-off date.[11] So the matter was moot. Although finding for McCallion on technical grounds, he wrote: "I reject the argument that the MCIA permits a member with an actual or deemed financial interest in a development to vote on the development charges applicable or potentially applicable to the development. In my opinion, the belief by Mayor McCallion that she could vote ... is contrary to common sense. It does not pass the 'smell' test.... Further, having a deemed financial interest in WCD, Mayor McCallion states that she made no inquiry as to the status of WCD's application for planning approval. In my opinion, this constitutes wilful blindness."

Again, a respected judge used strong words. More damning criticism. McCallion's belief she could vote was contrary to common sense. It did not pass the smell test. She was wilfully blind. But McCallion, ignobly, brushed off these findings and called the court's decision a win. Once more, the people agreed or were indifferent. Her approval rating went above 80 per cent.

•••

For most of her mayoralty, Hazel McCallion favoured real estate developers who took Mississauga from a collection of picturesque rural communities to a big and ugly city. She kept taxes low, relying on development fees to finance public infrastructure. Sprawl didn't bother her, because she was the people's mayor and the people (she said) wanted sprawl. They wanted spacious houses on large lots. What developer would build what he couldn't sell? With sprawl came a reliance on automobiles rather than public transport, and that was fine too, because that's what the people wanted. "Hazel McCallion had ... happened upon a formula for relatively easy governance and relatively easy popularity in a suburban context: be flamboyant and decisive, build new things, charge developers admission fees, and keep out of people's backyards," wrote Tom Urbaniak.[12] Toward the end, she experienced something of a conversion. She sensed that the winds were shifting. She was no longer so sure about development, and in any event Mississauga was pretty much built out. That meant that development fees were drying up, and tax hikes on residential property became inevitable. She converted into something of an environmentalist, vaguely green. And now the people seemed to want mass transit.

What to make of Tabasco-tongued Hurricane Hazel, the pint-sized dynamo, the extraordinarily popular people's mayor, for thirty-six years bouncing from banquet to banquet, from policy to policy, ignoring conflicts of interest, criticized severely by judge after judge, steamrolling everything in front of her, being everywhere and doing everything? Urbaniak says McCallion "had decided to be a mayor for all seasons. She has been honest in grasping the moods and sentiments of her people, and in giving voice to those moods and sentiments even before many of the people have figured out how to give voice themselves, or collected themselves sufficiently to do so."[13] French revolutionary Alexandre Auguste Ledru-Rollin is reputed to have said, "There go the people. I must follow them, for I am their leader." McCallion failed as a leader. When she became mayor, there was not much to Mississauga. She had a chance to plan imaginatively and create beautifully. Look what the people of Mississauga ended up with. She should not be fêted.

Reuters/Mark Blinch

Dubbed "absurdly handsome" by the *Edmonton Journal*, Mayor Don Iveson of Edmonton claims Abraham Lincoln as his political model. In 2013 *Maclean's* named Mayor Naheed Nenshi of Calgary the second most powerful person in Canada. A 2011 magazine survey voted him sexiest male Calgarian.

The Canadian Press/Don Denton

Gregor Robertson, mayor of Vancouver, apologized to the voters three days before the 2014 election for not listening to them enough.

THIRTEEN

Nenshi, Iveson, Robertson
The Western Triangle of Mayoral Goodness.

CONSIDER, for a moment, the recent mayors of Canada. In your mind's eye, move from the East Coast toward the centre of the country. Contemplate the dismal picture. Peter Kelly of Halifax was driven from office because of his incompetent and self-serving administration of a deceased friend's estate. Gérald Tremblay, mayor of Montreal, resigned when he became implicated in long-standing corruption of the city's administration. Tremblay's successor, Michael Applebaum, was arrested, charged with fraud and other crimes, and quit—all within a few months of becoming mayor. At about the same time, Laval's Gilles Vaillancourt was forced to resign and subsequently faced a plethora of criminal charges. Vaillancourt's successor, Alexandre Duplessis, left office when he became involved in a prostitution scandal. Ottawa's Larry O'Brien, a relative success in this sorry pantheon, spent the early months of his term defending himself in court against criminal charges (successfully) and then was easily defeated when he ran for re-election. Susan Fennell of Brampton was catastrophically defeated in the 2014 election after spending scandals and left office in ignominy. Hazel McCallion of Mississauga was found by a judicial inquiry to have had a conflict of interest in a proposed real estate development. Joe Fontana of London quit when he was convicted of fraud. Sam Katz of Winnipeg had trouble keeping his personal financial affairs and his civic duties separate, and faced with great and growing criticism, he decided not to run for mayor again. Then there's Rob Ford.

But as you move west from Winnipeg, things look different. Those suffering under incompetent or corrupt civic leaders in eastern or central Canada hear rumours that municipal administration is much better in the west. They hear about Naheed Nenshi of Calgary. They hear about Don Iveson of Edmonton. They hear about Gregor Robertson of Vancouver. They are told that these mayors are young, clever, well educated, imaginative, personable and honest. They ride bicycles (except for Nenshi). An article in the *Ottawa Citizen* tells us exuberantly, "These men seem to transcend today's politics.... Their success hints at an evolution of the framing of public issues that is coming as a new generation of leaders takes over.... A new wave of leadership is approaching the shore."[1] The *Globe and Mail* talks of a "western triangle of mayoral goodness."[2] Maybe now, with Brian Bowman the new mayor of Winnipeg, the western triangle of mayoral goodness has become a quadrangle.

Can it be true?

•••

Naheed Nenshi's parents came to Toronto from Tanzania in 1971, when they were both thirty years old. His mother was pregnant with Naheed, and he was born in Toronto in 1972. The family moved to Red Deer, Alberta, the following year. Soon, the Nenshis relocated again, to northeast Calgary, an ethnically diverse and poor neighbourhood. Naheed's mother, Noorjah, ran the lottery booth at a Superstore. His father,

Kurban, operated a string of small businesses, including a laundromat and a dry cleaner. Naheed's sister, Shaheen Nenshi Nathoo, is a married pharmacist with two children. Nenshi is an observant Shia Ismaili. It is often pointed out that he is the first Muslim mayor of a major North American city. Nenshi rejects this categorization; he regards being Muslim as irrelevant to his political career.

Nenshi was a smart and aggressive kid with a lot of self-confidence. In May 1989, he was prime minister in Queen Elizabeth High School's mock parliament. He was also president of the student council. He was active in high school drama (his love of the theatre remains). In June 1989, he went to London, England, for the World Public Speaking Championships and came in ninth. The *Calgary Herald* reported at the time that Nenshi had been debating, public speaking and participating in school drama productions since the ninth grade. "'I've never known him to be shy,' says teacher Camille Tribe, his speech and debate coach for the last four years. 'He's quite outspoken and likes to challenge what is being said. He's got an incredible mind.'"[3]

In the fall of 1989, Nenshi went to the University of Calgary to study business. In January 1990, he and fellow student Ezra Levant—an odd couple, to be sure—represented the university at the Inter-Collegiate Business Competition at Queen's University and won the debating prize. They won it again in 1991. Nenshi was awarded a gold medal at the competition in 1992. (Nenshi and Levant, now a well-known right-wing commentator for Sun News, were once friends but have fallen to rhetorical blows. On a September 2013 radio show, Nenshi said Levant is "creepily and weirdly obsessed with me.")[4] In 1993, Nenshi was elected president of the University of Calgary student union. His future campaign manager, Chima Nkemdirim, was his vice-president. When they graduated later that year, Nenshi and Nkemdirim backpacked together across Europe.

Back from Europe, Nenshi went to Harvard's Kennedy School of Government in 1996. He graduated in 1998 with a master's degree in public policy. He worked briefly for McKinsey & Company, the powerful international consulting company. For most of his twenties he lived in Toronto. Then, professing homesickness, he returned to Calgary. He became a consultant and professor with a special interest in municipal government and non-profit organizations. He was a prolific commentator on public affairs and an enthusiastic writer of op-ed articles and letters to the editor. He assumed the mantle of "urban thinker" and "city hall watchdog." He became well known in Calgary, and something of a media darling.

In 2004, Nenshi ran unsuccessfully for alderman (he came in fourth). In 2006, the *Calgary Herald* picked him as "an influential shaper of Calgary's second century." Said the newspaper: "The Harvard graduate, Mount Royal College instructor and urban critic gets the nod for his community involvement, his bold views on Calgary's ethnic mix and his passion for building a city where everyone lives in harmony. His keen intellect, backed by research, often jolts people into a new sense of their city."[5]

Nenshi was elected mayor of Calgary in October 2010. His campaign emphasized the virtues of high-density living ("high-density" is code for "not suburban") and public transport. He ran as an outsider. He used Facebook and Twitter, and was described by some of those he was running against as a "marginal social media candidate." His campaign director was his old university friend, Chima Nkemdirim, who had become a partner at the establishment law firm of Fraser Milner Casgrain (now Dentons). For much of the campaign, Nenshi trailed badly in the polls. He somehow ended up with 40 per cent of the vote. When he was elected, there was an avalanche of adulatory press coverage across the country. Canadians, particularly those who lived in the east, could not get over the brilliant choice Calgarians had unexpectedly made.

Nenshi got off to a rocky start. This was not particularly surprising. He was a novice and entered the job faced with high and unrealistic expectations. Early on, he let an architectural firm buy him a plane ticket to attend a conference in Toronto; this was widely seen as an error in judgment, although the trip itself was hugely successful. Christopher Hume wrote in the *Toronto Star*, "Though he has scrupulously avoided the obvious comparison during his triumphant Toronto homecoming this week, in these parts Nenshi can only be seen as everything this city's current mayor is not—i.e., articulate, urban, informed and, best of all, optimistic."[6] An early criticism was that Nenshi did little immediately to improve public transit, despite having called for changes for years and making transit enhancement an important campaign promise. He was seen by some as arrogant and over-bearing, too full of himself, bumptious. He was accused of being anti-suburban—a charge he routinely denies, but one that has substance. Nonetheless, his charm and cheekiness were seductive.

After one year in office, Nenshi, writing in the *Calgary Herald*, listed what he considered his achievements to date: creating a permanent community investment fund; the Calgary Poverty Reduction Initiative; keeping major crime rates low; making government more open, accountable, efficient and effective; changing the negative tone of council; cutting red tape.[7] These achievements may have seemed modest and routine, the usual tropes of a municipal politician, but Nenshi remained extraordinarily popular and the darling of the press. A one-year anniversary article in the *Calgary Herald* described a recent Nenshi speech as containing "a dash of cheeky self-deprecation, a flash of civic philosophy and a jarring smash to politicians or administrators he felt were harming the city's interests."[8] A 2011 magazine survey voted him sexiest male Calgarian, and an Ipsos Reid/Global News poll gave him an 86 per cent approval rating. In November 2012, the *Calgary Herald* observed, "With zero precincts reporting and polls about to close in 11 months, election watchers appear ready to declare Naheed Nenshi the winner of the 2013 mayoral election."[9] Strangely, despite his great public popularity (and perhaps a harbinger of things to come), Nenshi often lost votes on the fifteen-member council—much more often, in fact, than his far less charismatic predecessor, Dave Bronconnier. In October 2012, the *Calgary Herald* analyzed sixty key votes over Nenshi's first two years in office; he lost thirty-one times, including on issues that really mattered to him, such as reforming the rules about secondary suites (generally apartments in house basements) to make them legal in most circumstances.[10]

The disastrous June 2013 Calgary flood was a testing ground and an opportunity, the equivalent of Hazel McCallion's Mississauga train derailment. Nenshi was in Toronto when the crisis arose and immediately returned to Calgary, staying awake for thirty hours straight to help with emergency measures. The Twittersphere begged him to get some rest, using the hashtag #nap4nenshi. Mandatory evacuation orders were quickly issued to more than one hundred thousand people in neighbourhoods near the Elbow and Bow Rivers. Later, the evacuation of downtown Calgary was ordered. The consensus was that Nenshi rose to the occasion splendidly, showing panache and passion and inspiring citizens to help one another. The *Globe and Mail* editorialized: "Mr. Nenshi has been such a superbly effective leader during the flood that has devastated his city and other Alberta communities that he appears on his way to folk-hero status....

He has been such a warm and engaging presence. You can't help but be cheered up by him."[11] The *Regina Leader-Post* commented: "Nenshi appears to intuitively understand what a political leader should be, and what he should not be, in a time of crisis. He must be chiefly a tireless communicator and cheerleader, as opposed to any kind of disaster micro-manager."[12] There were many remarks of this kind. The words "hero" and "superman" were used. The accepted wisdom quickly became that no one stood a chance of beating Nenshi in the upcoming municipal election.

The 2013 campaign was flat. Perhaps it was because the outcome was considered a foregone conclusion. Nenshi got 74 per cent of the vote, with about 40 per cent of eligible voters turning out (compared to 53 per cent in 2010). Jon Lord, a video store owner, former city councillor and one-time member of the Alberta legislature, won a surprising 21 per cent. Nenshi did well, but it was not what you would expect from a superhero. Commentators pointed out that an incumbent Calgary mayor had not been beaten since 1980, when Ralph Klein defeated Ross Alger in a shocking upset. Not everyone, it seemed, was a Nenshi fan. Some voters didn't appreciate recent and substantial city property tax increases. There was post-flood fatigue, and perhaps Nenshi fatigue as well.

Nenshi is colourful, cheerful, clever, cheeky and charismatic. He is very likeable. He has a huge amount of energy. He has great self-confidence. He has considerable speaking skills. He's a good storyteller and quotes Jane Jacobs. He is quintessentially Canadian. He has become an important political figure. In 2013, *Maclean's* named him the second most powerful person in Canada, after Stephen Harper. "When Naheed Nenshi's name comes up, Torontonians have only one question: When is he coming to save us?"[13] Another question is asked *sotto voce*: Will he become prime minister?

But Nenshi is still a mayor in a weak mayor system. He can charm, but he cannot rule. His cockiness and penchant for grandstanding can sometimes get the better of him and obscure his judgment. In January 2015, he chastised city councillors with allegations of alcohol abuse. These allegations were received badly, and several councillors commented adversely on Nenshi's leadership skills. He is hobbled by lack of political power and inadequate sources of finance. His unimpressive voting record at council illustrates the consequences of not having political parties at the municipal level (although he rails against partisanship). Much of what he promised in his 2010 Purple Revolution campaign—if still remembered—remains in the "planning stages." After all is said and done, what has he accomplished and can he accomplish?

•••

Don Iveson was born in Edmonton in 1979. His mother was an education professor at the University of Alberta, his father a sculptor. In 2001, Iveson graduated from the University of Alberta with a B.A. in political science. He was managing editor of the university student newspaper, the *Gateway*. After gradu-ation, he worked briefly as president of Canadian University Press in Toronto, before moving back to Edmonton to be the *Gateway*'s business manager. He became the advocacy director of the University of Alberta's student union. He's six-foot-five and wears size 15 shoes. He has said that Abraham Lincoln, who was six-foot-four, is his political model. He's a policy wonk. He has revealed he draws inspiration from the White House drama *The West Wing* (he's also a fan of *Star Trek* and *The Wire*). He likes to garden. The *Edmonton Journal* reported in 2013 that he had transformed his entire front lawn into a diorama of Alberta: "Over the past three years, he and his father-in-law have created a mini-mountain with a boardwalk and a brook, conifer-covered foothills and a prairie featuring 40 types of native plants and grasses along with rocks to symbolize glacial erratics."[14]

In 2006, Iveson married Sarah Chan, whom he met when they both worked at the *Gateway*. Chan is a piano teacher, photographer and avid cyclist. Her parents came to Alberta from Hong Kong as students, and later went into the restaurant business. Chan has a blog called *Girls and Bicycles*, started in 2008. "It features charming photos of immaculate children," said the *Edmonton Journal*, "and of Chan, impeccably garbed not in sweats or cycle shorts, but chic skirts and dresses and heels, riding stylishly through city streets, never breaking a sweat.... Who can live up to such an example?"[15] The Ivesons have two small children, Dexter and Alice.

In 2007, Iveson ran for city council, upsetting an incumbent in a narrow but surprising victory. Incumbents are seldom beaten. Iveson was called a "giant-killer" and a "golden boy." He ran a slick campaign. Some described it as brilliant. He had a Facebook group, posted videos on YouTube explaining his policies on city planning, affordable housing, public transit and community consultation. He had a blog. He campaigned mostly by bicycle but sometimes used his 1992 Dodge Caravan. He called for "smart, sustainable growth."

Iveson began to become well known in his first term as a councillor, but not too well known. "I get the odd double-take in the grocery store," he told the *Edmonton Journal* in 2010. "But if I'm wearing sunglasses, shorts and haven't shaved, I fly completely under the radar."[16] He doesn't like to shave. In the 2010 municipal election, Iveson ran on the standard, dull platform routinely offered up by municipal politicians: affordable housing linked by public transit, investment in the infrastructure of mature neighbourhoods, crime reduction, etc. He won a landslide victory against an opponent who entered the race at the last minute.

In November 2011, he said in a radio interview that he would not run for council in 2013. One reason, he said, was that he and Sarah were expecting a second child. Another was that he was considering some interesting business opportunities. He said he had never seen being a councillor as a career.[17] But he carefully left open the possibility of running for mayor. Speculation about an Iveson mayoralty candidacy quickly began, but there were doubts. "Vast and varied life experience matters when it comes to leadership," wrote David Staples in the *Edmonton Journal*. "In the angriest of civic battles, when the debates and negotiations get tough and nasty, will Iveson be able to effectively play hardball?"[18]

In May 2013, the popular and fiery incumbent mayor, Stephen Mandel, announced he would not run again. Iveson declared his candidacy not long after. The media, generally favourable to Iveson, circled warily:

> He's outstanding at understanding and explaining city policy and urban growth concepts. He's also got a calculating side, which came out when he struggled to find just the right word when he talked about his ongoing push to have more affordable housing built in the city core, especially for young families.... Driving by [a] development recently, Iveson said he was glad to see families had, in fact, moved in. "I actually saw strollers, kids' bikes, little trikes, sand castle crap—I shouldn't say 'crap'—sand castle accoutrements—I shouldn't say 'accoutrements'— uh, toys, toys!—on people's front stoops on these cool three storey townhouses."[19]

The race for mayor was generally regarded as dull. As it wore on, Iveson slowly took the lead. His principal opponent, fellow city councillor Karen Leibovici, seen as competent but uninspiring and gruff, was endorsed by Alberta's deputy premier. Transit expansion was the key issue of the campaign, particularly a proposed southeast light rapid transit line and how it was to be funded. There was the usual talk about repairing streets and renewing infrastructure and improving housing. But Iveson had a grip on the public imagination. A few days before the election, Paula Simons wrote in the *Edmonton Journal*, "Tall, dark, and almost absurdly handsome, with a photogenic young multicultural family, he seems the Hollywood beau ideal of the rising politician. His campaign cleverly plays to all our preconceived notions, formed by hours in the dark with Jimmy Stewart or Robert Redford." But Simons also sounded a note of caution: "He's sometimes seemed thin-skinned and prickly, almost petulant, on the campaign trail, especially when his pet ideas are challenged, or when he's come under what he perceives as personal criticism."[20] Iveson won the election with 62 per cent of the vote.

Iveson has been friends with Naheed Nenshi for many years. It was Iveson, not Nenshi, who coined the phrase "politics in full sentences." The new mayor of Edmonton and the newly re-elected mayor of Calgary quickly spoke of getting together on the two key issues facing all Canadian cities: civic charters and inadequate sources of revenue. For Iveson, the magic seemed to fade faster than it did for Nenshi. Just a few months after being elected, in March 2014, Iveson gave a state-of-the-city speech to a Chamber of Commerce audience that included Premier Alison Redford and several provincial Cabinet ministers. Paula Simons, apparently having cooled on the absurdly handsome Iveson, wrote in the *Edmonton Journal*: "He had a remarkable opportunity to inspire. He failed.... Iveson's important words about child poverty and aboriginal relations seemed lost in a speech which ranged from open government to LRT funding to regional planning to the much vaunted big city charter. It felt as though he has made a list and was ticking off boxes.... People who had arrived prepared to cheer were left to clap politely."[21] But when the first anniversary of his win came along in October 2014, most comments on his performance were kind—"more shine than tarnish," said an editorial in the *Edmonton Journal*. The newspaper singled out Iveson's attempts to reach out to the aboriginal and gay communities. But, the paper asked, "What is the next new idea?"[22]

•••

Gregor Robertson was born in 1964. His father was a Vancouver corporate lawyer, his mother a physical education teacher. His parents divorced when he was six, and Gregor and his brother, Patrick, went with their mother to California. Gregor returned to Vancouver to go to high school.

In 1982, Robertson went to Colorado College in Colorado Springs, where he met his future wife, Amy. In 1986, he graduated with a degree in English. He and Amy travelled in Asia and then, in October 1988, after the University of British Columbia medical school rejected his application, left for New Zealand in a refurbished wooden sailboat. The trip took fourteen months. In New Zealand, they farmed briefly. In 1990, Gregor and Amy came to British Columbia and started an organic farm.

In 1991, Gregor's father disappeared. He was fifty-three, separated from his second wife, and—reports had it—having career difficulties. Four years later, John Robertson's bones were found in a forest. No one knows what happened to him. Gregor has said, "It was suicide, or it was diabetic shock, or it was a bear. But there is no proof. It's a total, absolute mystery."[23]

In 1994, Robertson co-founded a company called Happy Planet Foods, a successful business that makes fruit juices and organic smoothies. He has been called an "organic juice mogul," "hipster entrepreneur," "fruit juice peddler," "new age fruit juice tycoon" and "juice czar." In 1998, he moved with his family to Cortes Island. They returned to Vancouver in 2005. The Robertsons have four children, now grown; one of them, a foster child, was sentenced in 2013 to four years in jail for gun and drug offences (they stood by him). Robertson is an avid cyclist, and refers to bicycling as a "third form" of transportation. He has a cat and likes to play soccer. He's a jazz fan and plays the tuba. Like Don Iveson, he's good-looking—"matinee idol looks" is a phrase sometimes used. He occasionally wears a kilt in honour of his Scottish Highlands ancestry, and he supported the "Yes" side in the 2014 Scottish referendum on independence.

In November 2004, Robertson was picked by the provincial New Democratic Party to run in the riding of Vancouver-Fairview in the May 2005 election (not long before, he'd been a member of the Green Party). He won in a tight race. After a difficult start, Robertson came to be regarded as a reasonably effective MLA, although there were criticisms of his performance. An article in *Vancouver Magazine* commented, "He didn't shine brightly in his early years. Instead, he struggled to make effective points in question period, to focus on key issues, and to get media attention. He bemused his NDP colleagues with his focus on appearances.... And he had a tendency, still present, to get obsessed with sometimes minor causes, pursuing them well beyond anyone else's interest level."[24] Despite criticism of this sort, pundits picked him as a possible candidate for mayor in the November 2008 municipal election. Sure enough, in February 2008 he declared his intention to seek the Vision Vancouver nomination as a mayoralty candidate, saying homelessness had reached a state of emergency and he could no longer stand by. (Homelessness has been Robertson's signature issue ever since, to his cost.) In June, Vision chose Robertson over two other candidates. He resigned his seat in the provincial legislature.

In the subsequent election, Robertson ran against Non-Partisan Association (NPA) candidate Peter Ladner. The *Vancouver Province* commented: "Both Ladner and Robertson have been described repeatedly as near-twins. Decent men, with silver-spoon backgrounds, young families, brushes with bohemia and small business, they are equally bright, pleasant and somewhat bland. Either might make a perfectly good mayor.... They are well spoken and sufficiently versed in the vagaries of public office to do just enough to let people warm to you without making too many enemies."[25] The 2008 campaign was tepid, perhaps because the men were too decent. The central issues put forward by Robertson were homelessness, crime and a "green agenda." He said homelessness was his top priority. His goal, he said, was to end homelessness by 2015, a promise that was not fulfilled and now haunts him. He also made the routine promise—seemingly made, and then ignored, by all candidates for mayor in any city— of more open and accountable government. *Vancouver Magazine* said Robertson "seems wrapped in a thick blanket of Sister Moon niceness."[26] (He came to be known as Mayor Moonbeam.) Vision Vancouver won seven out of ten seats on council. (In Vancouver, council members are elected to represent the city at large rather than individual wards.) The NPA was reduced to a shadow of its former self. Gregor Robertson was now in charge.

The new mayor's biggest problem was the over-budget Olympic Village, a project inherited from the previous city administration. The Olympic Village was built for the 2010 Winter Olympics and 2010 Winter Paralympics to house athletes and officials, and is touted on the city's website as "one of the greenest communities in the world, making Vancouver a leader in sustainable development." Early on, the billion-dollar development fell behind schedule and costs soared. The city had to assume its financing. With the permission of the province (the Vancouver Charter, a provincial statute, had to be amended), the city obtained more than $500 million in debt financing, doubling its debt load. Debt-rating agencies downgraded the city from AAA to AA. The problem lingered on after the Olympics were over. Eventually the city's investment in the project, made in a variety of ways, was more than a billion dollars. Most of that was ultimately recovered through sale of residential units, but it has been estimated that the city lost more than $100 million at the end of the day. Many said the money could have been better spent on what was supposed to be Mayor Robertson's top priority: shelter for the homeless (euphemistically called "social housing").

Meanwhile, Robertson was seen as moving from the left to the centre, and becoming a friend and ally of the Liberal premier, Gordon Campbell; there was anguish over that in the left-of-centre Vision Vancouver ranks. But he showed tenacity on the homelessness issue and pursued the green agenda, promoting bicycling and bike lanes in particular (including a controversial bike lane over the Burrard Bridge), and promising to make Vancouver the greenest city on earth by 2020.

The Winter Olympics were considered a success. Columnist Gary Mason, a Robertson fan, commented in the *Globe and Mail*: "Now that his city has just presided over a smash-hit Olympic party that won raves around the world, his boyish grin is bigger than ever. His political ambitions may be as well."[27] A May 2010 poll gave him an approval rating of 78 per cent. The poll numbers eased off considerably later on, but Robertson still looked very strong as the November 2011 election came into view. His main opposition was the NPA's Suzanne Anton. The campaign followed the brutal June Stanley Cup riot, after the Vancouver Canucks were defeated in the seventh game of the series, and coincided with the Occupy Vancouver movement, which took over the grounds of the Vancouver Art Gallery; these were considerable distractions. Nonetheless, it was a dull campaign—some called it the least interesting in memory—and ended with a big Robertson win.

The mayor started to move on from homelessness and bike lanes. Mental health, a subject he'd always been interested in, emerged as the next top policy priority. But it was beginning to look as if the bloom was off the Robertson rose. There was acrimony in Robertson's second term. *Vancouver Magazine* columnist Frances Bula wrote in a May 2013 article, "Vision— supposedly somewhat leftish, definitely greenish—has been slapped with the label 'arrogant' in several of its own polls."[28] That same month, a survey of downtown Vancouverites found that more could name Toronto's mayor, Rob Ford, than could name the mayor of Vancouver.

At the beginning of April 2014, Robertson announced that he would run for a third term as mayor under the Vision Vancouver banner. Tongues were wagging in July when Robertson and his wife announced that they were separating after thirty years of marriage. (Amy Robertson is now an advocate of the local food movement, a doula and a basket weaver.) And in July, respected and well-known journalist Kirk LaPointe, who was the *National Post*'s first executive editor, became the NPA mayoral candidate. "The existing city government has over-reached," he said in an interview. "I think you have to ground yourself in realism and not insult people by being more than yourself. I'm not a flight of fancy, pie-in-the-sky pipe dream person."[29] Shortly before the November 15 election, there were rumours, denied by Robertson, that he intended to run as a Liberal candidate in the 2015 federal election. Some even speculated that he wanted to lose the mayoralty race so that he was freely available to Justin Trudeau.

As election day got closer, the mayoralty race got more interesting and increasingly bitter. The result was no longer a foregone conclusion. The polls showed LaPointe closing in on Robertson. Commentators suggested that people were tiring of Vision Vancouver's "paternalistic and sanctimonious attitude," as well as Robertson's anti-resource-industry ideology. A week before votes were to be cast, Robertson launched a defamation suit against LaPointe, who had described him as "corrupt," "unethical" and "given to dishonest practices." LaPointe's charges arose out of a promise made by Vision Vancouver councillor Geoff Meggs at a meeting with the Canadian Union of Public Employees (CUPE). Meggs promised that Robertson would not contract out more city services to non-unionized workers, and in an apparent exchange, CUPE made a $34,000 campaign contribution to Vision. A tone of desperation crept into the Robertson campaign. On November 12, three days before voting day, the mayor apologized to voters for not listening to them enough, not doing some things very well and not always meeting expectations. "A craven tactical decision," wrote Pete McMartin in the *Vancouver Sun*. "Could Gregor be a goner?" asked *Maclean's*.

In the end, he squeaked by.

•••

Nenshi, Iveson, Robertson, the western triangle of mayoral goodness—how different they are from those beefy, non-bicycling eastern mayors, how interesting and clever and handsome and sexy they seem. They ride to office on their charm. But does it matter? Without strong powers and a capacious treasury, what can Nenshi do that Kelly couldn't have done? What can Iveson achieve that O'Brien couldn't have? What can Robertson accomplish that Ford could not? Good and bad mayors alike, in the west and in the east, are equally hobbled by a dearth of constitutional powers and an inadequate treasury. There is only one difference: the mayor's ability to use the bully pulpit that belongs to him. A mayor is *the mayor*. He speaks for all the citizens of his city, and speaks first. If he is telegenic and articulate, if he captures and expresses the zeitgeist, he will be listened to and will influence events. Nenshi in particular is superb at this. If a mayor is clumsy, coarse and confrontational, he will be laughed at or ignored, or will provoke strife. That was Rob Ford.

Comedian, artist and self-proclaimed anarchist, Jón Gnarr became the mayor of Reykjavik in 2010 after forming a joke party meant to protest corruption and satirize Icelandic politics.

One commentator has said frequently dishevelled Mayor Boris Johnson of London, England, often looks like a man who has spent the night in a barn. Anne Hidalgo, mayor of Paris, has said she would like Parisians to be friendlier.

Mayor Bill de Blasio, the tallest mayor in the history of New York, made the political mistake of eating pizza with a fork.

FOURTEEN
JÓN, BORIS, ANNE AND BILL
The World Beyond.

WE CANADIANS are an insular lot. Some of us have never visited Scandinavia, Central Asia or sub-Saharan Africa. Some of us speak only one language. Because of our insularity, we may have few points of comparison when we judge our mayors, their political environment and their behaviour. Looking at foreign mayors provides context. I've picked for examination, guided by no particular principle, a recent mayor of Reykjavik, Iceland, and the current mayors of London, Paris and New York.

Jón Gnarr, Reykjavik's mayor until early 2014, and Boris Johnson, the current mayor of London, are surprisingly similar. Each man's appeal and political power depends, not on government structure or policy or competence, but on a powerful and eccentric personality and an irreverent sense of humour. Gnarr and Johnson have no Canadian equivalent. Their closest counterpart is Naheed Nenshi of Calgary, but Nenshi falls short of the mark. Anne Hidalgo of Paris and Bill de Blasio of New York, admirers of each other, are fairly new to the job. The Spanish-born Hidalgo initially seemed like a breath of fresh air, but she increasingly appears dull and humourless. De Blasio, a preternaturally tall man who takes himself very seriously, is already a disappointment, making unexpected blunders.

Gnarr, Hidalgo and de Blasio started on the left but tacked to the right as power accreted. Johnson is resolutely on the right, with Winston Churchill as his idol.

•••

In September 2013, I was in Reykjavik for the annual congress of PEN International, an organization that promotes freedom of expression. One night Jón Gnarr, eccentrically dressed (although not wearing lipstick, as he sometimes does), gave an after-dinner speech to delegates. "Being a mayor," he told us, "is like being a member of a book club that only discusses grammar."

Lady Gaga loves Gnarr. He was Noam Chomsky's favourite mayor. Björk is one of his best friends. Gnarr has two tattoos— the logo of a punk band on one arm and Reykjavik's coat of arms on the other. He's a devotee of punk rock and a self-described anarchist. He says he has "an insatiable appetite for any kind of comedy."[1] He's an occasional cross-dresser. He's almost fifty years old. He has five children and is devoted to his wife. By all accounts, he was a pretty good mayor.

It was Iceland's 2008 financial crisis that got Gnarr interested in politics. A lot of fishermen had decided they'd rather be investment bankers. They weren't good at it, unfortunately, and the króna lost half its value in no time at all. The country's three largest banks collapsed. The stock market lost 90 per cent of its value. There were violent demonstrations in Reykjavik— startling events in a generally peaceful and well-ordered society. Gnarr decided to start a new political party and pursue a new kind of politics: the politics of no politics. He called his party the Best Party. Its slogan was "More punk, less hell!"

Gnarr knew nothing about government. He described his campaign as "anarcho-surrealist." He promised free towels in swimming pools. He said farmers would be allowed to take animals into hotel rooms. There would be a polar bear at the zoo and a Disneyland at the airport. He promised "a drug-free Parliament by 2020." He said Jews would be imported into Iceland so the country would finally have people who understood money. The Best Party would fight corruption by indulging in it publicly. Gnarr said he wanted a job that paid a lot for doing nothing. He said the Best Party could promise more than any other party because it would break every promise.[2] Campaign manager Heiða Helgadóttir said, "Our strategy for the campaign was to present an alternative world. Politics is dominated by old men passing around poisoned chalices. We, on the other hand, emphasize life experience, decency, humor."[3]

Gnarr and the Best Party won the election with 35 per cent of the vote. They won six of the fifteen seats on the Reykjavik city council and formed a coalition government. (Gnarr said he would only form a coalition government with someone who had seen all five seasons of *The Wire*, his favourite television show.) After he became mayor, Gnarr said he was the victim of his own joke. The prime minister of Iceland, Jóhanna Sigurðardóttir, said, "This is a big shock, a crash landing." At a press conference, Gnarr said, "No one has to be afraid of the Best Party because it is the best party. If it wasn't, it would be called the Worst Party or the Bad Party. We would never work with a party like that." At his victory party, he raised his fist and said, "Hurray for all kinds of things!"

When reporters asked questions of Gnarr, he would often answer, "I don't know" or "I have no idea." Once he burst into tears at a press conference. Like Canada's more progressive mayors, he was interested in bike lanes and gay rights. And to the surprise of many people, he ran a sound administration performing the traditional tasks of civic government. He tried to balance the budget, showing an unexpected ruthlessness and a willingness to slash costs in an attempt to stop the Reykjavik gravy train. He emphasized human rights and promoted "feminine values." He protested the jailing of Pussy Riot. He said, "Most have a lot to lose, they have a career and a past.... But I don't care. I don't intend to get re-elected." When people said to him, "You'll be in trouble at the next election," he would say, "What election?"

The Icelandic constitution gives municipalities an unusually robust independent status. Article 78 says, "The municipalities shall manage their affairs independently as laid down by law. The income sources of the municipalities, and the rights of the municipalities to decide whether and how to use their sources of income, shall be regulated by law." There is no regional government interposed between the national government and local authorities. Commensurately, the financial powers of Icelandic municipalities are considerable. Iceland is a signatory of the 1985 European Charter of Local Self-Government, which among other things provides, "Local authorities shall be entitled, within national economic policy, to adequate financial resources of their own, of which they may dispose freely within the framework of their powers." Section 5 of article 3 of Iceland's Local Government Act states that municipal authorities shall have their own sources of revenue. The Local Government Finance Act authorizes local income taxes, and 63 per cent of municipal revenues come from this source (service fees account for 18 per cent and property taxes for 11 per cent).

In Iceland, municipalities have considerable political independence and significant financial muscle. Add to the mix a mayor like Jón Gnarr—an idealist (albeit an odd one), someone not interested in the next election, a strong and attractive personality—and you have a powerful recipe for government that emphasizes "life experience, decency, humor." Of course, not everyone is a fan of Gnarr and his political approach. Journalist

Aaron Bastani has written in the *London Review of Books* about Gnarr's "disdain for ideas."[4] Bastani argues that an emphasis on the process of democracy can be "a surrogate for advancing any actual objectives, an emphasis on form papering over an absence of content." Gnarr has said, "One of the most valuable lessons that I have learned is that ideas are dangerous, especially good ones. Because it is almost certain that some halfwit will pick them up and misinterpret them and misuse them. This is why it was so important that the Best Party presented no ideology, no solution.... Nothing that some idiot could then adopt and develop and use as a basis for something horrible, making us ideologues behind some atrocity."[5] Bastani comments, "The Best Party thought the solution was action without politics and practice without conflict."

Yoko Ono has the last word on Jón Gnarr. On October 9, 2014, he was given the Lennon–Ono Grant for Peace Award. The ceremony took place on Viðey Island, just off Reykjavik in Faxaflói Bay. The award is given to individuals who symbolize the continuing campaign for world peace. Yoko Ono said that Gnarr has shown the world "that governmental politics are for the people and by the people. He was a comedian who became a politician. That demands great courage and many did not take him seriously to begin with. But eventually the whole world did. I have great respect for him. Even the way he dresses."[6]

•••

Boris Johnson and Jón Gnarr are alike. They both rely on (often self-deprecating) humour. American humorist Calvin Trillin has observed, "Boris Johnson is ... likely to come up with something about himself that is marginally less flattering than the accuser had been willing to say."[7]

Boris Johnson's full name is Alexander Boris de Pfeffel Johnson. He is better known as Boris, or sometimes BoJo. Boris is mayor of London. He has said he would like to be a walrus, because he admires the marine mammal's ability "to lie on rocks and belch" and make "amazing migratory journeys." He admits that sometimes he drinks "an awful lot" at lunch. But then so did his hero, Winston Churchill. Boris plans to emulate Churchill by becoming prime minister of the United Kingdom, an ambition he has had from a very early age and may well achieve (although when asked about the prospect in 2010, he said, "I'm more likely to be decapitated by a Frisbee or locked in a disused fridge"[8]). When he announced his intention to seek a parliamentary seat in the 2015 general election, a journalist covering the event wrote, "Boris Johnson staggered on to the stage, looking more than ever like a man who has spent the night in a barn before being discovered and evicted by an irate farmer. Even by his own matchless standards, he was superbly dishevelled."[9] On September 12, 2014, Johnson was adopted as the Conservative Party candidate for the Uxbridge and South Ruislip constituency. He will aim for the prime ministership from there. Johnson, who was born in New York City and holds a U.S. passport as well as a British one, has also noted that he is eligible to be president of the United States (although he now says he plans to give up his U.S. citizenship).

Boris Johnson, like the current prime minister, David Cameron, comes from Britain's upper class (the country still has one, and it remains an object of both fascination and contempt). He was born in 1964. His father, Stanley, was a writer, environmental activist, politician and, like his son, serial philanderer.[10] His mother, Charlotte, long divorced from Stanley, is an esteemed painter and the daughter of the international lawyer Sir James Fawcett. Boris's wife, Marina, a barrister, is the daughter of the broadcaster Sir Charles Wheeler and his Indian wife, Dip Singh; she and Johnson have four children. Boris was briefly married before, to the beautiful Allegra Mostyn-Owen, who as a young woman appeared on the cover of *Tatler*, and who in 2010 married a Muslim half her age.

Johnson is a descendant of King George II. His great-grandfather, Ali Kemal Bey, was one of the last interior ministers of the Ottoman Empire. He went to Eton and to Balliol College, Oxford, where he studied classics. He is a keen cyclist, like so many mayors. Like Jón Gnarr, he is fond of jokes and has an unruly hairstyle that some say is the secret to his success (he is said to muss it up before public appearances). Unlike Gnarr, he is not too keen on gay people, although he now says he is in favour of same-sex marriage. Like Sam Katz, erstwhile mayor of Winnipeg, he's decked a child in a charity football match.[11] Many intensely dislike Johnson. He has been called a "bigoted, lying Old Etonian buffoon."

Johnson initially pursued a career in journalism, and in 1999, at the age of thirty-five, he became editor of the *Spectator*, a conservative weekly newspaper then owned (indirectly) by Conrad Black. For what it's worth, Black has described Johnson as the most interesting politician in Europe. Johnson sometimes resembles Black, particularly in his tendency to bloviate. He once called political opponents "great supine protoplasmic invertebrate jellies."

In 2001, Johnson was elected to Parliament from the constituency of Henley, near London, succeeding Michael Heseltine, a Conservative Party grandee popularly known as Tarzan. In 2004, he served briefly on the Conservative front bench, as shadow minister for the arts, but was fired over accusations that he lied to Michael Howard, the party leader, about an extramarital affair (Johnson described the accusations as "an inverted pyramid of piffle"). In 2008, he ran for mayor of London. It was widely reported that during the campaign he said, "If you vote for the Conservatives, your wife will get bigger breasts and your chances of driving a BMW M3 will increase." He won the election and resigned as a member of Parliament. In 2012, *The Economist* said, "Mr. Johnson has been a good mayor rather than a great one. His image of tousle-haired disorganisation is not merely a pose. He has a habit of fastening on social problems, setting up an advisory group, then losing interest."[12]

The job of mayor is a new one in the ancient city of London. It was created in 2000 and modelled loosely on the American mayoralty system (although the mayor of London has fewer powers than his typical American counterpart). Johnson is only the second person to hold the office (the first was Ken Livingstone, former leader of the Greater London Council, which was abolished by Margaret Thatcher in 1986). The mayor of London is directly elected. There is a twenty-five-member "scrutiny-oriented" London Assembly, whose members are also directly elected and run as representatives of political parties. Together, the mayor and the assembly compose the Greater London Authority (GLA), which controls transport, policing, economic development, and fire and emergency planning, although these functions are exercised day to day by separate and distinct authorities. The GLA does not have other powers traditionally associated with city government— for example, over health, education, social care, arts and culture, and environmental protection. By far the most important power of the GLA, and therefore the mayor, is over transport, which includes buses and the London Underground. Transport is always a mayor's most important file, in London or anywhere else.

Financially, the GLA has little independence. Ninety per cent of its funding comes from the central government, often with precise strings attached. Less than 10 per cent of its revenue comes from local property taxes. Boris Johnson constantly complains that he has insufficient taxing powers, championing what has become known as "fiscal devolution." He has said that the push for devolution following Scotland's independence referendum offers a political opportunity for English cities to acquire new taxing powers. Devolution for cities has become a significant political issue in the United Kingdom. But as things stand today, London has a mayor with little explicit political power and even less money.

Now Boris Johnson is running for prime minister. A columnist in the *Observer* wrote, "There is a low moan of desire for Boris Johnson. If only BoJo was leading us, so it goes, things would be looking much better for the blue team."[13] Why are his aspirations taken seriously? Perhaps it's because next to David Cameron, Boris Johnson seems down to earth and approachable. Perhaps it's because he's entertaining and funny. No one ever accused David Cameron of being those things. *The Economist* says, "Rarely, perhaps never, in the history of British politics has such an unlikely and unreliable politician been spoken of as prime ministerial material by so many, for so long."[14]

•••

Anne Hidalgo—the cautious, modest, left-leaning, pant-suited, newish mayor of Paris—defeated two conservative, flamboyant, exciting, glamorous and younger women candidates. Mix a bit of socialism with a bit of dullness, and apparently you have an agreeable formula for voters in the City of Light.

Hidalgo, a member of France's Socialist Party, once an obscure two-term deputy mayor and protege of her predecessor, Bertrand Delanoë, was elected mayor in March 2014. In an obscure and Byzantine indirect system, the mayor of Paris is elected not by the voters at large but by 163 councillors representing Paris's twenty arrondissements. The job has national prominence, and can be a stepping stone to greater things. Jacques Chirac was mayor of Paris from 1977 to 1995, and subsequently became president of France. The mayor's office in the Hôtel de Ville (city hall) is bigger than the president's in the Élysée Palace.

The three main 2014 Paris mayoralty candidates were all female—Rachida Dati, Nathalie Kosciusko-Morizet and Anne Hidalgo. Forty-nine-year-old Dati, a former justice minister in the Nicolas Sarkozy government, is often described as a volatile woman of great beauty. In 2012, in the course of litigation over the paternity of her daughter, it was alleged by a putative father that Dati had had eight boyfriends at the time the child was conceived, including a TV host, the chief executive officer of a huge company, a former Spanish prime minister, one of Nicolas Sarkozy's brothers, Sarkozy himself, the Qatari attorney general and the heir to a luxury goods empire. Her exciting private life appeared to be too much even for the French, and she soon disappeared as a serious candidate. That left Anne Hidalgo and the conservative Nathalie Kosciusko-Morizet, known as NKM.

Like Dati, the glamorous but arrogant forty-one-year-old NKM had once been a minister in the Sarkozy government. Sometimes called the Boris Johnson of Paris, she described herself during the election campaign as a "star," which won her no friends. The battle between Hidalgo and NKM soon became known as "the Heiress vs. the Harpist." The fifty-five-year-old Hidalgo, cozily anointed by her predecessor, Delanoë, was the

Heiress. NKM, who had posed for *Paris Match* in the middle of a forest with an abandoned harp nearby, was the Harpist. Hidalgo, who carefully eschewed bling and grand gestures, was said to be "honest, serious and modest." One newspaper described her as "a consensual, hardworking politician. Even supporters suggest that she would be a safe pair of hands rather than an imaginative leader."[15]

During the campaign, Hidalgo said she would turn the Avenue Foch, which runs from the Arc de Triomphe to the Bois de Boulogne and is home to some of Paris's richest residents, into an accessible green park for the masses—and for good measure, she promised to build housing for the poor there as well. Her housing policy was heavily influenced by her own childhood experiences in Vaise, a poor district of Lyon. Her parents, Spanish émigrés who settled in Lyon, had no money, and for a time the family lived in an apartment without a bathroom. She has described social housing as her "absolute priority."

Hidalgo, like many mayors around the world, loves the environment in general and bicycles in particular. She is strongly in favour of Vélib' and Autolib', the Parisian bike- and car-sharing programs, respectively, and has proposed Scooterlib', a free moped system. She has called for diesel cars, which have high particulate emissions, to be banned from Paris by 2020 as a public health measure, and has argued that most vehicles of any kind should be kept out of parts of the city centre (this has led to criticism that she caters to elite city dwellers who dislike traffic rather than poorer people who live in the outskirts but work in the centre as waiters or taxi drivers). She has a curious preoccupation with cults. In 2005, she was head of a government committee that monitored "cult-like groups," including the Church of Scientology, and she has participated in demonstrations outside Scientology buildings. Like many of us, she wants

Parisians to be friendlier. In a September 2014 interview, she said, "There is one thing I am not happy about: Paris ranks among the unfriendliest cities. Parisians may have strong personalities, but they aren't unfriendly. By the end of my mandate, I want us to be among the friendliest. Parisians must be known for their smiles."[16]

In her first few months in power, Hidalgo put in place a "participatory budget" project, proclaiming she was "handing the keys of the budget to the citizens." Five per cent of the city's 2014–20 investment budget—about €426 million (roughly $600 million Canadian)—was set aside for projects that were voted on directly by Parisians. Voters were invited to choose from a list of fifteen ideas. In a September 2014 vote, Parisians picked nine of the fifteen, choosing mostly environmental projects; a scheme to create vegetation walls that would improve biodiversity received the most votes. But the participatory budget project was controversial. In June, the city announced it had a €400-million budget deficit, and some Parisians wondered whether it had the funds to support Hidalgo's curious financial adventure.

Parisian political lines were strangely blurred in a 2014 dispute over the proposed development of a forty-two-storey office tower in the city's southwest corner.[17] Many think the building will disfigure the city's skyline, just as the 1973 Montparnasse Tower did. But Hidalgo, drifting to the centre-right as incumbents so often do, claiming she intends to reinvent Paris, has fiercely promoted the project as an engine of economic growth in a poorer part of the city, fighting environmentalists, once her natural allies, as part of her campaign. The principal opponent to the development is Hidalgo's old rival, the Harpist, Nathalie Kosciusko-Morizet.

Bill de Blasio, mayor of New York, has described Hidalgo as a soulmate. "It's absolutely amazing by the way, 3,000 miles apart, we have come up with such a similar vision of what our cities need," he said when he met Hidalgo in New York in May 2014. "What we want to do now is constantly communicate as we implement this vision and help each other figure out what's working and what's not. We have three areas where we have tremendous commonality and shared vision: Early childhood education, affordable housing and on environmental sustainability."[18]

Now Hidalgo wants to go to London to visit Boris Johnson. "Or perhaps Boris will come here," she says. "I met him many times when I was deputy mayor, he is ... er ... eccentric."[19]

•••

On Saturday, October 25, 2014, Bill de Blasio and his wife, Chirlane McCray, had lunch at the Meatball Shop in New York's West Village. A few days earlier, Dr. Craig Spencer had dined at the same restaurant. Shortly after his meal, Dr. Spencer was diagnosed with the Ebola virus. "It's an example of how New Yorkers deal with a challenge," said de Blasio, mayor of the world's most important city, tucking into a plate of meatballs. De Blasio came out of the Ebola crisis looking good. He played the "unfamiliar" role of "the coolheaded executive, stern and sober, urging New Yorkers to go about their lives."[20]

De Blasio, a Democrat and the tallest mayor in the history of New York, took office on January 1, 2014, after a huge victory in the November election. Virtually his entire career has been devoted, in one fashion or another, to New York City municipal affairs and politics. He served on city council for several years, and then as the city's public advocate. De Blasio was sworn in as mayor by the Big Dog himself, Bill Clinton. "Make no mistake," de Blasio said in his inaugural address, "the people of this city have chosen a progressive path." He replaced Michael

Bloomberg, whose net worth is $30 billion. Ironically, inequality, including inequality of wealth, was the focus of de Blasio's campaign. He is an economic populist. He was endorsed by actors Alec Baldwin, Susan Sarandon, Sarah Jessica Parker and Steve Buscemi. *The Economist* said New York had gone from Mr. Data to Mr. Dateable.[21]

Bill de Blasio's father, a Yale- and Harvard-educated economist called Warren Wilhelm, lost a leg fighting in the Second World War. Warren walked out on Bill's mother, a writer with two degrees from Smith College, and later, riddled with cancer, shot himself in a car parked outside a motel. Bill took the name de Blasio, his mother's maiden name, after he graduated from college. In 1988, then twenty-six, he visited Nicaragua. *The New York Times* reported, "He was tall and sometimes goofy, known for his ability to mimic a goose's honk. He spoke in long, meandering paragraphs, musing on Franklin D. Roosevelt, Karl Marx and Bob Marley. He took painstaking notes on encounters with farmers, doctors and revolutionary fighters." De Blasio went to Nicaragua to distribute food and medicine. He returned, said *The New York Times*, with an admiration for the Sandinistas, Nicaraguan revolutionaries, and "a vision of the possibilities of an unfettered leftist government."[22] In 1994, Bill married Chirlane McCray, an African-American feminist poet and politician. McCray says she was a lesbian before she met Bill. They honeymooned in Cuba, violating a U.S. travel ban.

De Blasio's mayoralty got off to a rocky and trivial start. His "first mistake as mayor," much derided, was eating pizza with a fork at a Staten Island pizzeria. In January and February, there was a lot of snow; residents of the wealthy Upper East Side complained about snow clearance and the mayor apologized. On February 13, 2014, there was a massive blizzard, but public schools were kept open, a decision criticized on safety grounds by teacher unions, parents and the media. Meanwhile, de Blasio was castigated by actor Liam Neeson and others for his plans to outlaw Central Park's horse-drawn carriages, which he considered inhumane (he had promised a ban to animal-rights activists who supported his campaign). He was also attacked for making a call to the police after one of his political supporters was arrested. Then his promise to roll back the stop-and-frisk policy of the New York Police Department came under fire. Under this Bloomberg policy, young men in rough areas, often black or Hispanic, are stopped, questioned and sometimes frisked to deter them from carrying guns. Some thought a roll-back would encourage crime.

De Blasio's calm response to the Ebola crisis mitigated this bad beginning, and he received kudos for implementing a universal pre-kindergarten program early in his mayoralty. But soon he blundered again. Wednesday, November 12, 2014, was the anniversary of the 2001 plane crash in Queens that killed 265 people. There was a memorial service that included the tolling of a bell at the exact minute of the crash. De Blasio arrived late, angering the victims' assembled relatives. They had observed a moment of silence without him. He explained he'd had "a very rough night. I woke up sluggish." Later, showing extraordinary political tone-deafness, de Blasio said New Yorkers didn't care that he'd shown up late. Average New Yorkers, he said, don't care about that "inside baseball."

This faux pas was dramatically eclipsed by the mayor's first major crisis, a standoff with some members and representatives of the New York Police Department following the murder on December 20, 2014, of two NYPD officers sitting in their police car. De Blasio was seen as generally unsympathetic to the police, who were particularly angry at the way he had reacted to a grand jury's decision earlier in December not to indict a police officer who had killed a black man with a chokehold. "Today's outcome is one that many in our city did not want," de Blasio said when the grand jury's decision was announced.[23] He expressed sympathy with street protesters and said that he had warned his bi-racial son about interacting with the police. After the murder of the two officers, Patrick Lynch, president of the Patrolmen's Benevolent Association, said, "There is blood on many hands.... That blood on the hands starts on the steps of city hall in the office of the mayor."[24]

New York's mayor cannot do much without the agreement of the state. John Cassidy of the *New Yorker* has commented, "He is only the second-most-powerful official in New York City. Because of the arcane tax and budgeting process, when the mayor wants to get things done he is largely beholden to the governor."[25] De Blasio needed the agreement of the state legislature to lower the city's speed limit to twenty-five miles an hour. (This reminds us that Sam Katz had to have the province of Manitoba's agreement to lower the speed limit in Winnipeg school zones.) De Blasio wants to raise New York's minimum wage, but he cannot do it without the consent of the state, and Governor Mario Cuomo, who believes minimum wage to be a state matter, is not agreeable. De Blasio and Cuomo have fought over the mayor's wish to raise taxes on the wealthy and over charter schools (de Blasio opposes these schools, which receive public funding but operate independently).

The mayor has called the state government "illogical" and "unknowable." He has said that he will shift his agenda toward things that cannot be killed at the state level. His relationship with Governor Cuomo is not good. The mayor and the governor, although they are both members of the Democratic Party, do not see eye to eye. They have been called "the most dysfunctional couple in New York politics" and "deeply incompatible." The irony is that although the New York council and its highest official are politically neutered, they preside over an enormous budget of $70 billion, bigger than that of most countries.

Bill de Blasio may not love Mario Cuomo, but he does love Anne Hidalgo. He also loves Ed Miliband, leader of the United Kingdom's Labour Party. Both are socialists. In September 2014, de Blasio was the star speaker at Labour's annual conference in Manchester, England. In a self-congratulatory speech, he spoke out against economic inequality and described his own election campaign. "It was never my intention to nibble around the edges with policies of timid maintenance; I ran to take dead aim at the crisis of our time. And I became Mayor because everyday New Yorkers, too, were hungry for a clean break from the status quo."[26]

De Blasio likes to strut the national and international stage as a leader of the left. He goes to Washington, D.C. He has met several times with Italy's foreign minister and is treated as a major celebrity in that country. He talks to heads of state. He talks to the mayors of cities around the world. He is "eager to spread his message of social equity to other nations that he believes, thanks to austerity budgets and economic woes, are newly receptive to his brand of populist liberalism."[27] But back home, there is not a lot he can do.

•••

What do the careers of Jón, Boris, Anne and Bill tell us? Jón Gnarr, mayor of the least consequential city of the four, had the most political and financial power. Boris Johnson, Anne Hidalgo and Bill de Blasio—leading great metropolises, prominent persons of national and international significance—are beholden politically and financially to senior governments, and consequently are strangely ineffective, forced to resort to trivial initiatives encased in overblown rhetoric. The more effective of the four, Gnarr and Johnson, rely on huge public appeal, personal allure, and an ability to amuse and entertain. In the case of Johnson, those qualities could propel him into his country's premiership. There are two lessons in this. First, internationally as well as in Canada, cities are woefully treated, deprived of the powers and funds they desperately need. London is no different from Calgary, New York no different from Halifax. Second, leadership depends more on personality than anything else. That is why Naheed Nenshi is so prominent. That explains Rob Ford.

CONCLUSION
DEVO-MAX

IT'S A SORRY TALE, the tale of Canadian mayors. I'm sure you agree (if you've read this far). No need for me to repeat the litany of failure and disappointment. But I will say again that the nub of the problem is the legal and financial powerlessness of municipalities. They can't do what they're expected to do. They can't do what must be done. They don't have the necessary legal authority. They don't have the money required. In this world of legal and financial impotence, what person of real talent and understanding would want to be chief magistrate, presiding over a forlorn and hollowed-out quasi-kingdom? When John Tory was elected mayor of Toronto in October 2014, a colleague and friend of his, and close observer of the municipal scene, told me, "He's finished before he's even sworn in. He can't possibly do what he's promised to do. The city can't afford it. The campaign and its promises were an illusion." The backtracking began almost immediately. In January 2015, Tory broke an important campaign promise and raised transit fares.

The way out of this horrible mess is devo-max, a neologism coined in the United Kingdom to describe the maximum devolution of powers and status from a superior to an inferior level of government—in our case, from the provinces to the cities. How should devo-max unfold in Canada? First, the country must collectively address the national urban crisis. The Canada Elections Act requires that a federal election be held no later than October 19, 2015 (it may, of course, be called earlier). Soon, if it hasn't happened already, Canada will be plunged into an election campaign. During that campaign, each of the major political parties should pledge that, if it forms a government, it will promptly convene a national conference of big-city mayors and provincial premiers, presided over by the prime minister. This national conference will lay out the components of a New Deal for cities. No legal commitments or changes could appropriately be made at such a meeting. Those will come later, as a result of bilateral negotiations at the provincial level. But at the national conference, each premier and each big-city mayor will acknowledge the problems that exist and commit to prompt negotiations in accord with the understandings reached on the Canadian stage.

Each big-city mayor will then meet with his or her provincial premier. Any city without a charter—Calgary or Edmonton, for example—will negotiate one. Those with a charter will renegotiate its terms. Each charter, new or renegotiated, must have certain key provisions. The most important is an entrenchment clause, containing special requirements for modifying or repealing the charter. The charter will no longer be considered an ordinary statute of the provincial legislature—one that the legislature can modify when and as it wishes. The charter entrenchment clause is essential to the reform of city governance. Everything depends on it.

The charter entrenchment clause could take many forms. It would make the most sense if the clause required that a city agree, by formal vote of council, to any change in its charter proposed by the province. (A requirement of this type is sometimes called "procedural entrenchment.") The entrenchment clause—the extra requirements for repeal or amendment of the charter—would, of course, be subject to itself (that is, it could not be removed or amended unless it complied with its own terms). The clause could also allow a city council, by majority vote, to propose changes to its charter to the province and oblige the province to present those proposed changes to the legislature for a vote.

What is to stop a legislature simply repealing such a provision, in the ordinary way, without meeting the additional requirement? After all, the conventional wisdom is that in a democracy there can be no such thing as an entrenched law unless it is part of fundamental constitutional provisions (such as the Canadian Charter of Rights and Freedoms). The conventional wisdom says that any provincial statutory provision—including one that requires the consent of a city council to change—can be amended or removed in the ordinary way, despite what it says. Democracy, so the argument goes, demands that no legislature can bind either itself or a future legislature.

A genuine constitutional provision enhancing the status of Canadian cities would be the best solution, but this will not happen, for a variety of political and technical reasons. Procedural entrenchment is an indirect and feasible way of roughly attaining the same objective. It is an informal way of rewriting the constitutional rules. It is analogous in purpose and effect to the "notwithstanding" clause of the Charter of Rights and Freedoms, which allows Parliament or a provincial legislature to declare that a law shall operate notwithstanding the human rights provisions of the Charter. The clause was put in the Charter to secure the provincial support necessary to amend the constitution, but the expectation (correct, as it turns out) was that it would seldom be used, simply because the political and public relations price for opting out of the Charter would be severe. Similarly, a city charter entrenchment clause could in theory be ignored, but the political price of doing so would be great. It would be a provincial slap in the face of the city, and cities are full of people who vote in provincial elections.

What would be the key provisions of an entrenched city charter? There are three. First, the financial shackles that bind the city would be released. Second, ethical requirements for municipal politicians, particularly those dealing with conflicts of interest, would be refined and developed. Third, any impediments to political parties operating at the municipal level would be removed.

Financial freedom is essential. The city would have the authority to impose whatever taxes it saw fit, including a city sales tax and a city income tax. To make this possible, existing statutory prohibitions would need to be removed in some cases, and specific permission for these new taxes should be given in the new or revised charter. The easiest way to implement these new taxes would be through a surtax on the GST or HST and on provincial income tax. Most who have considered the fiscal woes of Canadian cities—municipal politicians, academics, editorialists, unions—support such new revenue streams. The idea is not new. It has widespread and increasing support. Some have even proposed scrapping the property tax altogether and replacing it with income and sales taxes,[1] but this is utopian.

As well as giving cities new and unrestricted taxing powers, an entrenched charter would remove restrictions on the ability of cities to borrow. At present, cities can issue bonds to fund major capital investments, but usually the provincial government must agree and various restrictions are imposed on the borrowing. In most cases, cities are not allowed to run a deficit to cover operating costs. These limitations should be eliminated.

Revised and expanded ethical requirements for municipal politicians should be incorporated into city charters. A good beginning would be to implement the recommendations made by Justice Cunningham in his 2011 report on Hazel McCallion's egregious involvement with her son's real estate dealings. Cunningham's report is appropriately entitled "Updating the Ethical Infrastructure." He recommended, among other things, that the pecuniary and other private interests of a council member's relatives be deemed to be the member's interests; that conflict-of-interest rules apply to all meetings attended by a councillor in his or her official capacity (not just council meetings); and that a wide range of tailored sanctions be available for ethical breaches. A new sanctions framework should be sensitive to the nature and severity of the breach. It should provide for the suspension or removal of a councillor or mayor in some circumstances—subject, of course, to appropriate legal safeguards.

Finally, as I suggested in chapter 1, political parties should be allowed to operate at the municipal level. Views differ on this subject, with thoughtful people on both sides of the debate, but I believe that political parties would provide focused authority, political clarity, discipline and accountability—all of which are desperately needed at the municipal level.

These reforms to city government, and Canada's constitutional arrangements, are simple but substantial. They change the constitutional landscape. They would go far toward making city government the most important level of government in law, as it is in fact.

•••

The mayors I have written about are, to put it generously, a mixed bunch.

Gérald Tremblay and Gilles Vaillancourt, full of hubris, presided over corrupt administrations in Montreal and Laval. Their successors, Michael Applebaum and Alexandre Duplessis, who exited the mayoral stage almost as soon as they entered upon it, were compromised nobodies. Joe Fontana of London and Susan Fennell of Brampton displayed poor and self-serving judgment. Little or nothing redeems these mayors. We are well rid of them.

Others, despite their bewilderment in office and often-comical failures, sometimes elicit sympathy and even respect; at least they tried, in their own odd ways, to do what they thought best. Larry O'Brien of Ottawa and Sam Katz of Winnipeg fit into this category. I would also add Rob Ford, who in his own tortured way is a man of the people. But I would exclude Hazel McCallion. McCallion's main achievement was clinging to power for an absurdly long period of time through strength of personality; she presided over disastrous development in Mississauga, giving developers a free hand, and was guilty of flagrant conflict of interest. She got away with so much and retired to absurd accolades. Peter Kelly of Halifax is a difficult case. The mistake that sank his political career was made in his private life and not as part of his job as mayor of Halifax. He was a strangely inept and clumsy mayor much of the time, but he could rise to the occasion.

As for the western triangle of mayoral goodness, they exemplify the impotence of the office more than any other mayors. These three men are not crippled by personal weakness or inadequacy. They are limited only by their office. Their careers epitomize those limitations.

•••

My tour of cities is done. I'm going back to Port Medway, Nova Scotia.

There's a winter storm warning in effect as the plane lands in Halifax. It will be a long and tricky drive from the airport, down Highway 103 to Port Medway. What will I find when I get there? The power may be out (it often is when the weather is bad). The village store may be closed, and there's not much to eat in the house.

The drive offers a chance to reflect on what I've seen and heard about the cities of Canada over the last few months. It's a sad and depressing train of thought. Canadian city dwellers have not been in good hands. Even the most competent and best motivated of mayors can do little because of the way we have set things up; they don't have the power, and they don't have the money. And many mayors, as we have seen, fall far short when it comes to competence and motivation. By now, I don't have to give you chapter and verse.

After two hours on the highway in the snow, I turn off at Exit 17A. Almost there. A couple of years ago, the government of Nova Scotia repaved the road, which is just a few kilometres long, from the highway down to Port Medway and the Eastern Shore Road. The repaving cost well over a million dollars. The road serves not much more than a handful of households. Is there no better use, in the poor province of Nova Scotia, for all that money? I wonder what the politics of it were. Do things work the same way down here in the boondocks as they do back in the big city?

NOTES

INTRODUCTION: THE NAKED GLADIATORS

1. Christopher Hume, "Forget Federal and Provincial Politics: The Action Is Local," *Toronto Star*, 24 May 2013, www.thestar.com/news/gta/2013/05/24/forget_federal _and_provincial_politics_the_action_is_local_hume.html (accessed 18 December 2014).

2. Gary Dimmock, "O'Brien Offered Cash If I Quit: Kilrea," *Ottawa Citizen*, 10 February 2007, www.canada.com/ottawacitizen/news/story.html?id=60cbb55f0e20-42c2-bb4e -bf05cb4bfa3b&p=1 (accessed 11 November 2013).

ONE: TO THE CITY

1. Quoted by Marcus Gee, "It's Time to Re-examine the Scope of Municipal Powers," *Globe and Mail*, 22 October 2014, www.theglobeandmail.com/news/toronto/its-time-to -re-examine-the-scope-of-municipal-powers/article21251359/ (accessed 26 October 2014).

2. John Barber, "Bring Back Truly Local Government," *Toronto Star*, 13 October 2014, www.thestar.com/opinion/commentary/2014/10/13/bring_back_truly_local_ government.html (accessed 14 October 2014).

3. Bartley Kives, "City Has Wish List Amid Provincial Race," *Winnipeg Free Press*, 18 May 2007, www.winnipegfreepress.com/historic/32233084.html (accessed 18 December 2014).

4. Larry Kusch, "Mayors Frustrated with Province," *Winnipeg Free Press*, 26 April 2013, www.winnipegfreepress.com/local/mayors-frustrated-with-province-204810081.html (accessed 24 April 2014).

5. Quoted by Angus Gillespie, "How the West Is Winning with Calgary Mayor Naheed Nenshi," *Canadian Business Journal*, 14 May 2014, www.cbj.ca/how_the_west_is_ winning_with_calgary_mayor_naheed_nenshi/ (accessed 24 July 2014).

6. See Jason Magder, "Quebec Studies Greater Powers for All Municipalities," *Montreal Gazette*, 2 May 2014, http://montrealgazette.com/news/local-news/ quebec-studies-greater-powers-for-all-municipalities (accessed 24 May 2014).

7. See Haukur S. Magnússon, "What Happened? Mayor Jón Gnarr Explains Himself, a Little," *Rekyjavik Grapevine*, 26 May 2014, http://grapevine.is/mag/feature/2014/05/ 26/what-happened/ (accessed 17 October 2014).

8. David Brooks, "The Stem and the Flower," *The New York Times*, 2 December 2013, www.nytimes.com/2013/12/03/opinion/brooks-the-stem-and-the-flower.html?_ r=1& (accessed 4 December 2013).

9. See James Lightbody, *City Politics, Canada* (Peterborough, ON: Broadview Press, 2006), 155.

10. Edward Keenan, *Some Great Idea: Good Neighbourhoods, Crazy Politics and the Invention of Toronto* (Toronto: Coach House Books, 2013), 24.

11. Savas Fortis, "Je suis déçu," LavalNews.ca, 15 November 2012, http://lavalnews.ca/ editorial/Je-suis-decu-Gilles-Vaillancourt-202161 (accessed 11 February 2014).

12. Peggy Curran, "Has Montreal Had Enough of Political Parties?" *Montreal Gazette*, 17 May 2013, http://montrealgazette.com/news/local-news/has-montreal-had-enough -of-political-parties (accessed 9 November 2013).

13. Andrew Sancton, *Canadian Local Government: An Urban Perspective* (Don Mills, ON: Oxford University Press, 2011), 175.

14. Tammany Hall wasn't all bad. See Terry Golway, "The Forgotten Virtues of Tammany Hall," *New York Times*, 18 January 2014, www.nytimes.com/2014/01/18/opinion/ the-forgotten-virtues-of-tammany-hall.html (accessed 23 January 2014).

15. See Lightbody, *City Politics*, 238ff.

16. "Key Findings in the Leger–Yahoo Canada Leadership Poll," *Yahoo! Canada News*, 13 November 2013, https://ca.news.yahoo.com/key-findings-in-the-leger-yahoo -canada-leadership-poll-215701378.html (accessed 4 December 2013).

17. Alexander Panetta, "'Bang! I Accelerate': Quebec Mayor Forced to Apologize for Saying How Much He Enjoys Killing Kittens with His Car," *National Post*, 14 July 2013, http://news.nationalpost.com/2013/07/14/bang-i-accelerate-quebec-mayor -forced-to-apologize-for-saying-how-much-he-enjoys-killing-kittens-with-his-car/ (accessed 4 December 2013).

18. "Mayor Tells Police Why He Bought Drugs," *Vancouver Sun*, 2 May 2006, www.canada .com/vancouversun/news/story.html?id=70377688-d53f-4718-b23e-8ecedc7c21e7&k =53811 (accessed 5 December 2013).

19. Tu Thanh Ha, "Third Quebec Mayor Resigns Amidst Corruption Allegations,"*Globe and Mail*, 30 November 2012, www.theglobeandmail.com/news/national/third -quebec-mayor-resigns-amidst-corruption-allegations/article5833313/ (accessed 27 April 2014).

20. James Lightbody, "'Wild Bill' Hawrelak: 'Let's Get Edmonton Rolling Again,'" in Allan Levine (ed.), *Your Worship: The Lives of Eight of Canada's Most Unforgettable Mayors* (Toronto: James Lorimer & Company, 1989), 36.

21. Les Perreaux, "Chateauguay Mayor Celebrated as Hero for Turning Down Bribe," *Globe and Mail*, 1 January 2014, www.theglobeandmail.com/news/national/ chateauguay-mayor-celebrated-as-hero-for-turning-down-bribe/article16165328/ (accessed 24 May 2014).

22. Nick Wing, "24 U.S. Mayors Who Prove We're Also Better Than Canada at Electing Embarrassing Officials," *Huffington Post*, 6 November 2013, www.huffingtonpost .com/2013/11/06/worst-mayors_n_4221583.html (accessed 5 December 2013).

23. "Freshening New England's Armpit," *The Economist*, 5 July 2014, www.economist .com/news/united-states/21606316-ex-mayor-who-inspired-gangster-musical -returns-freshening-new-englands-armpit (accessed 17 July 2014).

24. Campbell Robertson, "Politicians Are Slowed by Scandal, but Many Still Win the Race," *The New York Times*, 17 July 2013, www.nytimes.com/2013/07/18/us/ politics/politicians-are-slowed-by-scandal-but-many-still-win-the-race.html (accessed 6 December 2013).

25. Calvin Trillin, "Capital Fellows," *New Yorker*, 14 April 2008, www.newyorker.com/ magazine/2008/04/14/capital-fellows (accessed 19 October 2014).

26. John Doyle, "Rob Ford, Lindsay Lohan and the Disappearance of Truth," *Globe and Mail*, 1 April 2014, www.theglobeandmail.com/arts/television/rob-ford-lindsay-lohan-and-the-disappearance-of-truth/article17726385/ (accessed 26 April 2014). The Galloway interview with Ford can be heard at www.cbc.ca/player/News/Canada/Toronto/ID/2445276405/.

27. "The Rob Ford Phenomenon: What's Going On in Toronto?" Canada Institute, Wilson Center, 16 May 2014, www.wilsoncenter.org/event/the-rob-ford-phenomenon-what's-going-toronto (accessed 10 August 2014).

28. Thom Ernst, "Mayors and the Movies," *Toronto Star*, 23 May 2014, www.thestar.com/entertainment/movies/2014/05/23/mayors_and_the_movies.html (accessed 23 May 2014).

29. Peter Howell, "Vodka-Soaked Satire Drips with Despair," *Toronto Star,* 23 January 2015, E5.

30. Richard Ouzounian, "Dreaming of Rob Ford Premieres at Crawl Festival," *Toronto Star*, 14 May 2014, www.thestar.com/entertainment/stage/2014/05/14/dreaming_of_rob_ford_premieres_at_crawl_festival.html (accessed 23 May 2014).

31. Victoria Ahearn, "Writer of Rob Ford Musical Says Toronto Mayor Is 'Very Shakespearean,'" CTV News, 15 June 2014, www.ctvnews.ca/entertainment/writer-of-rob-ford-musical-says-toronto-mayor-is-very-shakespearean-1.1869578 (accessed 17 June 2014).

32. Jeffrey Toobin, "Our Broken Constitution," *New Yorker*, 9 December 2013, www.newyorker.com/magazine/2013/12/09/our-broken-constitution (accessed 21 December 2014).

33. Reprinted in Philip B. Kurland and Ralph Lerner, eds., *The Founders' Constitution*, volume 1, chapter 2, document 23 (Chicago: University of Chicago Press, 2000), http://press-pubs.uchicago.edu/founders/documents/v1ch2s23.html (accessed 6 December 2013).

34. Benjamin R. Barber, *If Mayors Ruled the World: Dysfunctional Nations, Rising Cities* (New Haven, CN: Yale University Press, 2013).

35. Alan Broadbent, *Urban Nation: Why We Need to Give Power Back to the Cities to Make Canada Strong* (Toronto: HarperCollins, 2008), 80.

TWO: PETER KELLY OF HALIFAX

1. Tim Bousquet, "Peter Kelly: Mayor," *The Coast*, 10 May 2012, www.thecoast.ca/halifax/peter-kelly/Content?oid=3155363 (accessed 12 October 2013).

2. Ruth Davenport, "Peter Kelly Hoping to Be Remembered as a 'Mayor of the People,'" *Metro*, 5 November 2012, http://metronews.ca/news/halifax/429489/peter-kelly-hoping-to-remembered-as-a-mayor-of-the-people/ (accessed 2 October 2013).

3. You can see a clip of this at www.youtube.com/watch?v=vU_BRc-FNxA (accessed 9 October 2013).

4. Mary Vallis, "Halifax Mayor Peter J. Kelly Takes Bullet to Airport, Really Likes Cheetahs," *National Post*, 28 May 2010, http://news.nationalpost.com/2010/05/28/halifax-mayor-peter-j-kelly-takes-bullet-to-airport-really-likes-cheetahs/ (accessed 1 October 2013).

5. Michael MacDonald, "Halifax Mayor Fighting for Political Life," MSN News, 20 March 2011, www.msn.com/en-ca/news/canada?cp-documentid=28068341 (accessed 9 October 2013).

6. Tim Bousquet, "Two Decades of World-Class Delusion," *The Coast*, 11 July 2013, www.thecoast.ca/halifax/two-decades-of-world-class-delusion/Content?oid=3930595 (accessed 1 November 2013).

7. Tim Bousquet, "A Trust Betrayed: Peter Kelly and the Estate of Mary Thibeault," *The Coast*, 16 February 2012, www.thecoast.ca/halifax/a-trust-betrayed/Content? oid=2958898 (accessed 2 October 2013). My account of the Thibeault matter is substantially drawn from the Bousquet article. Bousquet and *The Coast* were 2012 Michener Award finalists for this story.

8. Tim Bousquet, "Judge Approves Settlement between Thibeault Heirs and Peter Kelly," *The Coast*, 11 March 2013, www.thecoast.ca/RealityBites/archives/2013/ 03/11/judge-approves-settlement-between-thibeault-heirs-and-peter-kelly (accessed 7 October 2012).

9. My account of the concert scandal relies in good part on Tim Bousquet's article "How Halifax's Concert Scandal Played Out," *The Coast*, 5 December 2011, www .thecoast.ca/halifax/how-halifaxs-concert-scandal-played-out/Content?oid=2786283 (accessed 9 October 2013).

10. Auditor General, Halifax Regional Municipality, "A Review of Concerts Held on the North Common—January 2006 to March 2011" (June 2011), www.halifax.ca/ auditorgeneral/documents/WebOKReviewConcertsonNorthCommonJune11.pdf. In 2012, the auditor general reported further on the scandal in "Review of the Transfer of Box Office Operations from the Halifax Metro Centre to Trade Centre Limited" (July 2012), www.halifax.ca/AuditorGeneral/documents/WebOKFinalTicket AtlanticcJuly12.pdf (accessed 9 October 2012).

11. Oliver Moore, "Halifax Mayor under Fire for Cash Advances to Promoters of High-Profile Concerts," *Globe and Mail*, 24 June 2011, www.theglobeandmail.com/ news/national/halifax-mayor-under-fire-for-cash-advances-to-promoters-of-high -profile-concerts/article598929/ (accessed 8 October 2013).

12. Laura Fraser, "A Year in the Life of Peter Kelly," *Halifax Chronicle Herald*, 31 December 2011, http://thechronicleherald.ca/metro/47775-year-life-peter-kelly (accessed 9 October 2013).

13. Bousquet, "Peter Kelly: Mayor."

14. Dan Leger, "Kelly's Fumbles and Deceptions Saved the Occupy Protest," *Halifax Chronicle Herald*, 21 November 2011, http://thechronicleherald.ca/opinion/34997 -kelly's-fumbles-and-deceptions-saved-occupy-protest (accessed 12 October 2013).

15. Tim Bousquet, "Peter Kelly's Laughable Claim That He Wants Less Secrecy," *The Coast*, 30 November 2011, www.thecoast.ca/halifax/peter-kelly-s-laughable-claim -that-he-wants-less-secrecy/Content?oid=2781745 (accessed 12 October 2014).

16. "Halifax Mayor Peter Kelly Coy about Possible Run for Council," CTV Atlantic News, 23 August 2012, http://atlantic.ctvnews.ca/halifax-mayor-peter-kelly-coy -about-possible-run-for-council-1.927409 (accessed 9 October 2013).

17. MacDonald, "Halifax Mayor Fighting for Political Life."

18.   You can listen to the speech at www.africville.ca/society/apology.html (accessed 1 November 2013).

19.   Tim Bousquet, "The Honest Truth," *Halifax Examiner*, 5 August 2014, www .halifaxexaminer.ca/featured/the-honest-truth-morning-file-friday-august-5-2014/ (accessed 5 September 2014).

20.   Doug Neuman, "County Union Files Complaint with Labour Relations Board," *Westlock News*, 14 October 2014, www.westlocknews.com/article/20141014/WES0801/ 310149988/-1/wes08/county-union-files-complaint-with-labour-relations-board (accessed 17 October 2014).

THREE: LARRY O'BRIEN OF OTTAWA

1.   "Inside Ottawa's New 'Power Address,'" *Ottawa Citizen*, 24 August 2007, www .canada.com/ottawacitizen/news/city/story.html?id=d9b621a3-58d4-4534-931f -c5773d68bea2 (accessed 24 November 2013).

2.   Larry O'Brien, *Ethical Entrepreneurship: A Guide to Surviving the Coming Economic Crisis* (St. Catharines, ON: Freedom Press, 2013), ix.

3.   Mohammed Adam, "O'Brien Looks on His Past from His High-Rise Window," *Ottawa Citizen*, 6 September 2010, www.ottawacitizen.com/Brien+looks+past+from+ high+rise+window/3486535/story.html (accessed 15 January 2014).

4.   "A Person of Substance," *Ottawa Citizen*, 21 March 2008, www.canada.com/story .html?id=001580f9-164e-4b7c-9dc0-8eda087739c2 (accessed 23 November 2013).

5.   "Mayor to Marry," *Ottawa Citizen*, 23 December 2007, www.canada.com/story_ print.html?id=912223cc-5208-4650-a991-3b357421fac3&sponsor= (accessed 23 November 2013).

6.   "Larry O'Brien, Successful Mayor," *Ottawa Citizen*, 22 October 2011, http://blogs .ottawacitizen.com/2011/10/22/larry-obrien-successful-mayor/#print (accessed 23 November 2011).

7.   Jordan Timm, "Mayor May Not," *Maclean's*, 25 October 2007, http://forum .skyscraperpage.com/showthread.php?t=140061 (accessed 18 November 2013).

8.   Ken Gray, "Mayor Larry O'Brien: Can He Govern?" *Ottawa Citizen*, 8 December 2006, www.canada.com/ottawacitizen/columnists/story.html?id=bbfd91cc-423f -4571-97bd-8b64001a2c5b (accessed 11 November 2013).

9.   Excerpts from a video of the interview are available on several websites—see, for example, www.ottawasun.com/videos/featured/featured-ott/1213592866001/ opp-interview-with-obrien/24311087001/page/10 (accessed 20 November 2013).

10.   Section 121 of the Criminal Code makes it an offence to pretend to have influence with the government and to offer to use that supposed influence in exchange for a benefit. Section 125 makes it an offence to offer a reward in connection with the seeking of an office.

11.   Gary Dimmock, "Mayor Booked at OPP Station," *Ottawa Citizen*, 7 January 2008, www2.canada.com/ottawacitizen/features/obrienfile/story.html?id=7a4e356f-7c22 -4d5e-9c95-a481e848ba57 (accessed 23 November 2013).

12.   Justice Cunningham's entire judgment can be seen at http://ici.radio-canada.ca/ regions/ottawa/dossiers/2009/proceslarryobrien/pdf/verdict.pdf (accessed 19 November 2013).

13. Quoted by Don Butler, "The Mayor Returns," *Ottawa Citizen*, 6 August 2009, www
.ottawacitizen.com/news/mayor+returns+strong+vindication/1861956/story.html
(accessed 20 November 2013).

14. Don Butler, "Exclusive: Larry O'Brien Interview," *Ottawa Citizen*, 11 January 2010,
www.ottawacitizen.com/news/Exclusive+Larry+Brien+interview/1862857/story.html
(accessed 20 November 2013).

15. Marcus McCann, "Acquittal of Mayor Larry O'Brien Still Leaves City in Crisis,"
Daily Xtra, 4 August 2009, http://dailyxtra.com/ottawa/news/acquittal-mayor-larry
-obrien-still-leaves-city-in-crisis-7304 (accessed 20 November 2013).

16. Mohammed Adam, "Larry's Party," *Ottawa Citizen*, 15 December 2007, www2
.canada.com/ottawacitizen/features/obrienfile/story.html?id= dfbaed38-58fb-487b
-8aa3-0fca4371ce02&p=1 (accessed 23 November 2013).

17. "Walter Robinson Resigns," *Ottawa Citizen*, 27 June 2007, www.canada.com/
story_print.html?id=b3fde2ba-21e7-4bdc-90ad-e6a414fc013c& sponsor= (accessed
23 November 2013).

18. "Mayor's Top Aide Resigns over Call to Radio Station," *Ottawa Citizen*, 20 March
2008, www.canada.com/ottawacitizen/news/city/story.html?id=bb2a48a2-e0eb
-4b10-a215-9c082b0ba978 (accessed 18 November 2013).

19. See "Councillors Bitter over Mayor's Blog," *Ottawa Citizen*, 27 June 2008, www
.canada.com/ottawacitizen/news/story.html?id=a31ade6b-7e15-4a02-8556
-d4f116740822 (accessed 18 November 2013).

20. Mohammed Adam, "Larry O'Brien's Mea Culpa: I Was a Lousy Mayor, but Not
Anymore," *Ottawa Citizen*, 5 October 2010, www.ottawacitizen.com/news/Larry+
Brien+culpa+lousy+mayor+anymore/3623183/story.html (accessed 19 December 2014).

21. Nancy Macdonald, "Canada's Lousy Mayors," *Maclean's*, 14 October 2010, www
.macleans.ca/news/canada/a-depository-for-the-truly-mad/ (accessed 11 November
2013).

22. Gloria Galloway, "Jim Watson Topples Larry O'Brien in Ottawa Mayoral Race,"
Globe and Mail, 23 August 2012, http://m.theglobeandmail.com/news/national/
jim-watson-topples-larry-obrien-in-ottawa-mayoral-race/article1215583/?service=
mobile (accessed 20 November 2013).

23. Mohammed Adam, "Councillors Pan Mayor's 'Happy Face' Budget Spin," *Ottawa
Citizen*, 28 December 2007, www2.canada.com/ottawacitizen/features/obrienfile/
story.html?id=6e1adc2a-5b9e-437a-b44b-206b80c85248&p=2 (accessed 23 November
2013).

24. O'Brien, *Ethical Entrepreneurship*, x.

25. Ibid., 73.

26. Ibid., 75.

FOUR: GÉRALD TREMBLAY OF MONTREAL

1. Quoted in "Quebec Corruption Inquiry's Star Witness Says He Donated Illegally to
Every Party: 'I Didn't Have a Choice,'" *National Post*, 15 October 2012, http://news
.nationalpost.com/2012/10/15/quebec-corruption-inquirys-star-witness-says-he
-donated-illegally-to-every-party-i-didnt-have-a-choice/ (accessed 10 December 2013).

2. Peter Rakobowchuk, "Quebec Corruption Inquiry: One Embattled Mayor Down and Maybe One to Go," *Canadian Press*, 25 October 2012, www.thestar.com/news/canada/2012/10/25/quebec_corruption_inquiry_one_embattled_mayor_down_and_maybe_one_to_go.html# (accessed 21 December 2014).

3. Paul Wells, "Bye Bye Mon Tremblay," *Maclean's*, 5 November 2012, www.macleans.ca/politics/ottawa/bye-bye-mon-tremblay/ (accessed 14 December 2013).

4. Lysiane Gagnon, "Montreal's History of Peculiar Mayors," *Globe and Mail*, 14 November 2012, www.theglobeandmail.com/globe-debate/montreals-history-of-peculiar-mayors/article5252826/ (accessed 12 December 2013).

5. Martin Patriquin, "When It Comes to the Chains of Office, Toronto's Got It Good," *Maclean's*, 14 August 2013, www.macleans.ca/news/canada/when-it-comes-to-the-chains-of-office-torontos-got-it-good/ (accessed 13 December 2013).

6. Linda Gyulai, "Mayor's Seat of Power a Laid-Back Easychair," *Montreal Gazette*, 4 November 2002, www.canada.com/montreal/news/story.asp? id={A6E84D67-15CC-4685-B718-22B7CB8E62A9} (accessed 12 February 2014).

7. "Gérald Tremblay: Quebec Inc.'s Chief Executive," *Toronto Star*, 16 February 1992, http://ezproxy.torontopubliclibrary.ca/login?url=http://search.proquest.com/canadiannewsmajor/docview/436573877/fulltext/14257F91E8681869FB/ (accessed 14 December 2013).

8. Quoted by David Johnston, "Ambition, Opportunity, Revisit: Tremblay Hinted He'd Be Back When He Resigned from Provincial Politics," *Montreal Gazette*, 28 February 2001, http://ezproxy.torontopubliclibrary.ca/login?url=http://search.proquest.com/canadiannewsmajor/docview/433687015/14280D366BC4F1A5BF3/ (accessed 22 December 2013).

9. Quoted by Linda Gyulai, "Tremblay's Mission to Serve; Montreal Mayor Says Catholic Faith Plays a Major Role in His Life and Drives His Quest to Win a Third Straight Term," *Montreal Gazette*, 1 October 2009, http://montrealgazette.com/news/local-news/from-the-archive-tremblays-mission-to-serve (accessed 19 December 2014).

10. Sarah Scott, "Liberals Eye Pierre Marc Johnson as Leader," *Montreal Gazette*, 29 May 1993, http://ezproxy.torontopubliclibrary.ca/login?url=http://search.proquest.com/canadiannewsmajor/docview/432436064/14257F91E8681869FB/ (accessed 14 December 2013).

11. Quoted by Robert McKenzie, "Favorite Quits Race to Succeed Bourassa," *Toronto Star*, 6 October 1993, http://ezproxy.torontopubliclibrary.ca/login?url=http://search.proquest.com/canadiannewsmajor/docview/436917115/14262CDCD5D74D0526E/ (accessed 16 December 2013).

12. Mike Boone, "The New, Gray Mayoral Candidate," *Montreal Gazette*, 28 February 2001, http://search.proquest.com.ezproxy.torontopubliclibrary.ca/canadiannewsmajor/docview/433686782/14262E9256222808438/ (accessed 16 December 2013).

13. Andrew Sancton, *Canadian Local Government: An Urban Perspective* (Don Mills, ON: Oxford University Press, 2011), 135.

14. Ibid., 158.

15. Sean Gordon, "Forget It, Mayors Urge Liberals," *Montreal Gazette*, 20 March 2003, http://ezproxy.torontopubliclibrary.ca/login?url=http://search.proquest.com/canadiannewsmajor/docview/433912525/142777962D3658A818C/ (accessed 20 December 2013).

16. Roberto Rocha, "Demerger Referendum Day," *Montreal Gazette*, 20 June 2004, http://ezproxy.torontopubliclibrary.ca/login?url=http://search.proquest.com/canadiannewsmajor/docview/434064748/14281EF5382A39C6B3/ (accessed 22 December 2013).

17. An intriguing film about the de-amalgamation movement is Ryan Young's *The Village Resists*. You can view it at www.youtube.com/watch?v=1KlNzgnuwpk (accessed 22 December 2013).

18. Sancton, *Canadian Local Government*, 164.

19. For Gyulai's attempt to explain the system, see "Making Sense of an Intricate System," *Montreal Gazette,* 2 November 2013, www.montrealgazette.com/news/Montreal+election+Making+sense+intricate+system/9115053/story.html (accessed 27 May 2014).

20. Sue Montgomery, "Tremblay Headquarters Is Not Exactly Party Central," *Montreal Gazette*, 7 November 2005, www.canada.com/story.html?id=ed83b411-5d8d-4385-929f-d546ba1d8e96 (accessed 23 December 2013).

21. Adam McDowell, "Tackling Corruption, One Step at a Time," *National Post*, 15 July 2010, http://ezproxy.torontopubliclibrary.ca/login?url=http://search.proquest.com/canadiannewsmajor/docview/613392952/1428667DAB242AF98C0/ (accessed 23 December 2013).

22. Henry Aubin, "Tremblay Mayoralty Built on Deceit; He Broke the Promise That Brought Him to Power, and Now Has Lost Credibility and Any Claim to the Benefit of the Doubt," *Montreal Gazette*, 1 November 2012, www.montrealgazette.com/Henry+Aubin+Tremblay+Gérald+Tremblay+mayoralty+built+deceit/7481476/story.html (accessed 21 December 2013). Aubin has been a consistent and eloquent critic of amalgamation. See, for example, *Who's Afraid of Demergers?: A Journalist Takes On Tremblay, Olivier, and Other Defenders of Quebec's Municipal Mergers* (Montreal: Véhicule Press, 2004).

23. Monique Muise, "Ex-Mayor 'Shocked' at Corruption; Montreal's Tremblay Offers Host of Denials," *Ottawa Citizen*, 30 April 2013, http://ezproxy.torontopubliclibrary.ca/login?url=http://search.proquest.com/canadiannewsmajor/docview/1347043141/142C48EA11B309EAF86/ (accessed 4 January 2014).

24. René Bruemmer, "Coderre, Bergeron Won't Speculate about Former Mayor Tremblay," *Montreal Gazette*, 15 September 2014, www.montrealgazette.com/news/Coderre+Bergeron+speculate+about+former+mayor+Tremblay/10206162/story.html (accessed 17 September 2014).

25. Peggy Curran, "Did Tremblay Really Stick His Head in the Sand?" *Montreal Gazette,* 15 September 2014, www.montrealgazette.com/news/Peggy+Curran+Tremblay+really+stick+head+sand/10208825/story.html (accessed 16 September 2014).

26. Linda Gyulai, "Gérald Tremblay on Corruption," *Montreal Gazette*, 14 September 2014, www.montrealgazette.com/news/Gérald+Tremblay+corruption/10205372/story.html (accessed 20 December 2014).

27. Quoted by Linda Gyulai, "Questions Only Tremblay Can Answer," *Montreal Gazette*, 24 April 2013, www.montrealgazette.com/news/corruption/questions-tremblay.html (accessed 3 January 2014).

28. Gyulai, "Gérald Tremblay on Corruption."

29. Quoted by Gyulai, "Questions Only Tremblay Can Answer."

30. Linda Gyulai, "2 Firms Split Work on Plants," *Montreal Gazette*, 26 September 2012, http://ezproxy.torontopubliclibrary.ca/login?url=http://search.proquest.com/canadiannewsmajor/docview/1081004655/142C4A733267104F7B3/ (accessed 4 January 2014).

31. Henry Aubin, "At Least Part of Tremblay's Background Smells Good," *Montreal Gazette*, 30 April 2013, www.montrealgazette.com/news/Henry+Aubin+least+part+Tremblay+background+smells+good/8323446/story.html (accessed 5 January 2014).

FIVE: MICHAEL APPLEBAUM OF MONTREAL

1. Ingrid Peritz, "Michael Applebaum: Montreal's Unconventional Choice for Mayor," *Globe and Mail*, 23 November 2012, www.theglobeandmail.com/news/national/michael-applebaum-montreals-unconventional-choice-for-mayor/article5622933/ (accessed 8 January 2014).

2. Sandra Phillips, "These Stores Have Staying Power," *Montreal Gazette*, 18 July 1993, http://ezproxy.torontopubliclibrary.ca/login?url=http://search.proquest.com/canadiannewsmajor/docview/432454190/E57332B6037A4255PQ/ (accessed 1 February 2014).

3. Peritz, "Montreal's Unconventional Choice for Mayor."

4. Janice Arnold, "Applebaum Now No. 2 at City Hall," *Canadian Jewish News*, 5 May 2011, http://archive.today/YEcJE (accessed 2 February 2014).

5. Linda Gyulai, "Tremblay 'Circling the Wagons,'" *Montreal Gazette*, 14 April 2011, www.montrealgazette.com/opinion/editorials/Analysis+Mayor+Gérald+Tremblay+circling+wagons/4611939/story.html (accessed 5 February 2014).

6. Lysiane Gagnon, "Montreal's New Mayor Is a Breath of Fresh Air," *Globe and Mail*, 21 November 2012, www.theglobeandmail.com/globe-debate/montreals-new-mayor-is-a-breath-of-fresh-air/article5502148/ (accessed 19 December 2014).

7. Peritz, "Montreal's Unconventional Choice for Mayor."

8. Sidhartha Banerjee, "Montreal's Mayor Refutes Suggestions He Has Mafia Ties," *Globe and Mail*, 15 January 2013, www.theglobeandmail.com/news/national/montreals-mayor-refutes-suggestions-he-has-mafia-ties/article7372152/ (accessed 9 January 2014).

9. This account of the police raid is drawn from René Bruemmer, Linda Gyulai, Marian Scott, Sue Montgomery, Peggy Curran, Janet Bagnall, Christopher Curtis and Allison Hanes, "UPAC Raids Montreal City Hall, Six Boroughs and Union Montreal Offices," *Montreal Gazette*, 18 February 2013, www.montrealgazette.com/news/UPAC+raids+Montreal+city+hall+boroughs+Union+Montreal+offices/7986522/story.html (accessed 19 December 2014).

10. Jack Todd, "Budding Optimism Drives Montreal's Resurgence," *Montreal Gazette*, 22 May 2014, http://montrealgazette.com/news/local-news/jack-todd-budding-optimism-drives-montreals-resurgence (accessed 24 May 2014).

11. Sophie Cousineau, "A City's Sad Tale," *Globe and Mail*, 19 June 2013, www
.theglobeandmail.com/report-on-business/a-citys-sad-tale-montreal-out-scandals-to/
article12659069/ (accessed 19 December 2014).

12. "Turns Out That We Could Do a Lot Worse Than Gregor Robertson," *Vancouver
Province*, 19 June 2013, http://blogs.theprovince.com/tag/michael-applebaum/
(accessed 1 February 2014).

13. Peritz, "Montreal's Unconventional Choice for Mayor."

14. James Mennie, "Applebaum Says He Rests Easy, Even as He Wields City's Axe,"
Montreal Gazette, 23 September 2011, http://ezproxy.torontopubliclibrary.ca/login?
url=http://search.proquest.com/docview/89398159 4/B1E5994F04A749DDPQ/
(accessed 5 February 2014).

SIX: GILLES VAILLANCOURT OF LAVAL

1. Martin Patriquin, "Is Gilles Vaillancourt Canada's Most Powerful Mayor?" *Maclean's*,
18 April 2011, www.macleans.ca/news/canada/the-king-of-laval/2/ (accessed
10 February 2014).

2. Bill Tierney, "It's a Long and Sad Way to Fall for Gilles Vaillancourt," *Montreal
Gazette*, 19 June 2013, http://ezproxy.torontopubliclibrary.ca/login?url=http://search
.proquest.com/docview/1369581123 (accessed 8 March 2014).

3. James Mennie, "Mayor," *Montreal Gazette*, 9 October 2009, http://ezproxy
.torontopubliclibrary.ca/login?url=http://search.proquest.com/canadiannewsmajor/
docview/434868252/FB7CD4EC99664B4DPQ/ (accessed 11 March 2014).

4. Quoted in "'King of Laval' Dethroned: Vaillancourt Quits as Mayor," CBC News,
9 November 2012, www.cbc.ca/news/canada/montreal/king-of-laval-dethroned
-vaillancourt-quits-as-mayor-1.1180789 (accessed 6 March 2014).

5. David Johnston, "In Laval, Two Upstart Parties Challenge Vaillancourt Dynasty,"
Montreal Gazette, 27 August 2009, http://ezproxy.torontopubliclibrary.ca/login?
url=http://search.proquest.com/docview/434849342/D23D74F291E64746PQ/
(accessed 9 March 2014).

6. Linda Gyulai and Allison Lampert, "How Laval 'Garden of Eden' Dream Was
Uprooted," *Montreal Gazette*, 26 July 2013, www.montrealgazette.com/business/
Laval+Garden+Eden+dream+uprooted/8708663/story.html (accessed 11 March 2014).

7. Henry Aubin, "Laval Mayor Vaillancourt Is My Person of the Year," *Montreal Gazette*,
20 December 2008, www.canada.com/story.html?id=5a55a92d-9f8e-4285-9dc4
-a86d6f8d1a50 (accessed 10 March 2014).

8. Christian Latreille, "Le maire Vaillancourt a offert 10 000 $ comptant à Serge Ménard,"
Radio-Canada, 16 November 2010, http://ici.radio-canada.ca/regions/montreal/2010/
11/15/007-vaillancourt-menard-argent.shtml (accessed 7 January 2015).

9. Henry Aubin, "When Good Guys Remain Quiet," *Montreal Gazette*, 18 November
2010, http://ezproxy.torontopubliclibrary.ca/login?url=http://search.proquest.com/
docview/807629005/20F5E3A04F93451CPQ/ (accessed 12 February 2014).

10. David Johnston, "Vaillancourt Holds Head High," *Montreal Gazette*, 17 November
2010, http://ezproxy.torontopubliclibrary.ca/login?url=http://search.proquest.com/
docview/807509617/20F5E3A04F93451CPQ/ (accessed 12 February 2014).

11.   Quoted by Anne Sutherland, "'No Clues, Only Rumours' in Laval; Police Chief Pleased Former Mayor Arrested," *Montreal Gazette*, 11 May 2013, http://ezproxy .torontopubliclibrary.ca/login?url=http://search.proquest.com/docview/1350006986 (accessed 9 March 2014).

12.   Kevin Dougherty and David Johnston, "Laval Mayor Asked to Quit Hydro Board," *Montreal Gazette*, 20 November 2010, www.montrealgazette.com/news/todays-paper/ Laval+mayor+asked+quit+Hydro+board/3859334/story.html (accessed 12 February 2014).

13.   "'King of Laval' Dethroned," CBC News.

14.   Savas Fortis, 'Je suis déçu'—Gilles Vaillancourt, LavalNews.ca, 15 November 2012, http://lavalnews.ca/editorial/Je-suis-decu-Gilles-Vaillancourt-202161 (accessed 11 February 2014).

15.   See Monique Muise, "'I Collected the Money,'" *Montreal Gazette*, 22 May 2013, http://ezproxy.torontopubliclibrary.ca/login?url=http://search.proquest.com/ docview/1353875838 (accessed 12 February 2014).

16.   Felix Seguin, "Ex-Laval, Que., Mayor Gilles Vaillancourt Allegedly Used Minors to Smuggle Cash to Europe," *Toronto Sun*, 27 May 2013, www.torontosun.com/2013/ 05/27/ex-laval-que-mayor-gilles-vaillancourt-allegedly-used-minors-to-smuggle-cash -to-europe (accessed 12 February 2014).

17.   Monique Muise, "Charbonneau Commission: Witness Implicates Laval's New Mayor," *Montreal Gazette*, 29 May 2013, www.montrealgazette.com/news/Charbonneau+ Commission+Witness+implicates+Laval+mayor/8455589/story.html (accessed 15 March 2014).

18.   Les Perreaux, "Recording Bolsters Allegations That Laval Ex-Mayor Offered Cash to Candidate," *Globe and Mail*, 8 October 2013, www.theglobeandmail.com/news/national/ mayoral-candidate-in-laval-calls-for-police-protection/article14741039/?cmpid=rss1 (accessed 8 March 2014).

SEVEN: ALEXANDRE DUPLESSIS OF LAVAL

1.   Quoted by René Bruemmer, "Alexander Duplessis Elected New Interim Mayor of Laval," *Montreal Gazette*, 24 November 2012, www.montrealgazette.com/news/ Alexandre+Duplessis+elected+interim+mayor+Laval/7600730/story.html (accessed 12 March 2014).

2.   See Les Perreaux, "Sex Scandal Forces Laval Mayor to Quit," *Globe and Mail*, 28 June 2013, www.theglobeandmail.com/news/national/interim-laval-quebec-mayor-resigns/ article12885483/ (accessed 15 March 2014).

3.   "Women Charged in Alleged Prostitution Scandal That Brought Down Laval Mayor," *Globe and Mail*, 29 July 2013, www.theglobeandmail.com/news/national/ women-charged-in-alleged-prostitution-scandal-that-brought-down-laval-mayor/ article13482830/ (accessed 15 March 2014).

4.   Kevin Dougherty, "Laval Comes Under Trusteeship of Quebec," *Montreal Gazette*, 4 June 2013, www.montrealgazette.com/news/Laval+comes+under+trusteeship+ Quebec/8472861/story.html (accessed 13 March 2014).

5.   Monique Muise, "Charbonneau Commission: Inquiry Casualties Mount," *Montreal Gazette*, 22 June 2013, www.montrealgazette.com/news/montreal/Charbonneau+ Commission+Inquiry+casualties+mount/8562536/story.html (accessed 26 May 2014).

6. See Les Perreaux, "As Scandal-Plagued Laval's New Mayor, an Ex-Cop Gets Ready for Cleanup Work," *Globe and Mail*, 6 November 2013, www.theglobeandmail.com/news/politics/as-scandal-plagued-lavals-new-mayor-an-ex-cop-gets-ready-for-cleanup-work/article15306468/ (accessed 27 April 2014).

EIGHT: SAM KATZ OF WINNIPEG

1. Quoted by Bartley Kives and Jen Sherritt, "Katz Defends Luncheon at Restaurant He Owns," *Winnipeg Free Press*, 23 February 2011, www.winnipegfreepress.com/local/katz-defends-luncheon-at-restaurant-he-owns-116719454.html (accessed 31 January 2015).

2. Quoted by Mike McIntyre, "Poor Judgment or Corruption?" *Winnipeg Free Press*, 3 April 2013, www.winnipegfreepress.com/local/poor-judgment-or-corruption-201190951.html (accessed 19 December 2014).

3. "Visionary Leader Juba 'Put 'Peg on the Map,'" *Winnipeg Free Press*, 12 July 2009, www.winnipegfreepress.com/local/visionary-leader-juba-put-peg-on-themap-50574972.html (accessed 3 April 2014).

4. "The Greatest Manitobans: #19 Steve Juba," *Winnipeg Tribune*, http://forum.skyscraperpage.com/showthread.php?t=157241 (accessed 3 April 2014). A somewhat different, and less amusing, story about the Pan Am Games is told by Allan Levine in *Your Worship*, 79–80.

5. David Roberts, "Winnipeg Wheeler Hits Winning Deals," *Globe and Mail*, 31 May 1994, http://ezproxy.torontopubliclibrary.ca/login?url=http://search.proquest.com/canadiannewsmajor/docview/385187329/DE052BD16B844EE1PQ (accessed 25 May 2014).

6. Bartley Kives, "Mayor Weathers Full-Time Scrutiny So He Can Fight for Improved Life in City," *Winnipeg Free Press*, 14 October 2006, http://newspaperarchive.com/ca/manitoba/winnipeg/winnipeg-free-press/2006/10-14/page-6 (accessed 19 December 2014).

7. Bartley Kives and Gabrielle Giroday, "Another Kick at the Can for Sam," *Winnipeg Free Press*, 26 October 2006, www.highbeam.com/doc/1P3-1151280051.html (accessed 26 March 2014).

8. Bartley Kives, "Katz in Command," *Winnipeg Free Press*, 10 July 2009, www.winnipegfreepress.com/local/katz-in-command-50459197.html (accessed 19 December 2019).

9. "Mayor's Excuse Divorced from Reality," *Winnipeg Free Press*, 18 October 2007, http://newspaperarchive.com/ca/manitoba/winnipeg/winnipeg-free-press/2007/10-18/page-3 (accessed 3 April 2014). Katz himself was paid $216,788 in 2005 as president of the Goldeyes, almost twice his salary as mayor.

10. See www.youtube.com/watch?v=H8xi_YwMOQM (accessed 25 March 2014). This supposed campaign advertisement was a fake posted by an unknown jokester.

11. Gordon Sinclair Jr., "Chewing Out the Mayor's Poor Attitude," *Winnipeg Free Press*, 25 May 2013, www.winnipegfreepress.com/opinion/columnists/chewing-out-the-mayors-poor-attitude-208927641.html (accessed 19 December 2014).

12. Mohammed Adam, "If the City Ran Like a Business …" *Ottawa Citizen*, 8 November 2007, www.canada.com/story_print.html?id=e3679776-6678-48ed-885d-d2368cf25305&sponsor= (accessed 19 December 2014).

13. Dan Lett, "No Self-Doubt about It," *Winnipeg Free Press*, 20 October 2007, http://newspaperarchive.com/ca/manitoba/winnipeg/winnipeg-free-press/2007/10-20/page-6 (accessed 19 December 2014).

14. Dan Lett, "Selinger Far from Keen to Step into Katz Flap," *Winnipeg Free Press*, 5 October 2012, www.winnipegfreepress.com/local/selinger-far-from-keen-to-step-into-katz-flap-172782451.html (accessed 19 December 2014).

15. "Winnipeg Mayor Buys House from Developer's Sister," CBC News, 27 September 2012, www.cbc.ca/news/canada/manitoba/winnipeg-mayor-buys-house-from-developer-s-sister-1.1163379 (accessed 7 April 2014).

16. "Winnipeggers Believe Mayor in Conflict of Interest, Poll Suggests," CBC News, 12 December 2012, www.cbc.ca/news/canada/manitoba/winnipeggers-believe-mayor-in-conflict-of-interest-poll-suggests-1.1290905 (accessed 7 April 2014).

17. Bartley Kives, "Mayor Weathers Toughest Year," *Winnipeg Free Press*, 29 December 2008, www.winnipegfreepress.com/opinion/columnists/mayor_weathers_toughest_year.html (accessed 19 December 2014).

18. Bartley Kives, "Sam Has His Say," *Winnipeg Free Press*, 16 October 2010, www.winnipegfreepress.com/special/civicelection2010/mayor/sam-has-his-say-105093489.html (accessed 20 December 2014).

19. Bartley Kives, "Chain of Office Is Heavy: Year in Review with Mayor Sam Katz," *Winnipeg Free Press*, 27 December 2011, www.winnipegfreepress.com/local/chain-of-office-is-heavy-136249743.html (accessed 20 December 2014).

20. Stephanie Findlay, "Poll Puts Hazel on Top, Ford near Bottom," *Toronto Star*, 25 October 2011, www.thestar.com/news/gta/2011/10/24/poll_puts_hazel_on_top_ford_near_bottom.html (accessed 20 December 2014).

21. Bartley Kives, "Mayor Katz Reflects on Accomplishments, Controversies and Hopes," *Winnipeg Free Press*, 22 December 2012, www.winnipegfreepress.com/local/sams-take-on-the-year-184528171.html (accessed 20 December 2014).

22. Aldo Santin, "Katz Turns the Page," *Winnipeg Free Press*, 30 December 2012, www.winnipegfreepress.com/special/yearinreview/katz-turns-the-page-237927971.html (accessed 20 December 2014).

23. Kristin Annable, "Nearing 10-Year Anniversary, Winnipeg Mayor Katz Says He's the Same Ol' Sam," *Winnipeg Sun*, 24 May 2014, www.winnipegsun.com/2014/05/24/nearing-10-year-anniversary-winnipeg-mayor-katz-says-hes-the-same-ol-sam (accessed 26 May 2014).

24. Tom Brodbeck, "Katz Failed the People of Winnipeg, End of Story," *Winnipeg Sun*, 24 May 2014, www.winnipegsun.com/2014/05/24/katz-failed-the-people-of-winnipeg-end-of-story (accessed 26 May 2014).

25. Ernst & Young, "City of Winnipeg, Real Estate Management Review, Findings and Recommendations Report, 19 June 2014," www.winnipeg.ca/clkdmis/ViewDoc.asp?DocId=13707&SectionId=&InitUrl= (accessed 4 July 2014).

26. Aldo Santin and Bartley Kives, "Gloves Off over City Hall Audit," *Winnipeg Free Press*, 3 July 2014, www.winnipegfreepress.com/local/gloves-off-over-city-hall-audit-265650131.html (accessed 5 July 2014).

27. See Bartley Kives and Aldo Santin, "Real Estate Audit Raises Serious Issues; Katz Questions Methodology," *Winnipeg Free Press*, 5 July 2014, www.winnipegfreepress.com/ local/City-councillors-taking-extra-time-with-audit-265555641.html (accessed 5 July 2014).

28. Bartley Kives, "Katz's Third-Term Stumbles Overshadow Earlier Accomplishments," *Winnipeg Free Press*, 20 June 2014, www.winnipegfreepress.com/opinion/columnists/ Katzs-third-term-stumbles-overshadow-earlier-accomplishments-264013941.html (accessed 3 July 2014).

29. "City Hall Needs an Overhaul," *Winnipeg Free Press*, 18 July 2014, www.winnipegfreepress .com/opinion/editorials/city-hall-needs-an-overhaul-267613851.html (accessed 20 July 2014).

30. Bartley Kives, "Call Inquiry into City Hall's Rotten, Fetid Mess," *Winnipeg Free Press*, 19 July 2014, www.winnipegfreepress.com/opinion/columnists/call-inquiry-into-city -halls-rotten-fetid-mess-267755621.html (accessed 20 July 2014).

31. Steve Lambert, "Winnipeg Mayoral Race Features Rob Ford References and Misspelt Names," CTV News, 10 August 2014, www.ctvnews.ca/politics/winnipeg-mayoral-race -features-rob-ford-references-and-misspelt-names-1.1953443 (accessed 19 August 2014).

32. Bartley Kives, "Defiant to the End: Outgoing Mayor Katz Discusses Legacy, Scandals and Future," *Winnipeg Free Press*, 4 October 2014, www.winnipegfreepress.com/special/ civicelection2014/mayor/Defiant-to-the-end-278055651.html (accessed 13 October 2014).

33. Bartley Kives, "Katz Never Dodged Media," *Winnipeg Free Press*, 4 October 2014, www.winnipegfreepress.com/opinion/analysis/katz-never-dodged-media-despite -adversarial--relationship-mayor--always-answered-queries-278105171.html (accessed 13 October 2014).

34. Bartley Kives, "Out with Old and in with New," *Winnipeg Free Press*, 23 October 2014, www.winnipegfreepress.com/local/out-with-old-and-in-with-new-280151902.html (accessed 26 October 2014).

NINE: JOE FONTANA OF LONDON

1. Joe Belanger, "Gleeson One of the Best," *London Free Press*, 11 May 2009, http://pbdba .lfpress.com/perl-bin/publish.cgi?x=articles&p=264686&s=remembered (accessed 14 May 2014).

2. Fan-Yee Suen, "Serial-Killer Capital of the World? A Look at London, Ont.'s Dark History," CTV News, 10 March 2014, www.ctvnews.ca/canada/serial-killer-capital -of-the-world-a-look-at-london-ont-s-dark-history-1.1721931 (accessed 15 March 2014).

3. Adam Radwanski, "The Long, Slow Decline of the Nation's Industrial Heartland," *Globe and Mail*, 30 May 2014, www.theglobeandmail.com/news/politics/after-the-gold -rush/article18923563/ (accessed 4 June 2014).

4. Rory Carroll, "Marconi Blocked Jews from Il Duce's Academy," *The Guardian*, 19 March 2002, www.theguardian.com/world/2002/mar/19/physicalsciences .humanities (accessed 11 May 2014).

5. Chip Martin, "The Real Story Behind the Joe Fontana Spending Scandal," *London Free Press*, 24 October 2012, www.lfpress.com/2012/10/23/the-real-story-behind-the-joe -fontana-spending-scandal (accessed 11 May 2014).

6. See, for example, "London Mayor Joe Fontana's RCMP Interview," www.therecord.com/news-story/4553540-video-london-mayor-joe-fontana-s-rcmp-interview/ (accessed 4 June 2014).

7. Canada Revenue Agency, "The Canada Revenue Agency Revokes the Registration of Trinity Global Support Foundation as a Charity," press release, 3 May 2013, http://news.gc.ca/web/article-en.do?nid=738169 (accessed 12 May 2014).

8. Joe Fontana, "A Message to Londoners," 24 July 2012, http://mayorfontana.ca/dear-londoners/ (accessed 9 May 2014).

9. Chip Martin, "London Mayor Joe Fontana's Boyhood Friend Vincent Ciccone Charged in $21 Million Fraud," *London Free Press*, 8 May 2014, www.lfpress.com/2014/05/07/london-mayor-joe-fontanas-boyhood-friend-vincent-ciccone-charged-in-21-million-fraud (accessed 13 May 2014).

10. Ken MacQueen, "Politicians, Pot and Problems at the Border," *Maclean's*, 4 September 2013, www.macleans.ca/news/canada/politicians-pot-and-problems-at-the-border/ (accessed 20 May 2014).

11. Greg Van Moorsel, "Fontana Turns a Fine Legacy into a Rap Sheet," *London Free Press*, 16 June 2014, www.lfpress.com/2014/06/16/van-moorsel-fontana-turns-a-fine-legacy-into-a-rap-sheet (accessed 18 June 2014).

12. Sean Meyer, "Fontana Not Surprised by Mixed Message of Environics Survey," LondonCommunityNews.com, 17 December 2013, www.londoncommunitynews.com/news-story/4275115-fontana-not-surprised-by-mixed-message-of-environics-survey/ (accessed 13 May 2014).

13. Richard J. Brennan, "Ontario Municipal Councils 'Addicted' to Secrecy, Ombudsman Says," *Toronto Star*, 12 December 2013, www.thestar.com/news/queenspark/2013/12/11/ontario_municipal_councils_addicted_to_secrecy_ombudsman_says.html (accessed 20 December 2014).

14. Ombudsman Ontario, "2012–2013 OMLET (Open Meeting Law Enforcement Team) Annual Report," 11 December 2013, www.ombudsman.on.ca/Files/sitemedia/Images/Reports/1590-OMLETAR-ENGLISH-WebResolution_1.pdf (accessed 26 May 2014).

15. "Desperate London Mayor Joe Fontana Went for Sizzle but Laid an Egg," *London Free Press*, 30 January 2014, www.lfpress.com/2014/01/30/desperate-mayor-went-for-sizzle-but-laid-an-egg (accessed 14 May 2014).

16. "Budget Defeats Suggest London Mayor Joe Fontana Losing Traction," *London Free Press*, 26 February 2014, www.lfpress.com/2014/02/26/budget-defeats-suggest-fontana-traction-gone (accessed 14 May 2014).

17. *R. v. Fontana*, 2014 ONSC 3546 (Ontario Superior Court of Justice, 13 June 2014). The judgment is available at www.scribd.com/doc/229551154/Reasons-for-Judgment-Fontana-trial#download (accessed 14 June 2014).

18. Jane Sims, "London Mayor Joe Fontana Found Guilty on All Charges," *London Free Press*, 13 June 2014, www.lfpress.com/2014/06/12/judgment-day-for-joe (accessed 14 June 2014).

19. "London, Ont. Mayor Joe Fontana Resigns after Fraud Conviction," *Toronto Star*, 16 June 2014, www.thestar.com/news/canada/2014/06/16/london_ont_mayor_joe_fontana_resigns_after_fraud_conviction.html (accessed 18 June 2014).

20. Debora Van Brenk, "Marconi Members Keep Political Views Quiet," *London Free Press*, 13 June 2014, www.lfpress.com/2014/06/13/marconi-members-keep-political-views -quiet (accessed 18 June 2014).

21. Allison Jones, "Ex-London Mayor Joe Fontana Sentenced to Four Months House Arrest," *Toronto Star*, 15 July 2014, www.thestar.com/news/canada/2014/07/15/ exlondon_mayor_joe_fontana_to_be_sentenced_today_for_fraud.html (accessed 17 July 2014).

TEN: ROB FORD OF TORONTO

1. Richard Florida, "How Toronto, Vancouver and Montreal Became Cities Split by Class," *Globe and Mail*, 6 November 2014, www.theglobeandmail.com/globe-debate/ the-new-class-divide/article21456139/ (accessed 13 November 2014).

2. Edward Keenan, *Some Great Idea: Good Neighbourhoods, Crazy Politics and the Invention of Toronto* (Toronto: Coach House Books, 2013), 113.

3. Ibid., 14, 16.

4. Victoria Ahearn, "Writer of Rob Ford Musical Says Toronto Mayor Is 'Very Shakespearean,'" CTV News, 15 June 2014, www.ctvnews.ca/entertainment/ writer-of-rob-ford-musical-says-toronto-mayor-is-very-shakespearean-1.1869578 (accessed 17 June 2014).

5. For the full text of the Ford apology, see "Rob Ford's Apology to Daniel Dale," *Toronto Star*, 18 December 2013, www.thestar.com/news/gta/2013/12/18/rob_fords_ apology_to_daniel_dale.html (accessed 12 July 2014).

6. See discussion by Hamutal Dotan, "Rob Ford, Daniel Dale, and Our Notions of Masculinity," *Torontoist*, 4 May 2012, http://torontoist.com/2012/05/rob-ford -daniel-dale-and-our-notions-of-masculinity/ (accessed 12 July 2014).

7. Anthony Furey, "In Defence of Mayor Rob Ford," *Toronto Sun*, 2 November 2013, www.torontosun.com/2013/11/01/in-defence-of-mayor-rob-ford (accessed 13 July 2014).

8. Quoted by Andre Mayer, "Toronto Mayor Rob Ford 'Could Easily Get Re-elected,'" CBC News, 5 November 2013, www.cbc.ca/news/canada/toronto/toronto-mayor -rob-ford-could-easily-get-re-elected-1.2355481 (accessed 13 July 2014).

9. Marni Soupcoff, "This Is Why People STILL Support Rob Ford," *Huffington Post*, 6 November 2013, www.huffingtonpost.ca/marni-soupcoff/rob-ford_b_4226960 .html (accessed 13 July 2014).

10. Marcus Gee, "Toronto's Rob Ford: A Resilient Mayor, a Tolerant City," *Globe and Mail*, 19 July 2013, www.theglobeandmail.com/news/toronto/a-resilient-mayor-a -tolerant-city/article13331003/ (accessed 20 December 2014).

11. Lorraine Mallinder, "Why Is Toronto Mayor Rob Ford Still Popular?" BBC News, 5 November 2013, www.bbc.com/news/world-us-canada-24824648 (accessed 6 June 2014).

12. Stephen Marche, "Toronto's Hot Mess," *The New York Times*, 5 November 2013, www. nytimes.com/2013/11/06/opinion/torontos-hot-mess.html (accessed 12 June 2014).

13. John Wright, "Approval Is Not Electability: Why Rob Ford Is 'Dead Mayor Walking,'" *Globe and Mail*, 27 November 2013, www.theglobeandmail.com/globe-debate/approval -is-not-electability-why-rob-ford-is-dead-mayor-walking/article15625876/ (accessed 12 June 2014).

14. Bob Hepburn, "Why Ford Won't Win Re-election," *Toronto Star*, 24 April 2014, www .thestar.com/opinion/commentary/2014/04/23/why_rob_ford_wont_win_reelection_ hepburn.html (accessed 14 June 2014).

15. Daniel Dale, "Toronto Election Poll: Rob Ford Still Competitive after Seven-Week Absence," *Toronto Star*, 25 June 2014, www.thestar.com/news/city_hall/ toronto2014election/2014/06/25/toronto_election_poll_rob_ford_still_ competitive_after_sevenweek_absence.html (accessed 2 July 2014).

16. Keenan, *Some Great Idea*, 106.

17. Ibid., 138.

18. Christopher Hume, "Rob Ford's Billion-Dollar Boast Not Worth a Dime," *Toronto Star*, 28 October 2013, www.thestar.com/news/gta/2013/10/28/rob_fords_billiondollar _boast_not_worth_a_dime.html (accessed 12 June 2014).

19. Christopher Hume, "2013 Was Toronto's Year of Living Disastrously," *Toronto Star*, 30 December 2013, www.thestar.com/news/gta/2013/12/30/2013_was_torontos_ year_of_living_disastrously_hume.html (accessed 12 June 2014).

20. Ann Hui, "Meet the Sobriety Coach Hired to Keep Rob Ford on Track," *Globe and Mail*, 14 July 2014, www.theglobeandmail.com/news/toronto/sobriety-coach-hired -to-keep-rob-ford-on-track-everyone-deserves-a-chance/article19582848/ (accessed 17 July 2014).

21. Kevin Donovan and Jennifer Pagliaro, "Rob Ford 'Disruptive' in Rehab, Sources Say," *Toronto Star*, 8 July 2014, www.thestar.com/news/canada/2014/07/08/rob_ford_ disruptive_in_rehab_sources_say.html (accessed 12 July 2014).

22. Royson James, "Journalists Should Take a Stand against Rob Ford's Bullying Behaviour," *Toronto Star*, 1 July 2014, www.thestar.com/news/gta/2014/06/30/ journalists_should_take_a_stand_against_rob_fords_bullying_behaviour_james .html (accessed 1 July 2014).

23. "Rob Ford: Full Text of Toronto Mayor's Speech," CBC News, 30 June 2014, www .cbc.ca/news/canada/toronto/rob-ford-full-text-of-toronto-mayor-s-speech-1.2692459 (accessed 20 December 2014).

24. David Nickle, "Ford 'Fatigue' May Be Taking Hold as Poll Shows Majority of Torontonians Not Satisfied with Apology," InsideToronto.com, 4 July 2014, www .insidetoronto.com/news-story/4615350-ford-fatigue-may-be-taking-hold-as-poll -shows-majority-of-torontonians-not-satisfied-with-apology/ (accessed 12 July 2014).

25. Betsy Powell and Jennifer Pagliaro, "John Tory Has the Lead in New Toronto MayoralPoll," *Toronto Star*, 7 July 2014, www.thestar.com/news/city_hall/toronto2014election/2014/07/ 07/john_tory_has_the_lead_in_new_toronto_mayoral_poll.html (accessed 12 July 2014).

26. "Rob Ford on Drug Use: 'You Name It, I Pretty Well Covered It,'" CBC News, 2 July 2014, www.cbc.ca/news/canada/toronto/rob-ford-on-drug-use-you-name-it-i-pretty -well-covered-it-1.2693774 (accessed 12 July 2014).

27. Ivor Tossell, "Ford Nation: At Its Heart, an Army of the Alienated," *Globe and Mail*, 28 July 2014, www.theglobeandmail.com/globe-debate/ford-nation-at-its-heart-an -army-of-the-alienated/article19802047/ (accessed 24 February 2015).

28. Josh Visser, "Rob Ford Tied in Three-Way Lead for Toronto Mayoral Race as Olivia Chow Support Drops: Poll," *National Post*, 23 July 2014, http://news.nationalpost.com/ 2014/07/23/rob-ford-tied-in-three-way-lead-for-toronto-mayoral-race-as-olivia-chow -support-drops-poll/ (accessed 9 August 2014).

29. Kaleigh Rogers, "Rob Ford Takes Lead in Scarborough, but Trails Rivals in Rest of Toronto: Poll," *Globe and Mail*, 31 July 2014, www.theglobeandmail.com/news/toronto/rob-ford-takes-lead-in-scarborough-but-trails-rivals-in-rest-of-toronto-poll/article19881386/ (accessed 23 August 2014).

30. Daniel Dale, "Forum Poll Shows Sudden Decline with Women Has Olivia Chow 10 Points Behind John Tory," *Globe and Mail*, 8 August 2014, www.thestar.com/news/city_hall/toronto2014election/2014/08/08/toronto_poll_sudden_decline_with_women_has_chow_10_points_behind_tory.html (accessed 9 August 2014).

31. See Enid Stack and André Côté, "Is Toronto Fiscally Healthy?" *IMFG Perspectives*, no. 7 (2014), Institute on Municipal Finance and Government, Munk School of Global Affairs, University of Toronto, http://munkschool.utoronto.ca/imfg/uploads/288/1581fiscallyhealthyr5final.pdf (accessed 20 December 2014).

32. Josh Visser and Natalie Alcoba, "Rob Ford Says Threatening Email Has Given Him 12 Hours to Resign or City Hall Will Be Blown Up," *National Post*, 11 August 2014, http://news.nationalpost.com/2014/08/11/rob-ford-says-threatening-email-has-given-him-12-hours-to-resign-or-city-hall-will-be-blown-up/ (accessed 19 August 2014).

33. Natalie Alcoba, "Rob Ford Makes a New Enemy, Says He Has Been in 'Standoffs' with Fearless Raccoons Outside His Home," *National Post*, 18 August 2014, http://news.nationalpost.com/2014/08/18/rob-ford-makes-a-new-enemy-says-he-has-been-in-standoffs-with-raccoons-outside-of-home/ (accessed 19 August 2014).

34. Jill Mahoney and Elizabeth Church, "Rob Ford Only a Few Points behind Tory in a New Mayoral Poll," *Globe and Mail*, 28 August 2014, www.theglobeandmail.com/news/toronto/rob-ford-only-a-few-points-behind-leading-tory-in-new-mayoral-poll/article20231613/ (accessed 29 August 2014).

35. Dan Rath, "Why Rob Ford Will Win Again in Toronto," *Toronto Star*, 28 August 2014, www.thestar.com/opinion/commentary/2014/08/27/why_rob_ford_will_win_again_in_toronto.html (accessed 29 August 2014).

36. Rex Murphy, "As Olivia Chow Flounders, Rob Ford's Fans Show Us That the Common Man Still Matters," *National Post*, 30 August 2014, http://fullcomment.nationalpost.com/2014/08/30/rex-murphy-as-olivia-chow-flounders-rob-fords-fans-show-us-that-the-common-man-still-matters/ (accessed 31 August 2014).

37. Marcus Gee, "The Next Few Weeks in T.O. Mayoral Race Promise to Be a Corker," *Globe and Mail*, 1 September 2014, www.theglobeandmail.com/news/toronto/the-next-few-weeks-in-to-mayoral-race-promise-to-be-a-corker/article20295340/ (accessed 5 September 2014).

38. Quoted by Marcus Gee, "This Is a Time When Toronto Should Pull for Rob Ford," *Globe and Mail*, 11 September 2014, www.theglobeandmail.com/news/toronto/this-is-a-time-when-the-whole-city-should-pull-for-mayor-ford/article20527819/ (accessed 11 September 2014).

39. Marcus Gee, "Even Foes Hope Ford Wins This Fight," *Globe and Mail*, 17 September 2014, www.theglobeandmail.com/news/toronto/even-mayor-fords-foes-hope-he-wins-this-fight/article20652741/ (accessed 21 September 2014).

40. Edward Keenan, "Rob Ford's Fight Strikes Home for So Many of Us," *Toronto Star*, 11 September 2014, www.thestar.com/news/city_hall/toronto2014election/2014/09/11/rob_fords_health_fight_strikes_home_for_us_all_keenan.html (accessed 11 September 2014).

41. Marcus Gee, "Rob Made Us Care about the City's Fate," *Globe and Mail*, 13 September 2014, www.theglobeandmail.com/news/toronto/its-a-sad-ending-to-the-captivating-rob-ford-show/article20586355/ (accessed 13 September 2014).

42. Heather Mallick, "If Olivia Chow Fails, Blame Her," *Toronto Star*, 13 September 2014, www.thestar.com/news/gta/2014/09/12/if_olivia_chow_fails_blame_her_mallick.html (accessed 13 September 2014).

43. Gee, "Even Foes Hope Ford Wins This Fight."

44. Marcus Gee, "A Sense of Finality Hovered over Ford Fest," *Globe and Mail*, 28 September 2014, www.theglobeandmail.com/news/toronto/a-sense-of-finality-hovered-over-ford-fest/article20820006/ (accessed 12 October 2014).

45. Lauren Pelly, "Doug Ford Closes on John Tory in Latest Forum Poll," *Toronto Star*, 6 October 2014, www.thestar.com/news/city_hall/toronto2014election/2014/10/06/doug_ford_closes_on_john_tory_tied_in_latest_forum_poll.html (accessed 13 October 2014).

46. You can see Ford and Barber's exchange on YouTube at www.youtube.com/watch?v=z8EpSdyB0zY (accessed 13 November 2014).

47. John Barber, "Boredom Replaces Noise and Strife at Toronto City Hall," *Toronto Star*, 27 October 2014, www.thestar.com/opinion/commentary/2014/10/27/boredom_replaces_noise_and_strife_at_toronto_city_hall.html (accessed 13 November 2014).

ELEVEN: SUSAN FENNELL OF BRAMPTON

1. Jim Coyle, "Brampton Hockey Dynamo Ready for Her Breakaway," *Toronto Star*, 2 November 2000, www.thestar.com/editorial/toronto/20001102NEW01b_CI-COYLE.html (accessed 14 July 2014).

2. Jane Jacobs, *Dark Age Ahead* (Toronto: Vintage Canada, 2005), 92.

3. San Grewal, "Secrecy Clouds Brampton Mayor's Gala," *Toronto Star*, 12 October 2010, www.thestar.com/news/gta/2010/10/12/brampton_mayors_private_community_fund_not_registered.html (accessed 15 July 2014).

4. Royson James, "Fennell and Backers Need a Wake-Up Call," *Toronto Star*, 20 October 2010, www.thestar.com/news/gta/2010/10/20/james_fennell_and_backers_need_a_wakeup_call.html (accessed 15 July 2014).

5. San Grewal, "Rose Theatre Audit Alarms Brampton Councillors," *Toronto Star*, 6 June 2012, www.thestar.com/news/gta/2012/06/06/rose_theatre_audit_alarms_brampton_councillors.html (accessed 15 July 2014).

6. San Grewal, "Brampton's Susan Fennell Highest Paid Mayor in Canada," *Toronto Star*, 26 March 2013, www.thestar.com/news/gta/2013/03/26/bramptons_susan_fennell_highest_paid_mayor_in_canada.html (accessed 20 December 2014).

7. Christopher Hume, "Brampton, Like Mississauga, Has Hit the Fiscal Wall," *Toronto Star*, 1 November 2013, www.thestar.com/news/gta/2013/11/01/brampton_like_mississauga_has_hit_the_fiscal_wall_hume.html (accessed 20 December 2014).

8. San Grewal, "Brampton Mayor Susan Fennell Racks Up $186,000 in Expenses," *Toronto Star*, 12 November 2013, www.thestar.com/news/gta/2013/11/12/brampton_mayor_susan_fennell_racks_up_186000_in_expenses.html (accessed 20 December 2014).

9. "Curb Brampton Mayor Susan Fennell's Spending," *Toronto Star*, 15 November 2013, www.thestar.com/opinion/editorials/2013/11/14/curb_brampton_mayor_susan_fennells_spending_editorial.html (accessed 20 December 2014).

10. San Grewal, "'Close Friend' of Mayor Susan Fennell Got $1.1M in Brampton City Contracts," *Toronto Star*, 27 May 2014, www.thestar.com/news/gta/2014/05/27/close_friend_of_mayor_susan_fennell_got_11m_in_brampton_city_contracts.html (accessed 17 July 2014).

11. San Grewal, "Brampton Councillors Shocked by List of Contracts That Broke Rules," *Toronto Star*, 3 July 2014, www.thestar.com/news/gta/2014/07/03/list_of_bramptons_solesource_contracts_shocks_councillors.html (accessed 17 July 2014).

12. For the full text of the audit report, see www.theglobeandmail.com/news/toronto/article19927861.ece/BINARY/Brampton+Audit.pdf (accessed 8 August 2014).

13. Royson James, "Brampton Now Defined by Its Flawed Mayor," *Toronto Star*, 7 August 2014, www.thestar.com/news/gta/susanfennell/2014/08/07/brampton_now_defined_by_its_flawed_mayor.html (accessed 8 August 2014).

14. Todd Coyne, "Brampton Residents Say Mayor Susan Fennell's Behaviour 'Unacceptable,'" *Toronto Star*, 8 August 2014, www.thestar.com/news/gta/2014/08/08/brampton_residents_say_mayor_susan_fennells_behaviour_unacceptable.html (accessed 10 August 2014).

15. Shawn Jeffords, "Brampton Mayor Vows to Stay in Election," *Toronto Sun*, 10 September 2014, www.torontosun.com/2014/09/10/brampton-mayor-vows-to-stay-in-election (accessed 12 September 2014).

TWELVE: HAZEL McCALLION OF MISSISSAUGA

1. Jim Coyle, "Hazel's World Reigns Supreme," *Toronto Star*, 11 October 2000, www.thestar.com/thestar/editorial/toronto/20001011NEW01_CI-HAZEL.html (accessed 23 August 2014).

2. Tom Urbaniak, *Her Worship: Hazel McCallion and the Development of Mississauga* (Toronto: University of Toronto Press, 2009), 106.

3. Ibid., 3–4.

4. Christopher Hume, "High Time for Change in Mississauga," *Toronto Star*, 5 October 2009, www.thestar.com/opinion/2009/10/05/high_time_for_change_in_mississauga.html (accessed 23 August 2014).

5. Christopher Hume, "Until McCallion Goes, Mississauga Won't Grow Up," *Toronto Star*, 5 October 2011, www.thestar.com/news/gta/2011/10/04/hume_until_mccallion_goes_mississauga_wont_grow_up.html (accessed 24 August 2014).

6. Christopher Hume, "Mississauga on the Eve of McCallion's Departure," *Toronto Star*, 21 February 2014, www.thestar.com/news/gta/2014/02/21/mississauga_on_the_eve_of_hazel_mccallions_departure_hume.html (accessed 24 August 2014).

7. *Graham v. McCallion*, 1982 CanLII 2014 (Ontario High Court of Justice, 30 September 1982). The judgment is available at www.canlii.org/en/on/onsc/doc/1982/1982canlii2014/1982canlii2014.html?searchUrlHash=AAAAAQAJbWNjYWx saW9uAAAAAAE (accessed 21 August 2014).

8. Urbaniak, *Her Worship*, 113.

9. You can download the report at www.mississaugainquiry.ca (accessed 27 August 2014).

10.   Richard Cuthbertson, "No. 2 Nenshi to Meet Canada's Most Popular Mayor," *Calgary Herald*, 25 October 2011, www2.canada.com/calgaryherald/news/city/story.html?id=5f15d3d9-e184-44a7-9f35-7c3bfeb21d30 (accessed 26 August 2014).

11.   See *Hazineh v. McCallion*, [2013] O.J. No. 2696 (Ontario Superior Court of Justice, 14 June 2013). The judgment is available at www3.quicklaw.com/cgi-bin/LNC-prod/lnetdoc.pl?DOCNO=943 (accessed 26 August 2014).

12.   Urbaniak, *Her Worship*, 140.

13.   Ibid., 231.

THIRTEEN: NENSHI, IVESON, ROBERTSON

1.   Chad Park and Tim Draimin, "Meet the New Generation of Politicians," *Ottawa Citizen*, 28 October 2013, www.naturalstep.ca/ottawa-citizen-meet-the-new-generation-of-politicians (accessed 20 December 2014).

2.   Stephen Quinn, "Inside Western Triangle of Mayoral Goodness," *Globe and Mail*, 25 October 2013, www.theglobeandmail.com/news/british-columbia/inside-western-triangle-of-mayoral-goodness/article15098105/ (accessed 8 August 2014).

3.   Alan Boras, "A Class Act," *Calgary Herald*, 17 June 1989, http://ezproxy.torontopubliclibrary.ca/login?url=http://search.proquest.com/canadiannewsmajor/docview/244005012/152A1A9D0ADB4024PQ/ (accessed 26 July 2014).

4.   "Naheed Nenshi Calls Ezra Levant 'Creepily and Weirdly Obsessed,'" *Huffington Post*, 13 September 2013, www.huffingtonpost.ca/2013/09/13/nenshi-calls-ezra-levant-creepy-obsessed_n_3921261.html (accessed 1 August 2014).

5.   Don Braid, "Cultural Awareness: Harvard Grad Sees an Ethnic Divide That Can Make or Break Calgary," *Calgary Herald*, 1 October 2006, http://ezproxy.torontopubliclibrary.ca/login?url=http://search.proquest.com/canadiannewsmajor/docview/245442382/152A1A9D0ADB4024PQ/ (accessed 26 July 2014).

6.   Christopher Hume, "'Canada's Mayor' Sees the City Positively," *Toronto Star*, 10 February 2011, www.thestar.com/news/gta/2011/02/10/hume_canadas_mayor_sees_the_city_positively.html (accessed 27 July 2014).

7.   Naheed Nenshi, "After One Year as Mayor, I'm Still Excited," *Calgary Herald*, 14 October 2011, www2.canada.com/calgaryherald/news/story.html?id=33218c56-e368-4377-b03e-7173af197bd8 (accessed 27 July 2014).

8.   Jason Markusoff, "Mr. Mayor, Mr. Popular," *Calgary Herald*, 16 October 2011, www2.canada.com/calgaryherald/news/story.html?id=26231ce2-3699-4799-b79d-f9f54c1f44a5&p=5 (accessed 27 July 2014).

9.   Jason Markusoff, "Nenshi Launches Bid to Extend Purple Reign," *Calgary Herald*, 8 November 2012, www2.canada.com/calgaryherald/news/story.html?id=5b9c33cb-060e-4df7-9b8a-801edaf65780 (accessed 30 July 2014).

10.   Jason Markusoff, "Nenshi Often on Losing Side of Council Votes," *Calgary Herald*, 20 October 2012, www2.canada.com/calgaryherald/news/city/story.html?id=5e28c2da-e53a-4376-8a6a-74ebcdf1db94 (accessed 30 July 2014).

11.   "Leadership and the Flood," *Globe and Mail*, 24 June 2013, www.theglobeandmail.com/globe-debate/editorials/leadership-and-the-flood/article12786839/ (accessed 28 July 2014).

12. Michael Den Tandt, "Alberta Disaster Brings Out Best in Canada's Leaders," *Regina Leader-Post*, 26 June 2013, http://o.canada.com/news/politics-and-the-nation/0626-col-dentandt (accessed 20 December 2014).

13. "The 50 Most Important People in Canada," *Maclean's*, 20 November 2013, www.macleans.ca/news/canada/the-most-important-people-in-canada/ (accessed 25 July 2014).

14. Kent Gordon, "Iveson Likes to Get 'Dirt under His Fingernails' as Respite from Council," *Edmonton Journal*, 12 October 2013, www.edmontonjournal.com/news/insight/Iveson+likes+dirt+under+fingernails+respite+from+council/9027153/story.html (accessed 3 August 2014).

15. "Miss Sarah Chan Rides into New Role with Signature Style," *Edmonton Journal*, 5 November 2013, www.canada.com/story.html?id=aa74b4e1-4ee4-4a91-ad48-52aacd4b0a45 (accessed 2 August 2014).

16. Scott McKeen, "The Heady Rush of Celebrity That Surrounds a City Councillor," *Edmonton Journal*, 28 June 2010, www.canada.com/story.html?id=1bbe9bc1-8f3b-49a7-9762-61f31760769b (accessed 20 December 2014).

17. Kent Gordon, "Iveson, Anderson Bow Out of 2013 Councillor Race," *Edmonton Journal*, 18 November 2011, http://ezproxy.torontopubliclibrary.ca/login?url=http://search.proquest.com/canadiannewsmajor/docview/905044302/F69B3322ACD1490APQ/ (accessed 2 August 2014).

18. David Staples, "Council Full of Strong Candidates for Mayor," *Edmonton Journal*, 6 February 2013, www2.canada.com/edmontonjournal/news/story.html?id=3895cc31-882d-433c-818d-01d2bb61d725 (accessed 2 August 2014).

19. David Staples, "Don Iveson Answers Tough Questions," *Edmonton Journal*, 12 July 2013, www2.canada.com/edmontonjournal/story.html?id=07645d02-e777-4283-af54-01cc38bfba57 (accessed 8 August 2014).

20. Paula Simons, "Iveson Offers Edmonton a Fresh New Vision—but Can He Make That Image a Reality?" *Edmonton Journal*, 19 October 2013, www.edmontonjournal.com/news/Simons+Iveson+offers+Edmonton+fresh+vision+make+that+image+reality/9054903/story.html?__federated=1 (accessed 4 August 2014).

21. Paula Simons, "Iveson's Clark Kent Speech Safe, Dull," *Edmonton Journal*, 6 March 2014, www2.canada.com/edmontonjournal/news/story.html?id=bebfb2a4-9337-42d1-be1e-3917fd664f2e (accessed 3 August 2014).

22. "Where to Now, Mr. Mayor?" *Edmonton Journal*, 21 October 2014, www.edmontonjournal.com/opinion/editorials/Editorial+Where+Mayor/10308539/story.html (accessed 26 October 2014).

23. Quoted by Frances Bula, "The Next Mayor," *Vancouver Magazine*, 2 September 2008, www.vanmag.com/News_and_Features/The_Next_Mayor (accessed 7 August 2014).

24. Ibid.

25. David Berner, "Ladner's Self-Assurance Convinces Me He's Best Choice as Vancouver's Mayor," *Vancouver Province*, 31 October 2008, www.canada.com/story.html?id=0ffe566e-facb-4b86-ac62-ab277da96a2c (accessed 20 December 2014).

26. Bula, "The Next Mayor."

27. Gary Mason, "Mayor's Big Smile Matches His Big Ambitions," *Globe and Mail*, 9 March 2010, www.theglobeandmail.com/news/national/mayors-big-smile-matches-his-big -ambitions/article4316796/ (accessed 20 December 2014).

28. Frances Bula, "The People vs Gregor Robertson," *Vancouver Magazine*, 2 May 2013, www.vanmag.com/News_and_Features/The_People_vs_Gregor_Robertson (accessed 7 August 2014).

29. Quoted by Brian Hutchinson, "Kirk LaPointe Frames His Campaign to Be Mayor of Vancouver around Government Transparency," *National Post*, 22 July 2014, http:// fullcomment.nationalpost.com/2014/07/22/brian-hutchinson-kirk-lapointe-frames -his-campaign-to-be-mayor-of-vancouver-around-government-transparency/ (accessed 7 August 2014).

FOURTEEN: JÓN, BORIS, ANNE AND BILL

1. Jón Gnarr, *Gnarr!: How I Became the Mayor of a Large City in Iceland and Changed the World* (Brooklyn: Melville House Publishing, 2014), 33.

2. Gnarr's campaign video is worth watching. You can find it at www.youtube.com/ watch?v=xxBW4mPzv6E. It has been called "the most delightful political video ever made" (see www.tagesanzeiger.ch/ausland/europa/More-punk-less-hell/story/ 10069405).

3. Quoted by Constantin Seibt, "More Punk, Less Hell!" *Tages-Anzeiger*, 24 June 2014, www.tagesanzeiger.ch/ausland/europa/More-punk-less-hell/story/10069405 (accessed 16 October 2014).

4. Aaron Bastani, "The World According to Gnarr," LRB [*London Review of Books*] Blog, 1 September 2014, www.lrb.co.uk/blog/2014/09/01/aaron-bastani/the-world-according -to-gnarr/ (accessed 17 September 2014).

5. See Haukur S. Magnússon, "What Happened? Mayor Jón Gnarr Explains Himself, a Little," *Rekyjavik Grapevine*, 26 May 2014, http://grapevine.is/mag/feature/2014/ 05/26/what-happened/ (accessed 17 October 2014).

6. "Yoko Ono Has 'Great Respect' for Jón Gnarr, the Comedian and Former Mayor of Reykjavík," *Icelandic Magazine*, 9 October 2014, http://icelandmag.com/article/yoko -ono-has-great-respect-jon-gnarr-comedian-and-former-mayor-reykjavik (accessed 15 October 2014).

7. Calvin Trillin, "Capital Fellows," *New Yorker*, 14 April 2008, www.newyorker.com/ magazine/2008/04/14/capital-fellows (accessed 19 October 2014).

8. Kylie MacLellan and William James, "Colourful London Mayor, Potential Cameron Successor, Plans Return to Parliament," Reuters, 6 August 2014, http://uk.reuters .com/article/2014/08/06/uk-britain-politics-johnson-idUKKBN0G60T820140806 (accessed 19 October 2014).

9. Michael Deakin, "Boris Is Back," *Telegraph*, 6 August 2014, www.telegraph.co.uk/news/ politics/11016747/Sketch-Boris-is-back.html (accessed 5 November 2014).

10. The sexual escapades of Boris and his father, Stanley, are amply documented. For an introduction, see Geoffrey Levy, "Affairs, Wives Left in Anguish and How Boris Johnson Learned about Adultery at His Father's Knee," *Daily Mail* online, 26 September 2011, www.dailymail.co.uk/femail/article-2041220/Affairs-wives -left-anguish-Boris-learned-adultery-fathers-knee.html (accessed 21 October 2014).

11. You can see the video of this event, which happened on October 15, 2014, at www .telegraph.co.uk/comment/columnists/borisjohnson/11164689/Boris-Johnson-fouls -boy-in-childrens-football-match.html (accessed 18 October 2014).

12. "Right Man, Wrong Job," *The Economist*, 28 April 2012, www.economist.com/node/ 21553441 (accessed 20 October 2014).

13. Andrew Rawnsley, "Why Both the Tories and Labour Are Vainly Yearning for Fantasy Leaders," *The Guardian*, 19 October 2014, www.theguardian.com/commentisfree/ 2014/oct/19/boris-johnson-alan-johnson-fantasy-leaders-tories-labour (accessed 19 October 2014).

14. "Boris Is Back," *The Economist*, 25 October 2014, www.economist.com/news/britain/ 21627668-boris-johnson-unfit-be-compared-his-hero-winston-churchill-yet-may -emulate-him-boris (accessed 5 November 2014).

15. John Lichfield, "Anne Hidalgo Elected as Paris's First Female Mayor," *The Independent*, 30 March 2014, www.independent.co.uk/news/world/europe/anne-hidalgo-elected -as-pariss-first-female-mayor-9224766.html (accessed 25 October 2014).

16. Laure Gilbaut, "Madame Mayor: Anne Hidalgo Preps for Paris Fashion Week," *Women's Wear Daily*, 23 September 2014, www.wwd.com/eye/people/madame-mayor-7935774 (accessed 24 October 2014).

17. See Suzanne Daley, "In a City Wary of Skyscrapers, a New Tower May Rise," *The New York Times*, 19 November 2014, www.nytimes.com/2014/11/19/world/europe/in -paris-a-city-wary-of-skyscrapers-a-new-tower-may-rise.html? (accessed 6 December 2014).

18. Ross Barkan, "'We Have Such Similar Priorities': Bill de Blasio Bonds with Paris Mayor," *New York Observer*, 30 May 2014, http://observer.com/2014/05/we-have-such -similar-priorities-bill-de-blasio-bonds-with-paris-mayor/ (accessed 23 October 2014).

19. Kim Willsher, "Anne Hidalgo: 'I Am Who I Am. I Don't Play a Role,'" *The Guardian*, 23 June 2014, www.theguardian.com/lifeandstyle/2014/jun/23/ anne-hidalgo-first-female-mayor-paris-interview (accessed 23 October 2014).

20. Matt Flegenheimer and Michael M. Grynbaum, "De Blasio Takes a Businesslike Approach as Ebola Arrives in New York," *The New York Times*, 27 October 2014, www.nytimes.com/2014/10/28/nyregion/with-ebolas-arrival-de-blasio-stands -tall-as-christie-and-cuomo-falter.html?_r=0 (accessed 3 November 2014).

21. "Where Will You Go, Bill de Blasio?" *The Economist*, 9 November 2013, www .economist.com/news/united-states/21589419-big-apple-has-been-well-run-20 -years-mayor-elect-promises-change-where-will (accessed 29 October 2014).

22. Javier C. Hernández, "A Mayoral Hopeful Now, de Blasio Was Once a Young Leftist," *The New York Times*, 22 September 2013, www.nytimes.com/2013/09/23/nyregion/a -mayoral-hopeful-now-de-blasio-was-once-a -young-leftist.html (accessed 27 October 2014).

23. J. David Goodman and Al Baker, "Wave of Protests after Grand Jury Doesn't Indict Officer in Eric Garner Chokehold Case," *The New York Times*, 3 December 2014, www.nytimes.com/2014/12/04/nyregion/grand-jury-said-to-bring-no-charges-in -staten-island-chokehold-death-of-eric-garner.html (accessed 2 January 2015).

24. Al Baker and J. David Goodman, "After Shootings, Police Union Chief Deepens Rift with de Blasio," *The New York Times*, 23 December 2014, www.nytimes.com/2014/12/24/ nyregion/after-shootings-police-union-chief-in-new-war.html (accessed 2 January 2015).

25. John Cassidy, "The Education of Bill De Blasio," *New Yorker*, 31 March 2014, www
     .newyorker.com/news/john-cassidy/the-education-of-bill-de-blasio (accessed
     5 November 2014).

26. Patrick Wintour, "New York Mayor Urges UK Labour Party to Be Bold in Tackling
     Inequality," *The Guardian*, 24 September 2014, www.theguardian.com/politics/2014/
     sep/24/new-york-mayor-british-labour-party-inequality-bill-de-blasio (accessed
     2 January 2015).

27. Michael M. Grynbaum, "De Blasio Walks Tightrope between Municipal Politics and
     International Influence," *The New York Times*, 24 September 2014, www.nytimes.com/
     2014/09/25/nyregion/de-blasio-walks-tightrope-between-municipal-politics-and
     -international-influence.html?_r=0 (accessed 3 November 2014).

CONCLUSION: DEVO-MAX

1.   See, for example, Andrew Coyne, "Time to Scrap Property Taxes and Give Cities Power
     to Raise Their Own Income or Sales Taxes," *National Post*, 29 October 2014, http://
     fullcomment.nationalpost.com/2014/10/29/andrew-coyne-time-to-scrap-property
     -taxes-and-give-cities-power-to-raise-their-own-income-or-sales-taxes/ (accessed
     23 November 2014).

ACKNOWLEDGMENTS

An important source for this book was the written word, particularly newspapers. My belief in the great importance of newspapers to our democracy has been strongly reaffirmed. It is reporters across the country who tell us what is really going on in government. Often their toil is tedious and complicated, but it is essential to revealing the truth. Sometimes they are accused of bias, and occasionally they may be unreasonably dogged. But the work they do is of inestimable value to all of us. They are the cops on the beat. Without them, our system of government and way of life would be in serious trouble.

I particularly have in mind people like Tim Bousquet, formerly of Halifax's alternative weekly *The Coast* and now publishing the online *Halifax Examiner*; Linda Gyulai and Henry Aubin of Montreal's *Gazette*; Chip Martin of the *London Free Press*; San Grewal and Kevin Donovan of the *Toronto Star*; and Bartley Kives of the *Winnipeg Free Press*. There are others. A special tip of the hat goes to the *Toronto Star*'s Christopher Hume, who, although a bit grumpy sometimes, almost always gets it right. Our democracy cannot function properly without journalists like these.

Thanks to Gabrielle Domingues for her excellent and unflagging research help; to my agent, Beverley Slopen, for her sage advice on many things; to my long-time editor at Penguin Random House, and friend, Diane Turbide; and to editor Janice Weaver, who, in her gentle way, kept me on the straight and narrow.

And, of course, I owe more to Cynthia than I can ever explain.

INDEX